IMAGES
of America

TRIMBLE COUNTY

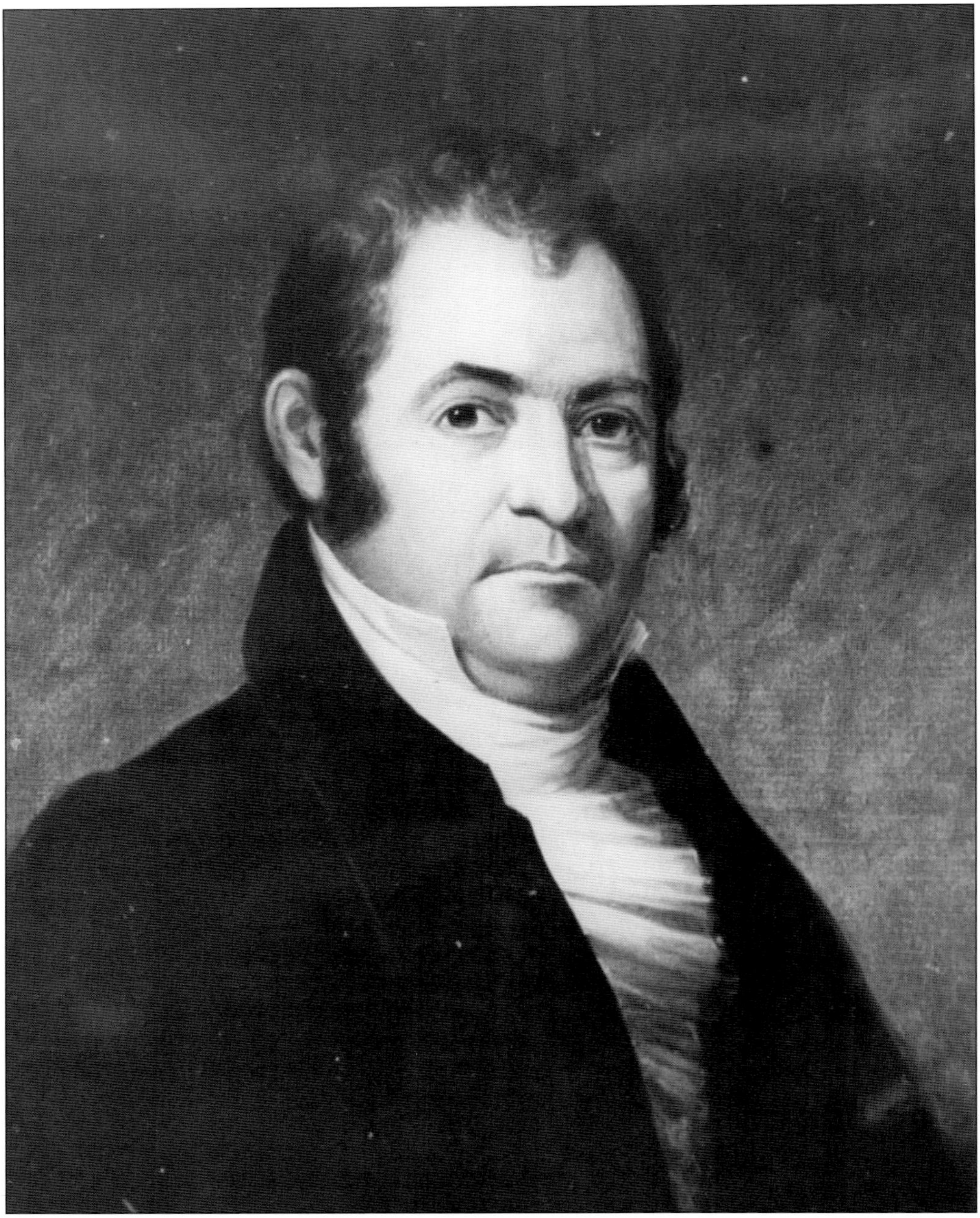

Robert Trimble was a native of Virginia before his family settled in Kentucky. He practiced law in Paris, Kentucky, in 1800 and served in the General Assembly from 1802 to 1804. He advanced to US district attorney before becoming a US district judge in 1817. Trimble was appointed to the US Supreme Court in 1826 by Pres. John Quincy Adams and died two years later in Washington, DC, at age 52. (Courtesy of Gary Greenwood.)

On the Cover: The Milton ferry landing was where travelers went to cross the Ohio River to Madison, Indiana, before the original Milton-Madison Bridge opened in December 1929. Here, George Green waves his hat to the photographer. Henry Wingham, far right, talks to another man on the dock. (Courtesy of Ted Taylor.)

IMAGES
of America

TRIMBLE COUNTY

Phyllis Codling McLaughlin

ARCADIA
PUBLISHING

ISBN 978-1-4671-1362-5

Published by Arcadia Publishing
Charleston, South Carolina

Printed in the United States of America

Library of Congress Control Number: 2014949513

For all general information, please contact Arcadia Publishing:
Telephone 843-853-2070
Fax 843-853-0044
E-mail sales@arcadiapublishing.com
For customer service and orders:
Toll-Free 1-888-313-2665

Visit us on the Internet at www.arcadiapublishing.com

I am indebted to everyone who contributed photos and stories and to my husband, Andrew "Patter" McLaughlin, whose love and encouragement made this book possible.

Contents

ACKNOWLEDGMENTS

I sincerely thank everyone who took the time to go through their personal collections to find photographs to help tell the story of Trimble County: Mike Gross, Carolyn Crafton Adams, Sue Ralston Reid, Betty Burkhardt, Bill and Darrell Henderson, Bob Stewart, Gary Greenwood, Mildred Pardo Pruitt, Ted Taylor and Peg Wainscott, Kim Vittitow, JoDeva Ogden, Mac and Linda Gordon, Gary Rowlett, Hilda Parrish, Diane Perrine Coon, the wonderful folks at the Trimble County Senior Center, and the Trimble County Public Library. My thanks to Janice Barnes and the Madison Jefferson County Public Library for providing me access to the original photographs of the Harry Lemen Collection. These provided a wonderful glimpse into early-20th-century Trimble County.

Special thanks to Frederica Congleton, who, late in the fourth quarter, went above and beyond to recruit contributors.

I appreciate being allowed into your homes, scanner and laptop in hand, to choose the photographs used in this book. I enjoyed getting to know all of you. I hope you enjoy this book as much as I've enjoyed putting it together. In the end, I collected far more photographs than I could use, of course. But that was a blessing, and the book is all the better for it.

I want to thank my editor, Maggie Bullwinkel, and the team at Arcadia for being patient—and tremendously flexible—throughout this project.

Finally, thank you to my dear husband, Andrew "Patter" McLaughlin, for all your love, support, and endless patience.

Introduction

Trimble County is the 86th of Kentucky's 120 counties, established by the General Assembly in 1836 and formally organized in 1837. Formed from sections of Oldham, Henry, and Gallatin Counties, it was named for Robert Trimble, a Paris, Kentucky, attorney who would rise to become a member of the US Supreme Court under Pres. John Quincy Adams.

In 1851, the eastern portion of Trimble County was given to neighboring Carroll County, which was formed in 1838. According to Richard A. Edwards, whose county history was published in a special section of the *Trimble Banner* in 1974, Benjamin M. Hitt, Trimble County's representative in the state legislature, chose an inopportune time to take a nap during a session in the statehouse. While Hitt slept, a bill was introduced and passed that moved the county's boundary five miles farther east—from Spillman Lane just outside of Milton city limits to Locust Creek, an area that included the rich farmland of Hunter's Bottom.

"When questioned about it at home, Ben said he would have it corrected at the next session of the Legislature," wrote Edwards, who served as Trimble County High School's first principal in 1910. " 'No you won't,' was the reply, 'another representative will be there.' " Ironically, Hitt is buried in the Fearn family cemetery in Hunter's Bottom, which remains within Carroll County to this day.

All along the Ohio River, several main routes of the Underground Railroad traversed Trimble County, most leading to Madison, Indiana, which was a major station and destination for fugitives. Hundreds of escaped slaves crossed into southern Indiana under cover of night, including Henry Bibb, who had been a slave on the Gatewood Plantation near Bedford. Bibb eventually became a leader of the antislavery movement, publishing a newspaper, writing a memoir of his years as a slave, and establishing a town for fugitives in Ontario, Canada, across the river from Detroit.

Slaveowners from Carroll, Trimble, Henry, and surrounding counties met at the Kings Tavern on Carrollton Pike (US 42) in 1847 to draft a resolution to the legislature regarding the case of the Adam Crosswhite family, fugitives from the Francis Giltner plantation on Hunter's Bottom near Locust Creek. Attempts by representatives of the Giltners to reclaim the family were halted by the townspeople of Marshall, Michigan, where the Crosswhites were living as free people. The affair was a major influence leading to Sen. Henry Clay's revisions to the Fugitive Slave Act in 1850, meant to coerce free states into allowing slaveowners to reclaim their property or face stiff penalties.

Despite that, Delia Webster, known as the "Petticoat Abolitionist," bought a 600-acre farm in Trimble County in 1854 and, for a time, operated a station there. She was arrested by local authorities for her efforts, but that case never went to trial. She was accused by local slaveowners of helping their slaves to escape. Vandalism and arson eventually drove her away from her farm, which she lost to creditors in 1869. She moved to Indiana, and later to Iowa, where she lived with a niece until her death in 1904.

Milton was the first town in what would become Trimble County. Located on the southern bank of the Ohio River across from Madison, Indiana, it was incorporated by the Virginia legislature in 1789, three years before Kentucky became a state. An adjacent town known as Kingston has since vanished.

Once a flourishing town with a flour mill, distillery, and numerous groceries and other businesses, nearly all of the historic buildings in Milton are gone, ravaged over the years by several major floods. The worst flood in recent memory hit in January 1937, when floodwaters destroyed many homes and other buildings and reached high into the second floors of taller buildings. Fire later destroyed the flour mill and other downtown buildings.

At 11:00 a.m. on December 20, 1929, the Milton-Madison Bridge was opened when Milton's Marguerite Pecar, crowned Queen of the Bridge, cut the ribbon during the dedication ceremony. The private crossing, built by J.G. White Engineering Corp., required a toll of 5¢ for pedestrians and 45¢ for vehicles until it was discontinued on the 20th anniversary of its dedication. The 20-foot-wide structure has been replaced by a 40-foot-wide span that rests on the original piers. The new bridge was built on temporary piers and, using hydraulic jacks, slid into place on the reinforced piers in the spring of 2013.

Some of Hollywood's elite, including Frank Sinatra, Dean Martin, and Shirley MacLaine, filmed portions of *Some Came Running* in Milton. The 1958 film opens as Sinatra's character rides a Greyhound bus down Milton Hill on his way to fictional Parkman, Indiana, set in Madison. A funeral scene takes place in Milton's Moffett Cemetery, which sits on a hill overlooking the river.

Nearby Preston Plantation was home to Sondra Rodgers, who found her own fame in Hollywood, landing roles on several TV shows, including *The Many Loves of Dobie Gillis*, *Alfred Hitchcock Presents*, and *Wagon Train*.

Juxtaposed with the former splendor of plantation life is nearby Payne Hollow, the primitive homestead of painter Harlan Hubbard and his wife, Anna. They were close friends of renowned author Wendell Berry of neighboring Henry County, who wrote Hubbard's biography in 1990.

The county seat of Bedford was incorporated in 1816. The town was established by Robert Bell, who named it for his hometown of Bedford, Virginia, when he built a cabin there in 1805. In the 1840s, Bedford became known for its medicinal mineral springs, drawing visitors from hundreds of miles away. The Bedford Springs Hotel was a top destination until 1851, when an outbreak of cholera closed it down.

While Milton was plagued by the floodwaters of the Ohio River, Bedford was plagued by numerous fires. Nearly all of the town's original buildings around the courthouse square were destroyed by fire in the 1930s through the 1950s. In March 1952, the courthouse was severely damaged by fire and rebuilt.

Both towns continue to thrive. The total population of Trimble County in 2010 was about 8,800. Bedford has a population of about 600 and Milton about 500.

Trimble remains almost entirely rural. Its biggest employer is the Wise's Landing Generating Station, a coal-fired power plant owned by Louisville Gas & Electric that began commercial operation in 1990.

The county is known for its production of peaches and apples, still sold at several roadside stands along US 42 and US 421. Tobacco is also a leading crop.

One

MILTON

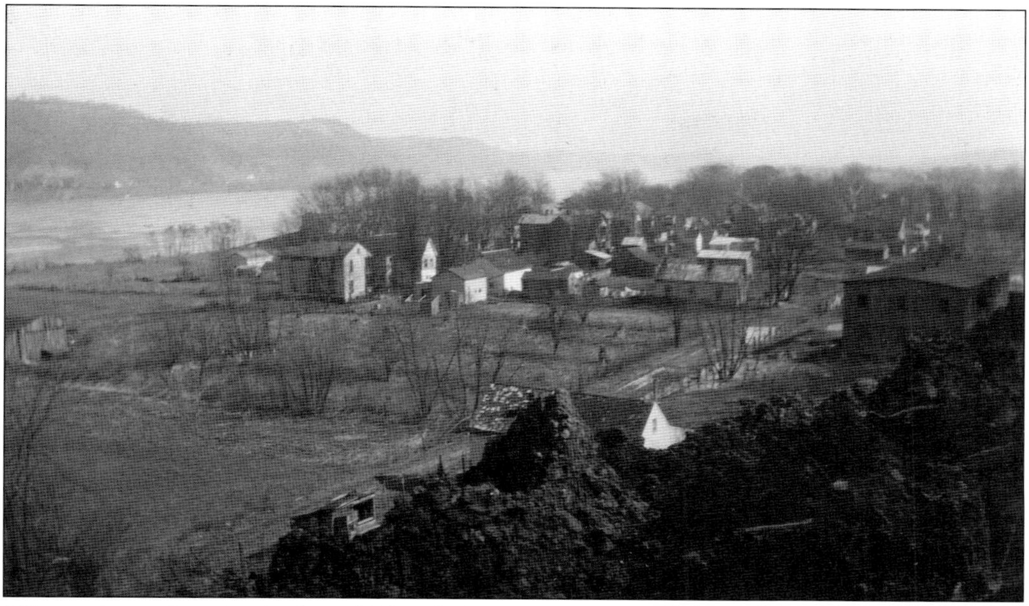

Milton, shown here in the late 1920s—before construction of the Milton-Madison Bridge—is one of just two incorporated towns in Trimble County. Established in 1789 when the region was still part of Virginia, Milton once flourished with a flour mill, distillery, and numerous grocery and dry goods stores. Most of the very old buildings have been destroyed by floods and fires, but the town continues to thrive. (Courtesy of Madison Jefferson County Public Library.)

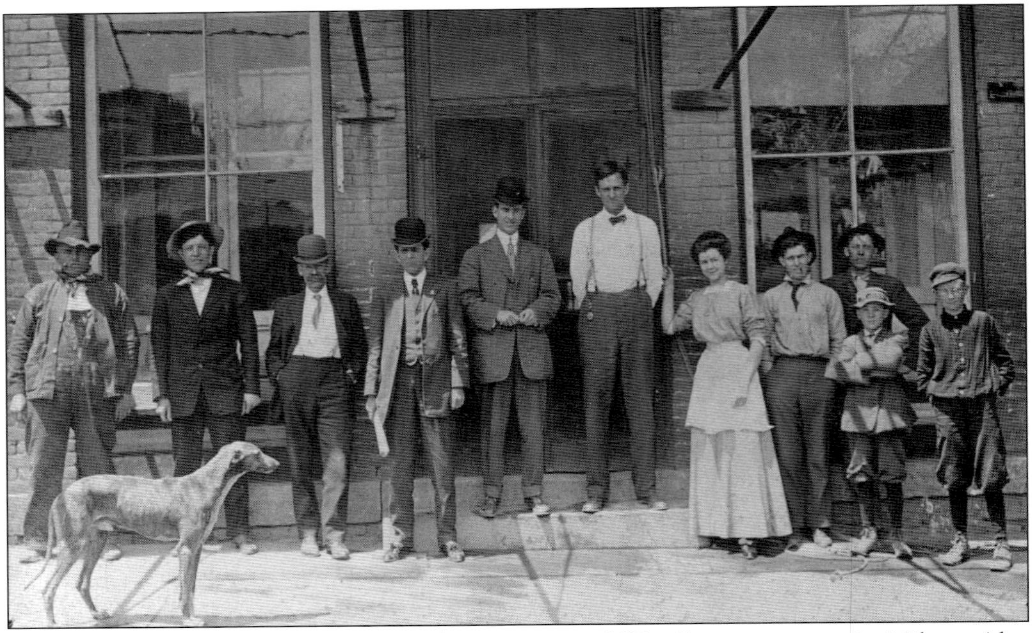

James Wood (center, white shirt) was the proprietor of Wood's grocery store in Milton. Also pictured is employee Nell Taylor and Wood's sons (in knickers), Wilber and Deward Wood. Wilbur Wood later established the Wood Funeral Home, now the Wood-Oakley Funeral Home. Deward Wood became a newspaperman in Indianapolis. (Courtesy of Gary Rowlett.)

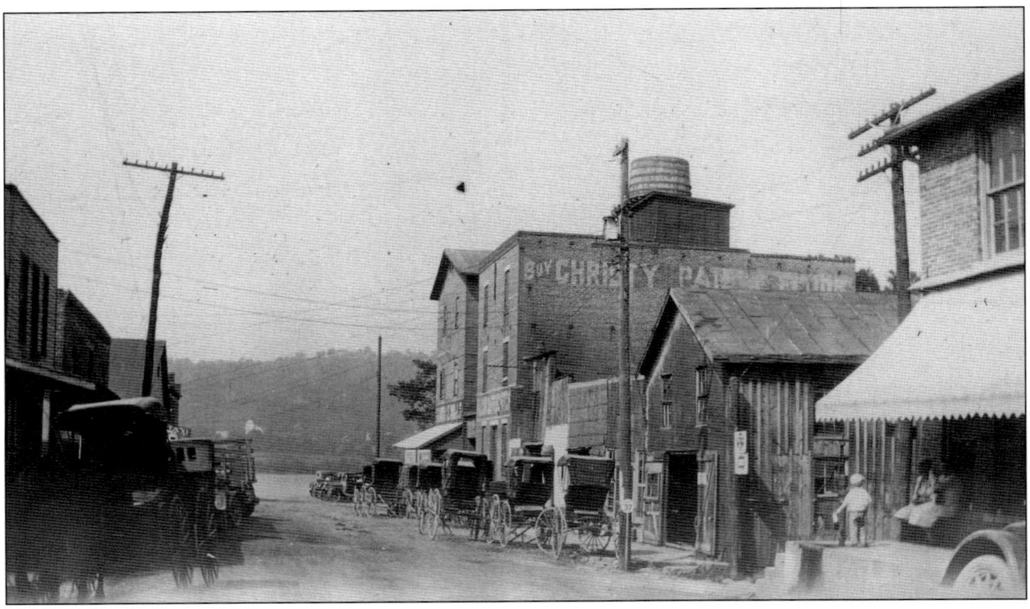

This image shows Ferry Street looking north toward Madison, Indiana. The Christy Flour Mill buildings stood at the far end of the street facing west, surrounded by shops and the Milton post office. Most of the buildings, except for the one at far right, were destroyed by a fire in the 1930s. (Courtesy of Madison Jefferson County Public Library/Lemen Collection.)

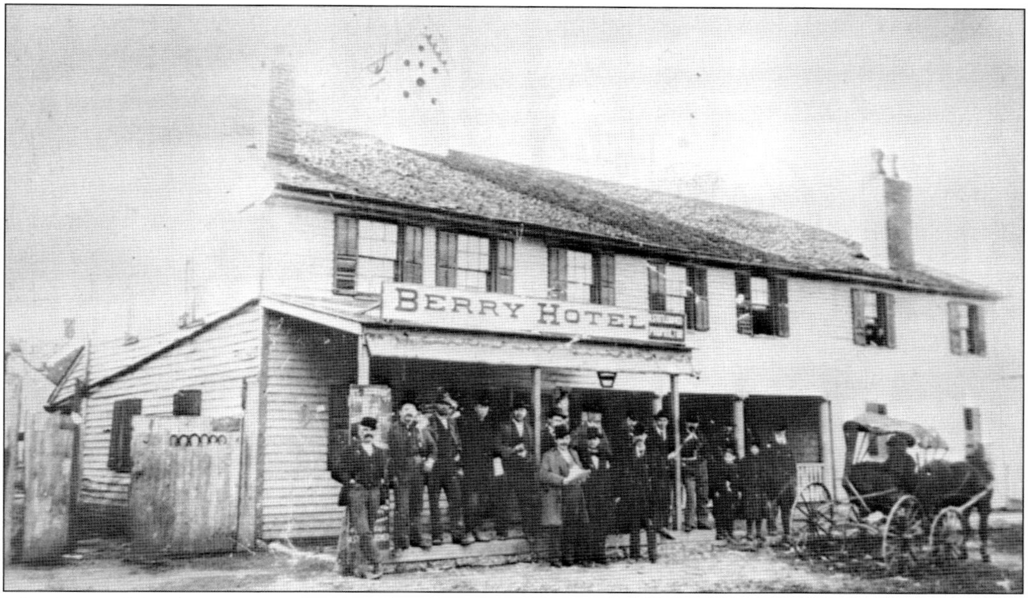

The Berry Hotel was one of many bustling businesses in Milton's early days. In 1837, Trimble County fiscal court set the price of one night of lodging at 12.5¢; the cost of stabling a horse was 50¢ per night, plus 18¢ for feed. Meals were 25¢, and a half pint of whisky was 6.5¢. (Courtesy of Gary Greenwood.)

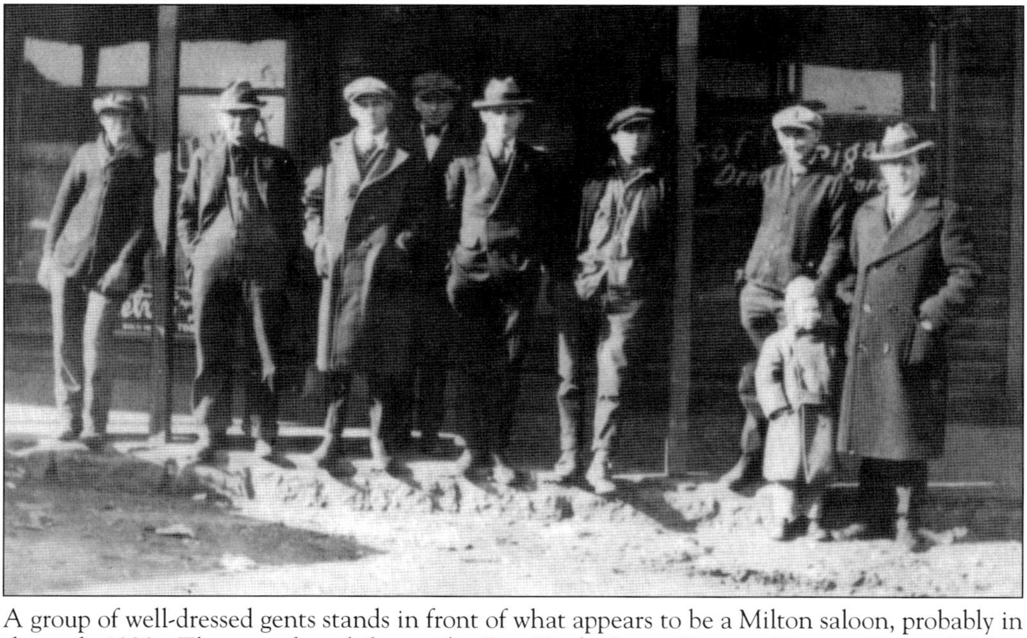

A group of well-dressed gents stands in front of what appears to be a Milton saloon, probably in the early 1930s. They are, from left to right, Roy Neal, Henry Gossom, Truman Bayne, Wilber Wood, Gobel Bayne, and Virgil Bayne. The little boy is Darrell Carder, who would group up to join the US Navy during World War II. (Courtesy of Bill Henderson.)

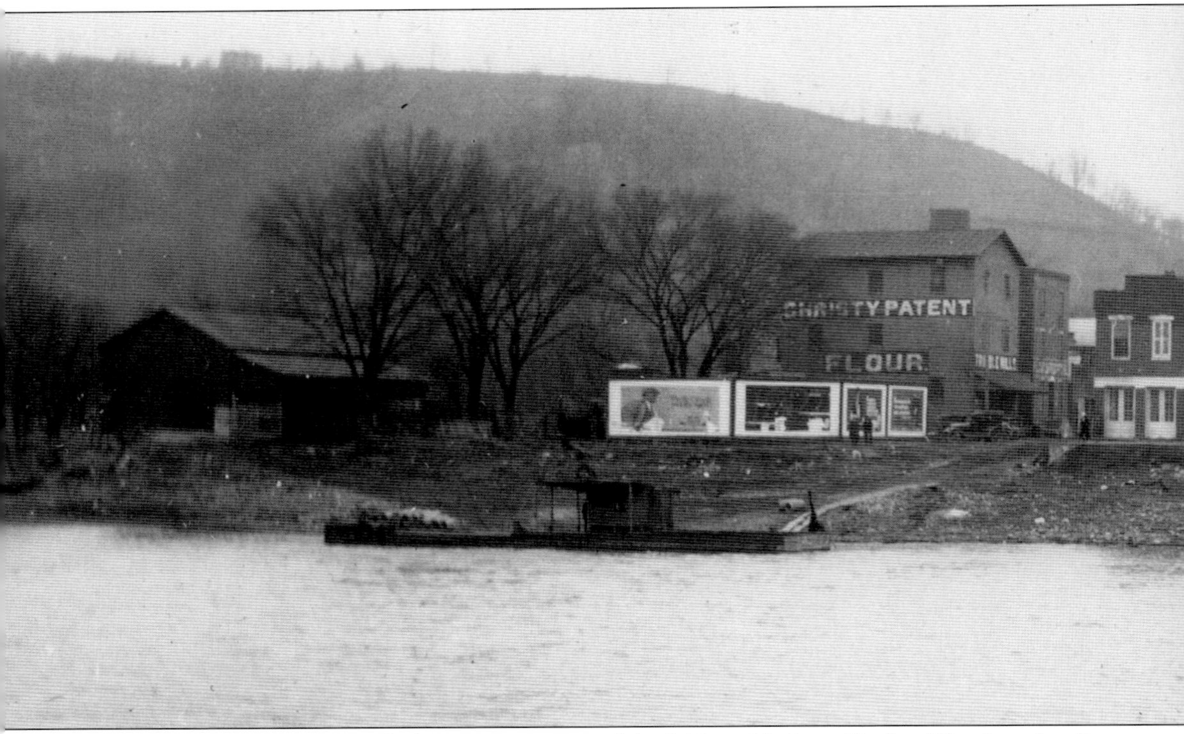

This is Milton's waterfront before construction of the Milton-Madison Bridge. The ferry landing was used for 125 years until the bridge made it obsolete. (Courtesy of Madison Jefferson County

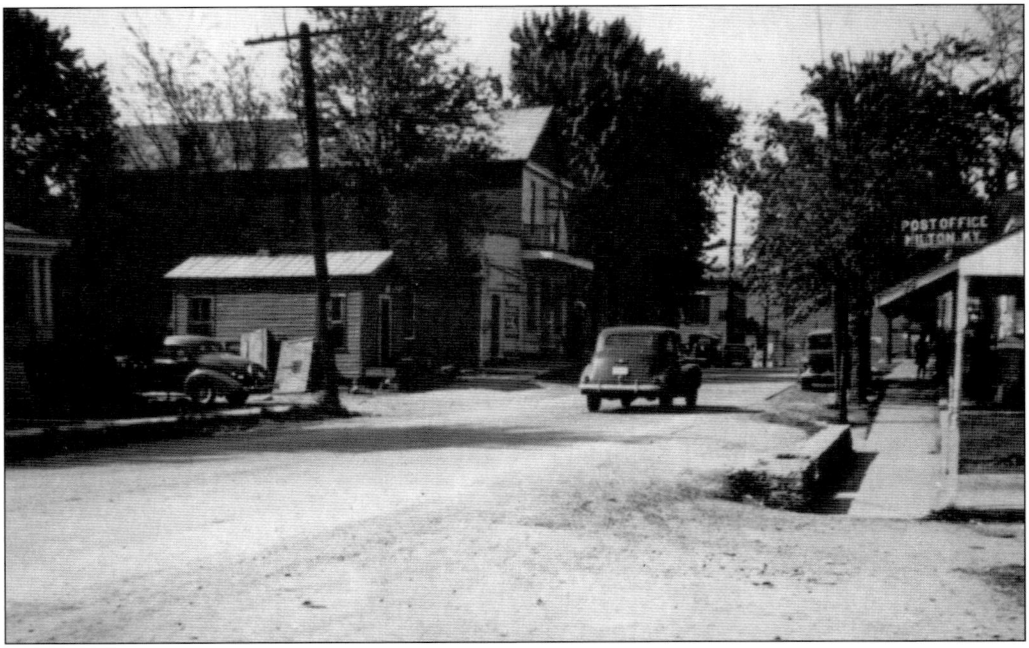

Here is a later view of Milton's Ferry Street, looking north toward the river. Before the bridge, the main route into town was School Hollow Road. In the late 1920s and early 1930s, a new road was built that curved up Milton Hill. This route started out as Kentucky 37 but later became US 421, which connects Milton with Bedford and Campbellsburg. (Courtesy of Darrell Henderson.)

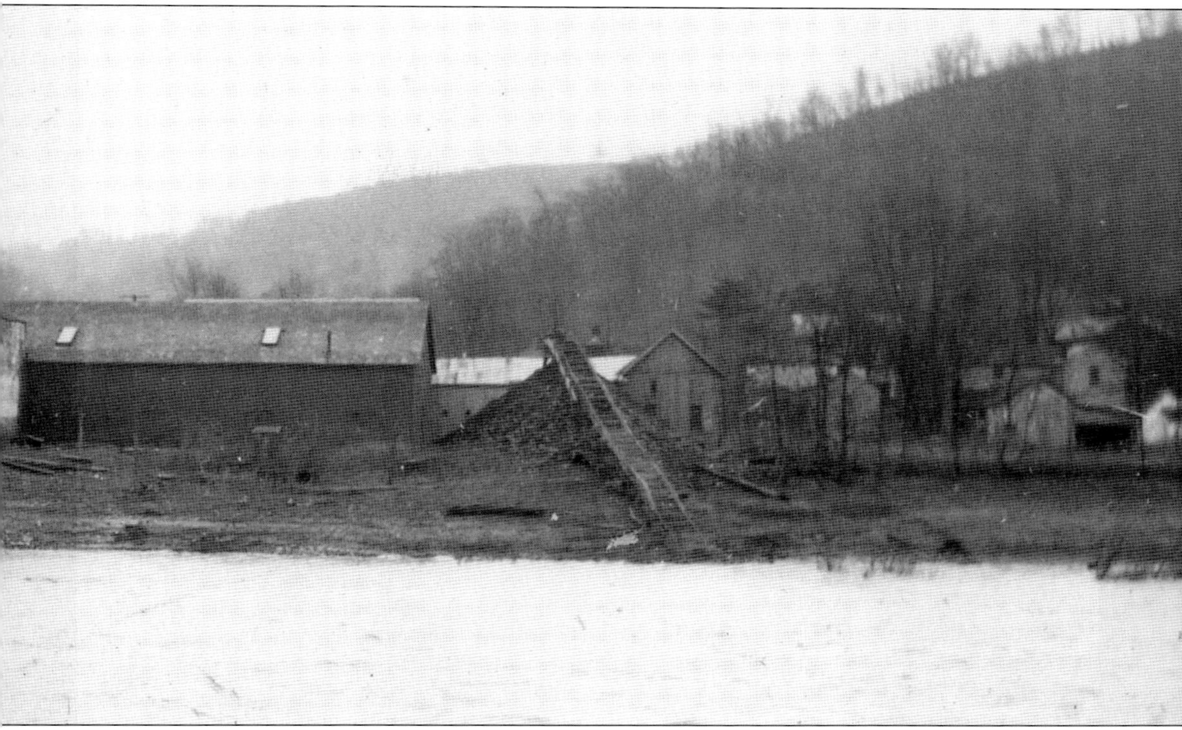

Public Library/Lemen Collection.)

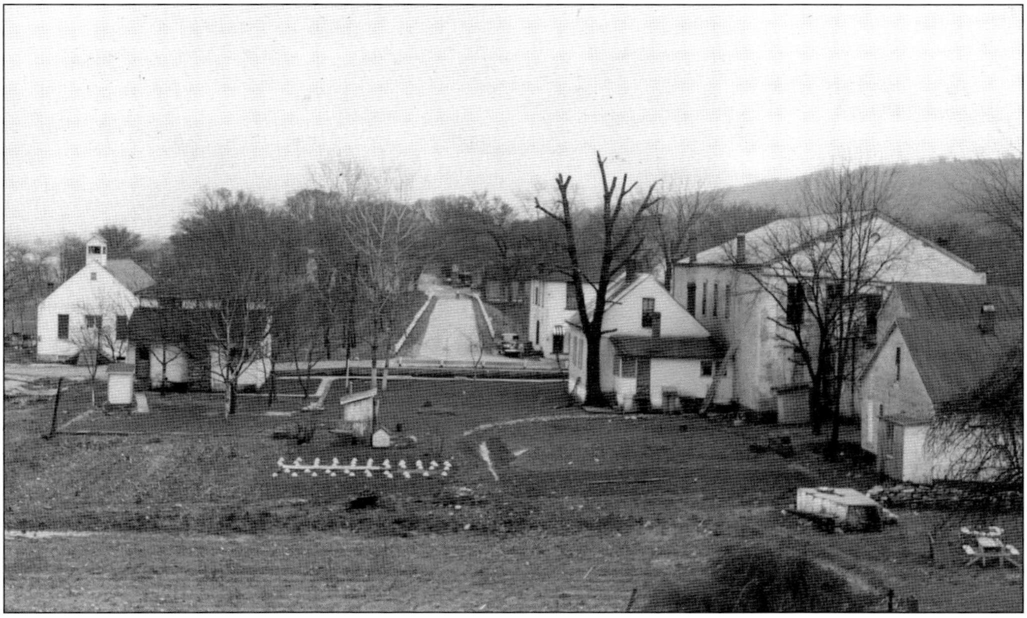

Standing on the approach to the Milton-Madison Bridge and looking west, the new Kentucky Highway 36, which connects Milton and Carrollton, Kentucky, is visible. Previously, that road was closer to the riverbank. To the left, across Ferry Street, is where the Christy Flour Mill once stood. It has been replaced with a church. (Courtesy of Madison Jefferson County Public Library/Lemen Collection.)

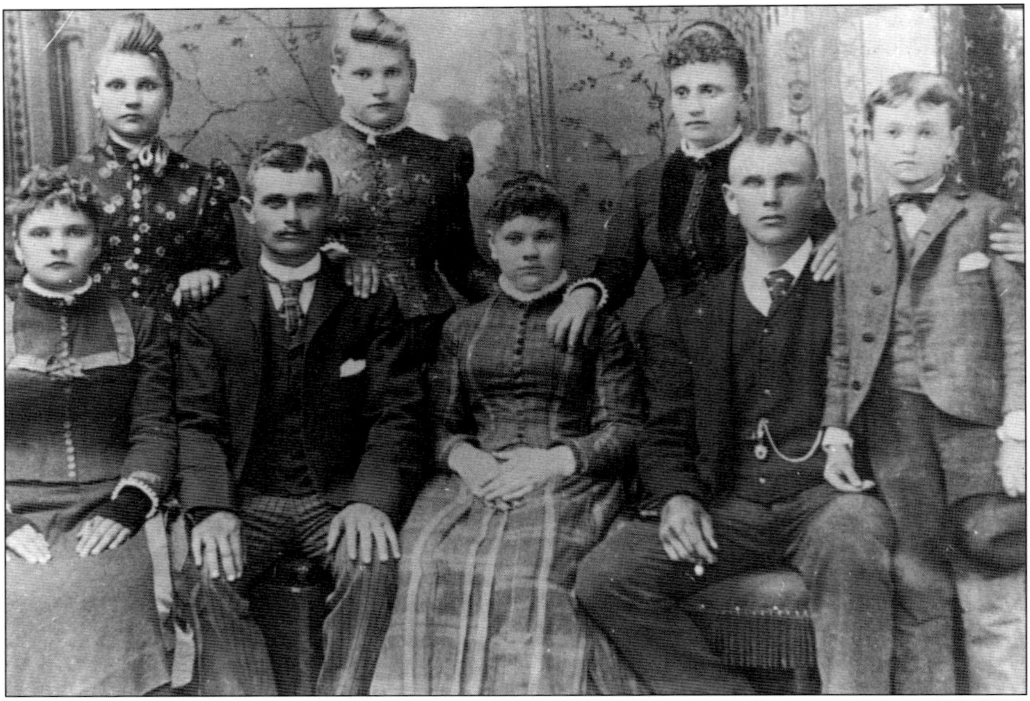

The Burkhardt family came from Germany, where they ran a successful bakery, and settled along the bottom a few miles west of Milton that is still known as Burkhardt's Bottom today. Frederick Burkhardt is the boy at far right. His descendants continue to farm the land where he once grew watermelon and other produce. The land is across the river from Hanover, Indiana. (Courtesy of Betty Burkhardt.)

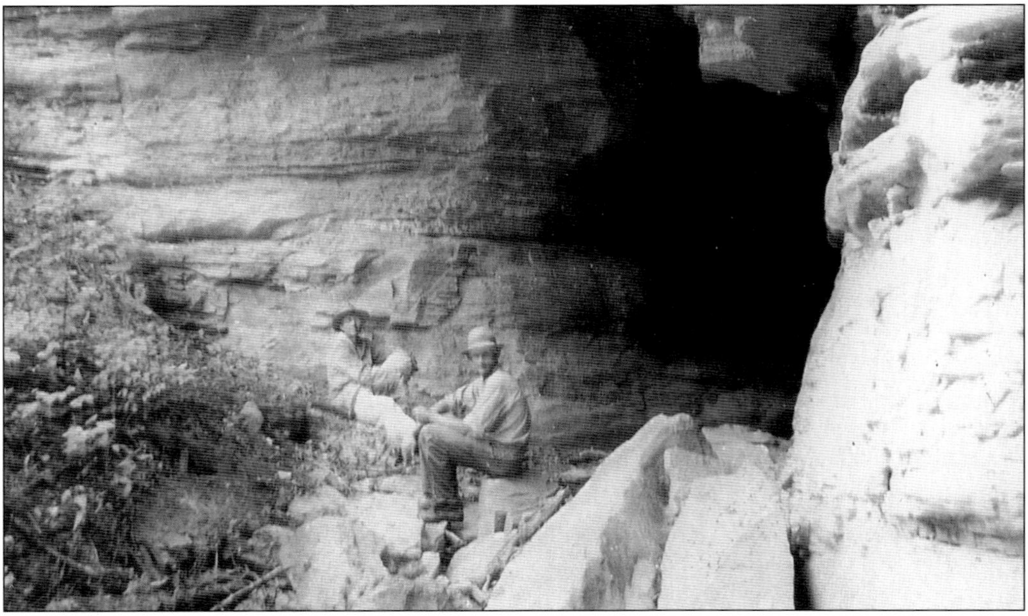

The old Richmond Cave is one of many that can be found in Trimble County overlooking the Ohio River. Bernard Buchanan (left) and Evans Wright pose at the entrance to the cave, which is located on private property. (Courtesy of Ted Taylor.)

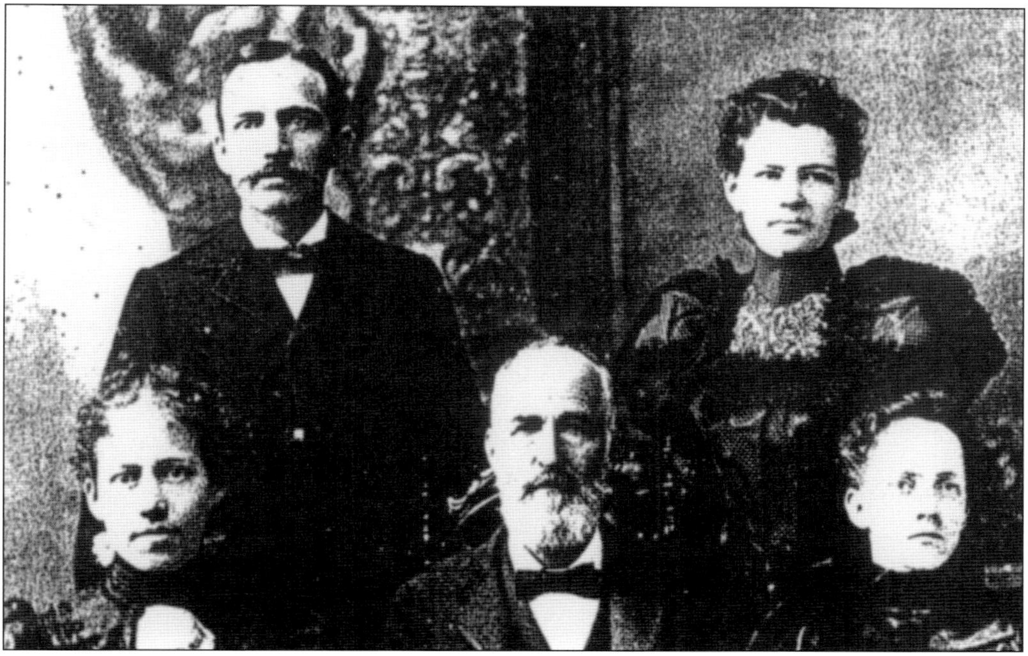

The Fearn family was one of the first to settle Hunter's Bottom, buying 1,000 acres in then Gallatin County, starting just east of Milton. Successful in business, the family built several fine homes along the river, including Richwood Plantation, home of Samuel Fearn Jr. (center) and his family. In 1886, the *Fannie Fearn* (below) succeeded the *Maggie Harper* in the family's packet steamboat business with Capt. S.S. Fearn (standing) at the helm. Competition from other steamboat companies forced the family to liquidate soon after. (Both, courtesy of Diane Perrine Coon.)

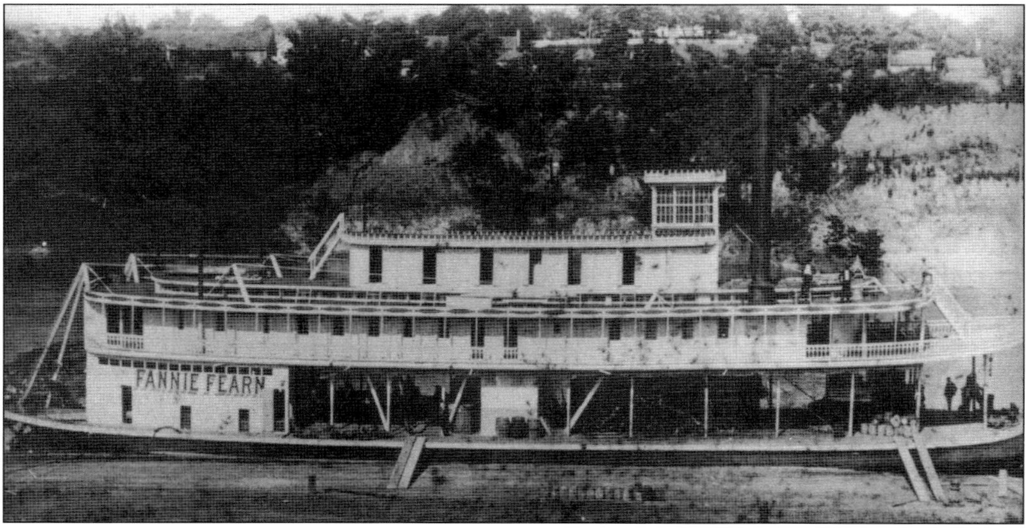

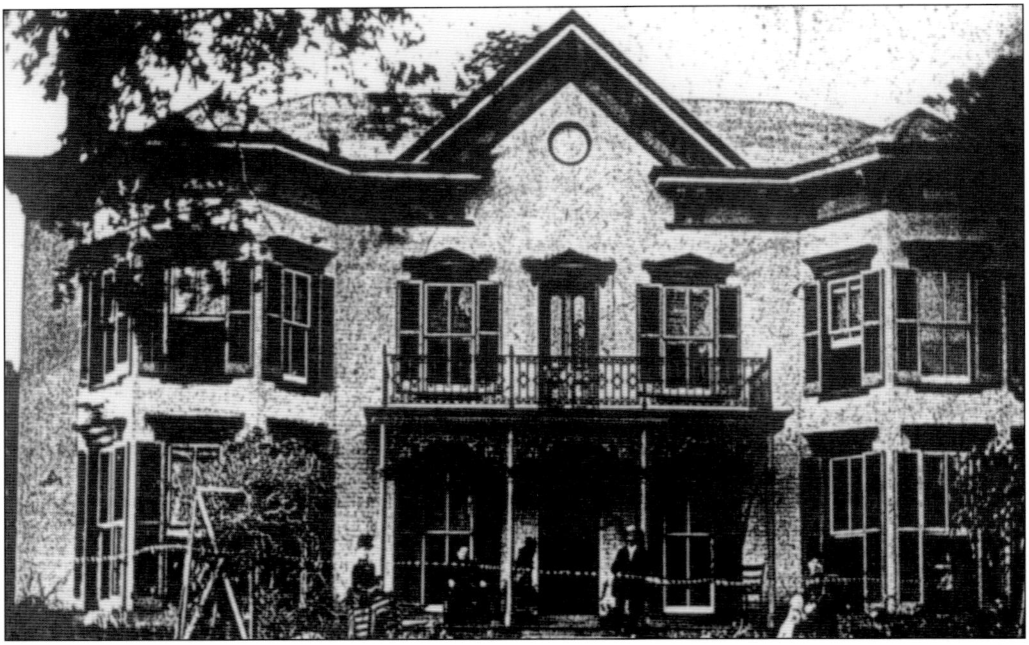

Richwood Plantation features a grand Italianate home built in 1857 by Samuel Fearn III. The plantation got its name from the Snyder family, who owned the Richwood Distillery. In the late 20th century, it was home to the Richwood Riding School for Girls. In 2001, Bill and Susan Hysinger bought the mansion, restored it, and turned it into a bed-and-breakfast and popular wedding venue. (Courtesy of Diane Perrine Coon.)

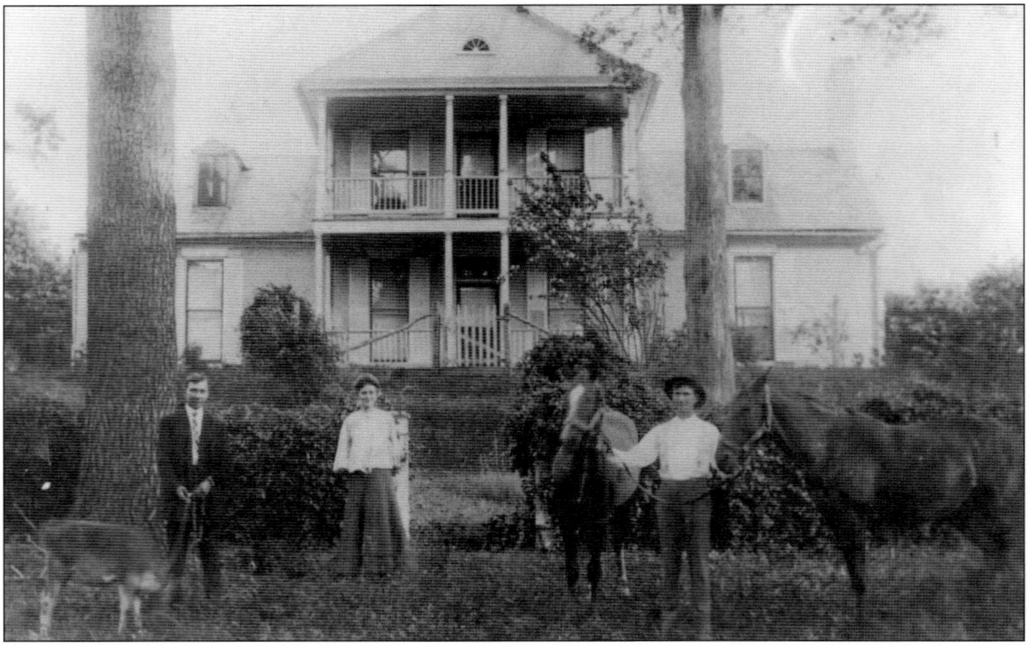

This house, also built by the Fearn family, is located in the portion of Hunter's Bottom that was handed over to Carroll County in 1851. Possibly the oldest house in the bottom, it was purchased from the Fearns by the Thieman family. Pictured are Frank and Flora Thieman with their son, Andrew. (Courtesy of Diane Perrine Coon.)

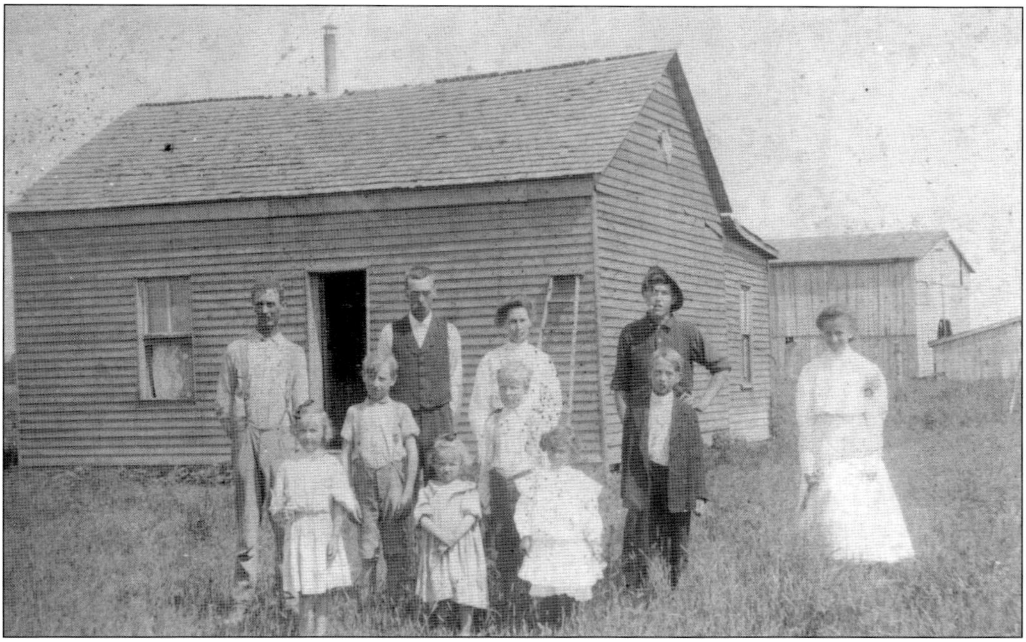

John Edward Hamilton (back row, second from left) stands with his wife, Carrie, and members of the family in front of his home in Trout's Bottom near Milton. Next to him is William Hamilton; next to Carrie are their children, Nolan and Nora. In front from left to right are Mable Wood, Charlie Hamilton, Oather Hamilton, Lula Hamilton, Della Hamilton, and Tullie Handlon. (Courtesy of Mike Gross.)

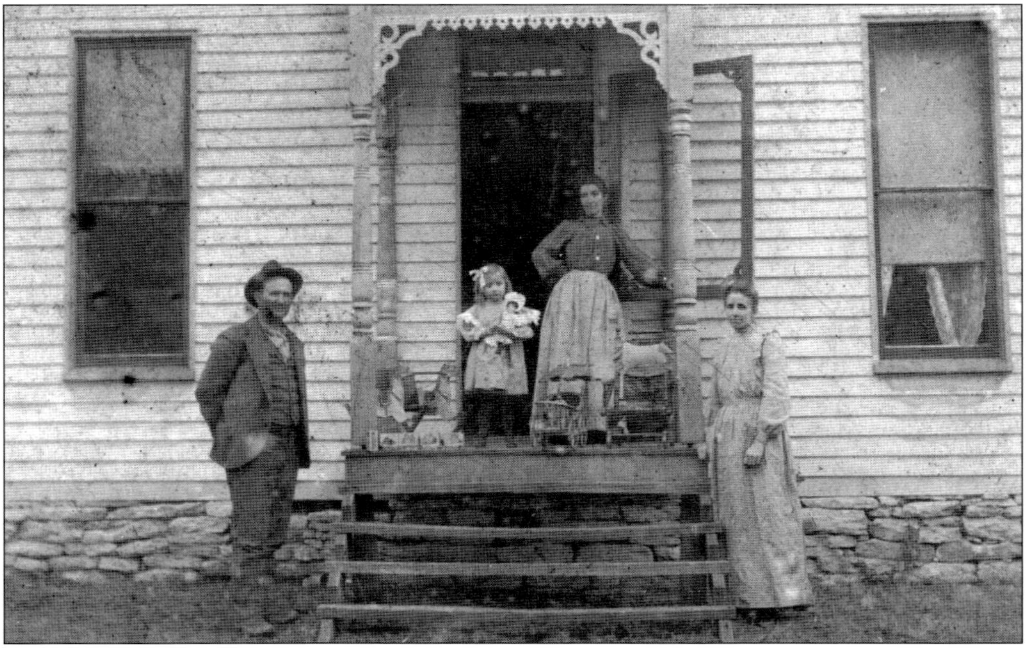

Charles A. Meek and his family lived in the Palmyra district of Trimble County, near the Carroll County line. He married Mary E. Cull. The couple had a daughter, Carrie, who married James Corbet Banks. The other woman may be Charles's sister, Ellie, who married Charles M. Driskell. (Courtesy of Mike Gross.)

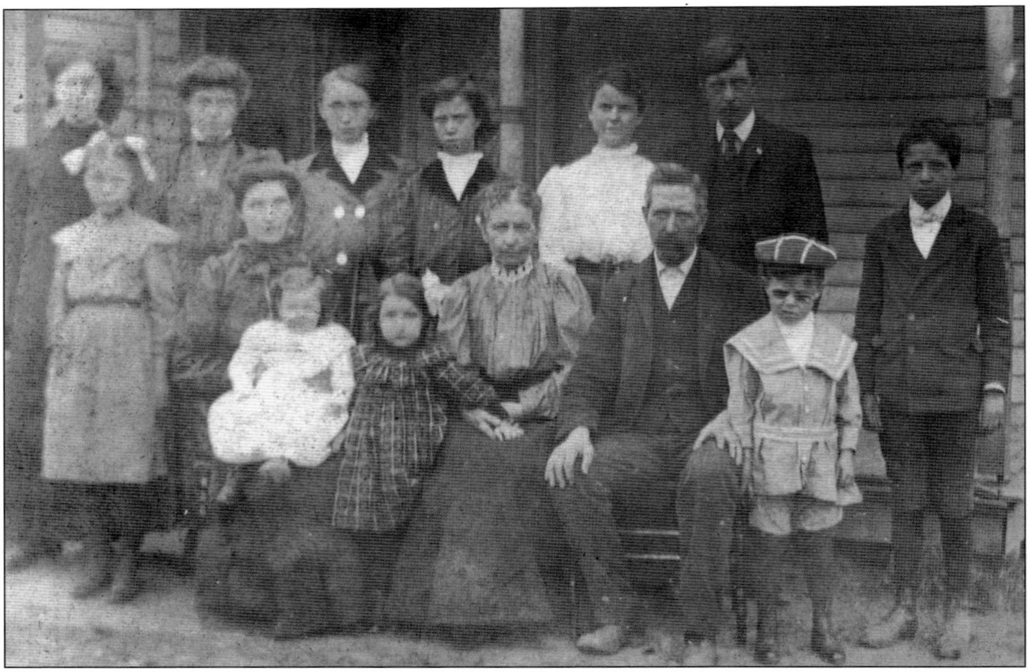

James and Susan Ogden Wood, seated, pose with their family. Son George, standing behind James, was born in the Corn Creek area on the hilltop near Milton. Next to him is his second wife, Ida, who helped him operate a dry good store in Greenwood, Indiana. Among the others pictured are George's children from his first marriage to Bettie Handlon: Roy, William, Clara, Pearl, and Clifford. (Courtesy of Charlene Boatwright Ellis.)

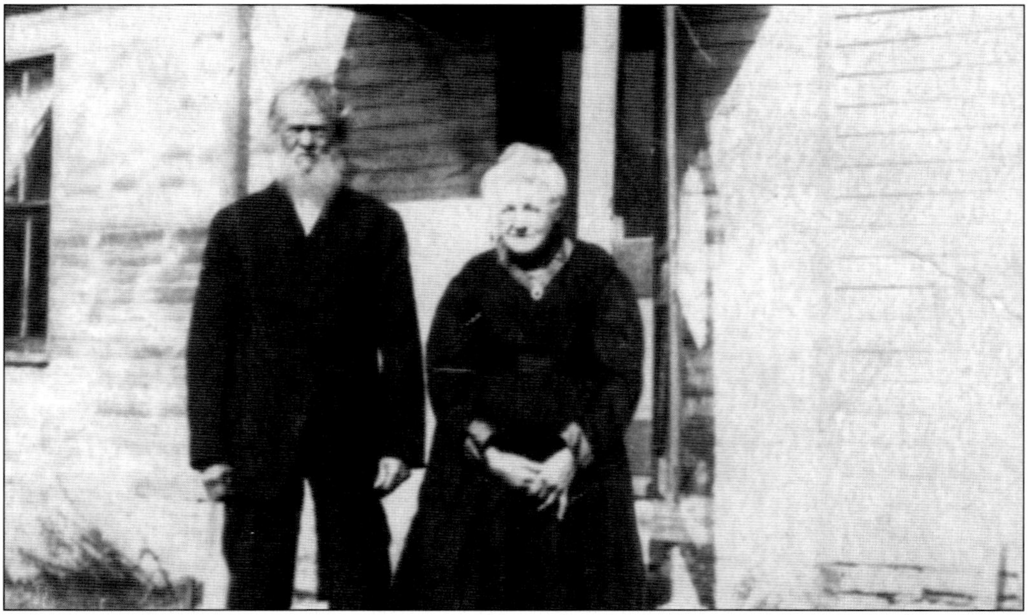

William and Frances (Joyce) Culver pose in front of the home on their farm in the Carmel district near Milton. Born in 1842, Culver served in the 82nd Indiana Volunteer Infantry during the Civil War, fighting in battles at Perryville, Murfreesboro, and Stones River. (Courtesy of Gary Greenwood.)

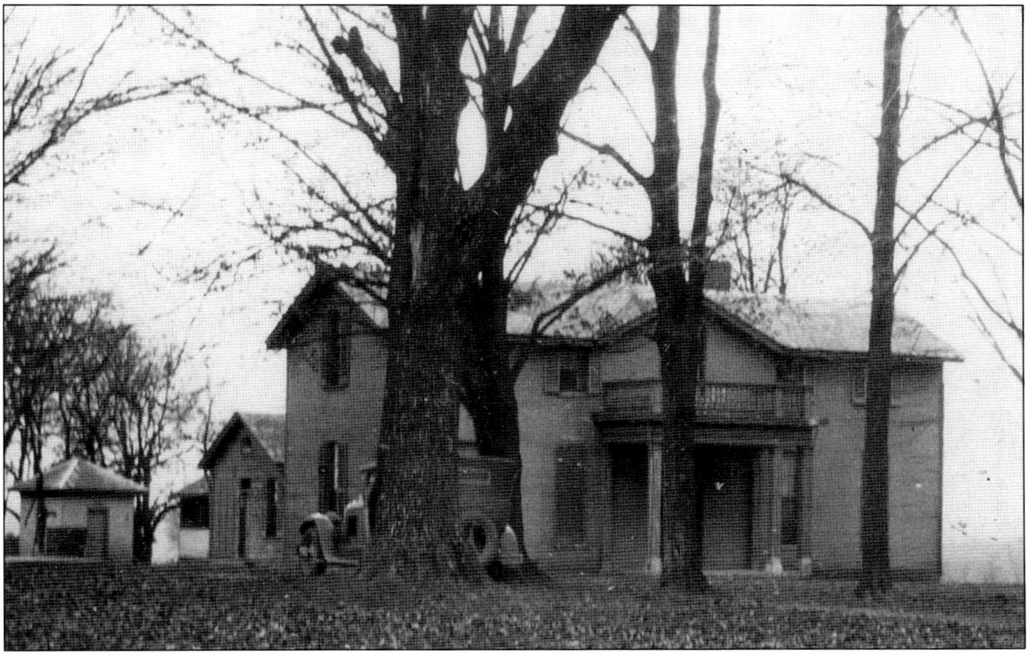

Preston Plantation sits on the northwest side of Trimble County at Watson Landing on the Ohio River. Originally part of John Howard's 8,000-acre tract known as the Norfolk Farm, the 3,300 acres eventually became home to his daughter, Margaret Preston Howard, and later his granddaughter, Mary Wickliffe Preston. While living in Lexington in the 1840s, Mary Wickliffe befriended Delia Webster, an abolitionist who later purchased a farm north of Preston Plantation. Below is Preston Plantation's last remaining slave cabin and, behind it, the overseer's house, still standing in the late 1920s. The photographs were taken by Harry Lemen, a Madison, Indiana, insurance agent and avid photographer whose extensive collection of regional photographs is kept in Madison. (Both, courtesy of Madison Jefferson County Public Library.)

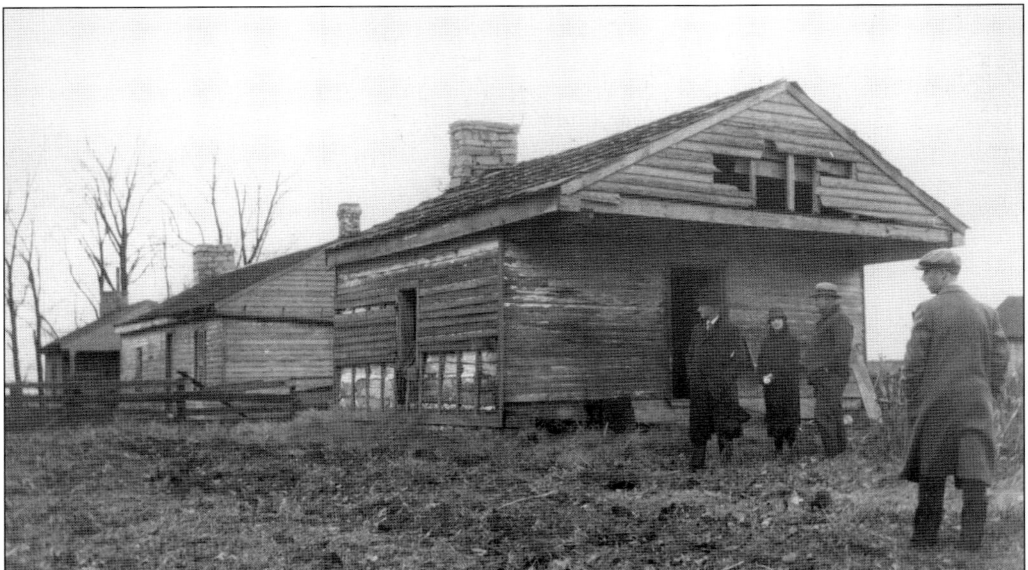

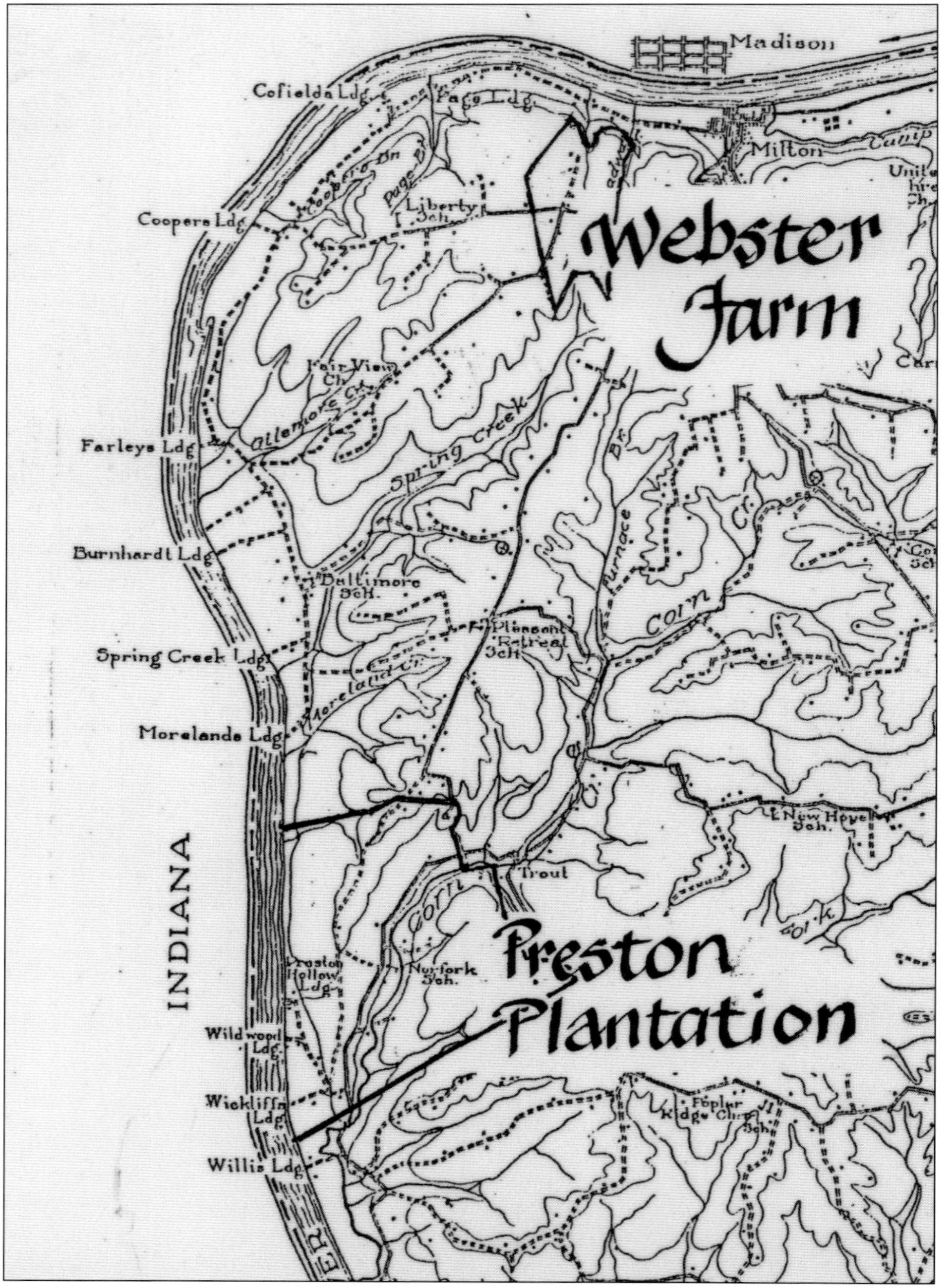

This 1929 geological survey map marks the location of Preston Plantation and, to the north, Preston Place, a portion of the plantation owned at one time by the "Petticoat Abolitionist" Delia Webster, believed by local slaveowners to have aided in the escape of as many as 50 slaves. In a 1938 letter to the *Madison Courier*, Susan Moffett Inglis wrote of her father, John H. Moffett, who owned a farm next to Webster's: "My own family and all in the county hated the name of 'Delia Webster' and looked upon her as a demon, or worse. She was so much despised that any one living on that farm for many years after had no social standing with the majority of the citizens." (Courtesy of Pam Vernard.)

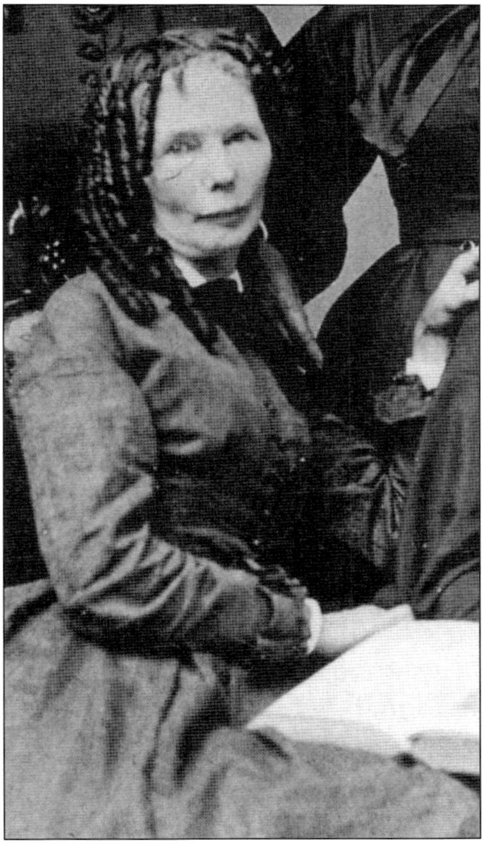

Delia Webster poses with her sisters in the only known portrait of the abolitionist to exist. Webster's plans for her Kentucky farm, which she named Mount Orison, included building a school based on her alma mater, Oberlin College in Ohio. Vandalism and arson by local slaveholders helped bring about the demise of the farm, which she sold in 1869. She died in 1904 in Des Moines, Iowa, where she lived with her niece. (Courtesy of Diane Perrine Coon.)

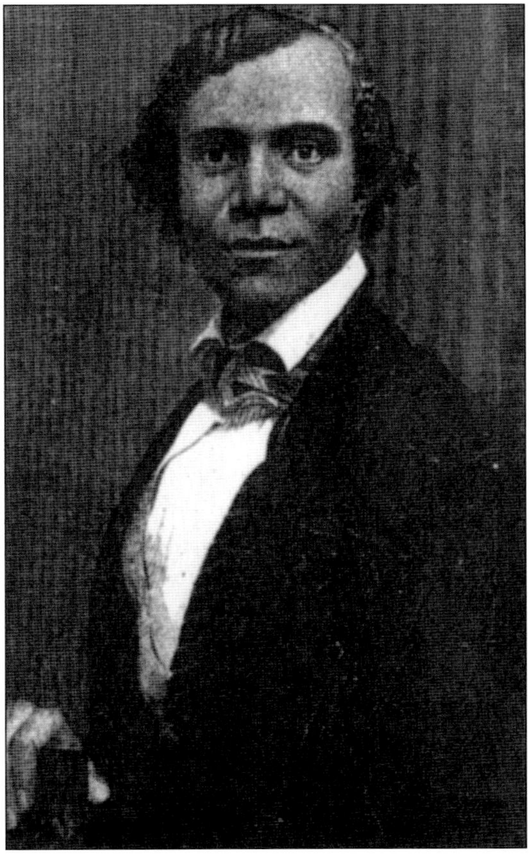

Henry Bibb, born to a slave mother in Shelby County, Kentucky, was sold to William Gatewood, owner of a slave named Malinda, whom Henry later married. Bibb escaped from the Gatewood Plantation, near Bedford, to freedom across the Ohio River. Eventually, he moved to Ontario, Canada, where he was editor of an abolitionist newspaper and started a community for other escaped slaves. (Courtesy of Trimble County Fiscal Court.)

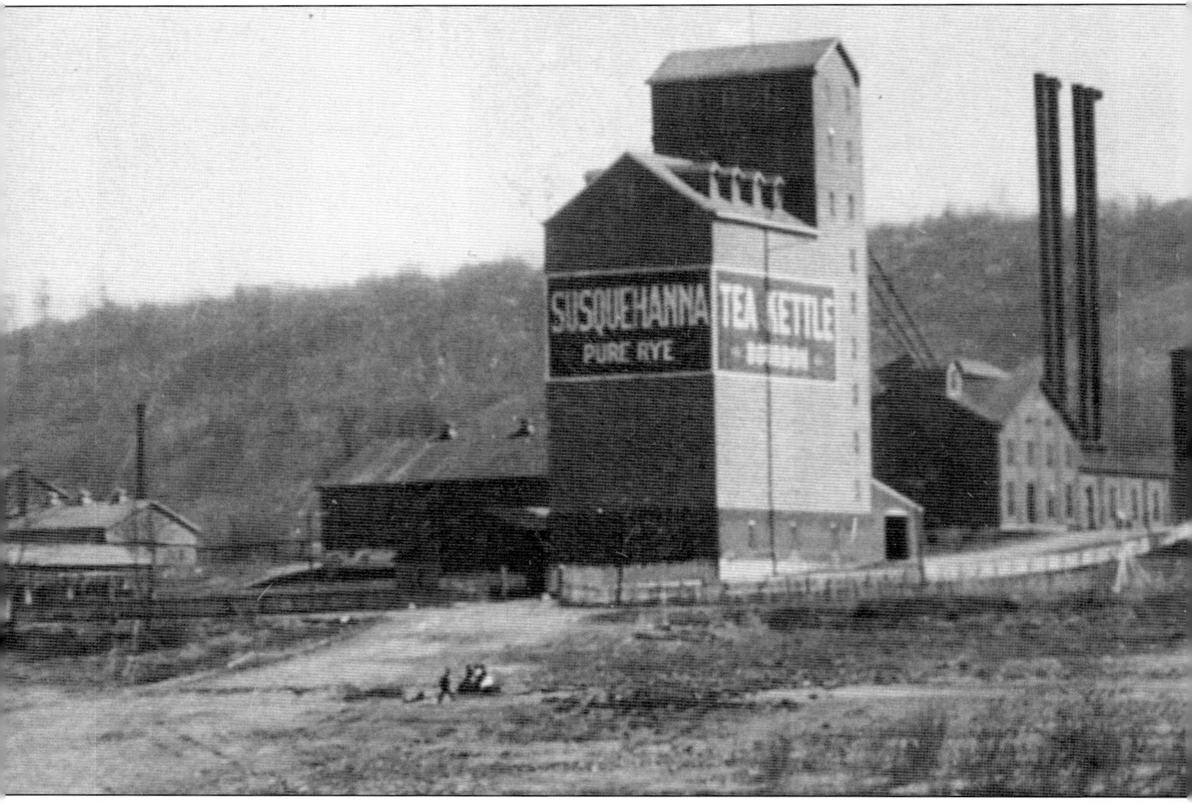

The Richwood Distillery produced Susquehana Rye and Tea Kettle brand bourbon on the banks of the Ohio River, just east of the city limits of Milton. Founded in 1840 by James Snyder, the distillery was a large operation that survived fires and Prohibition but saw its demise after the

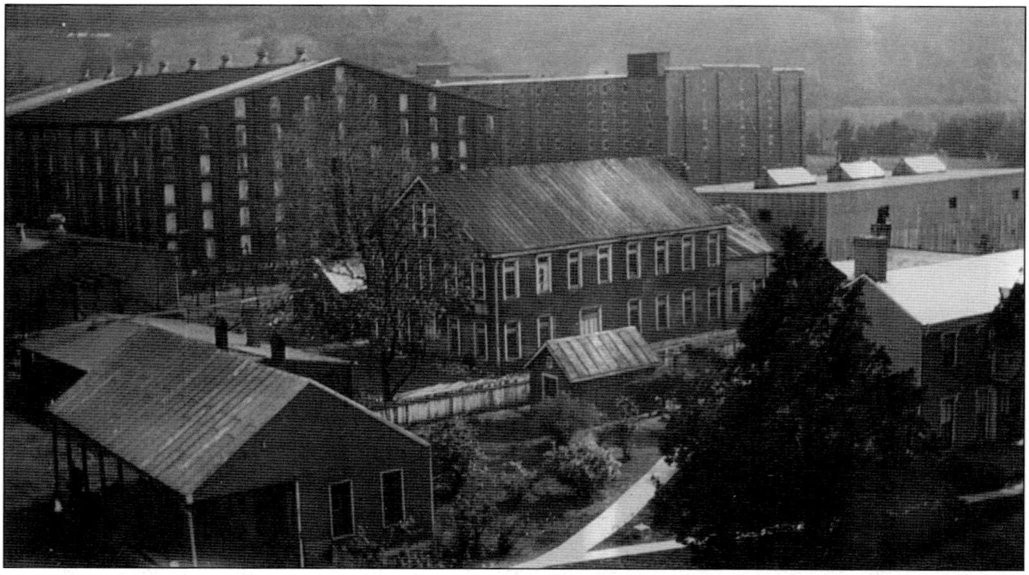

The house on the right still stands, but all the other buildings have long since disappeared. An apartment complex and other homes now stand on the site along Richwood Road, a dead-end lane named for the distillery and neighboring plantation. (Courtesy of Mac and Linda Gordon.)

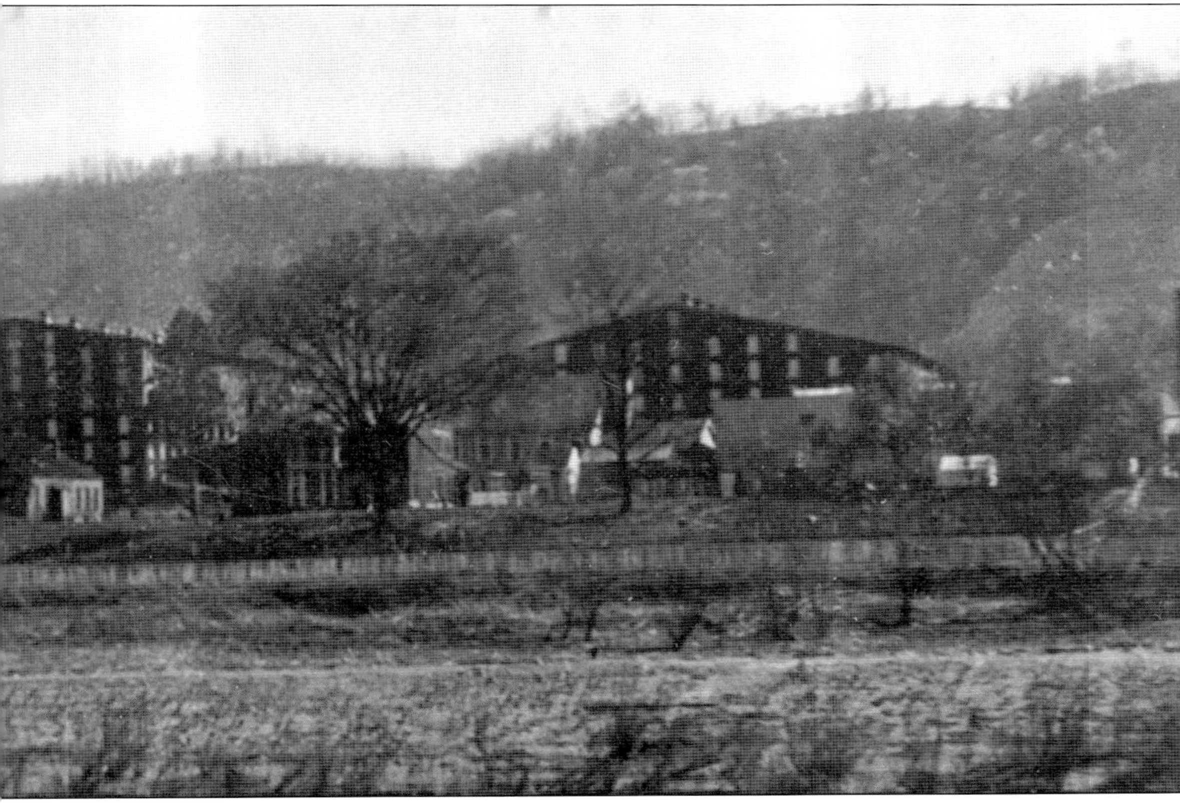

1937 flood. Only a portion of the original building remains and has been incorporated into a small apartment complex. (Courtesy of Mac and Linda Gordon.)

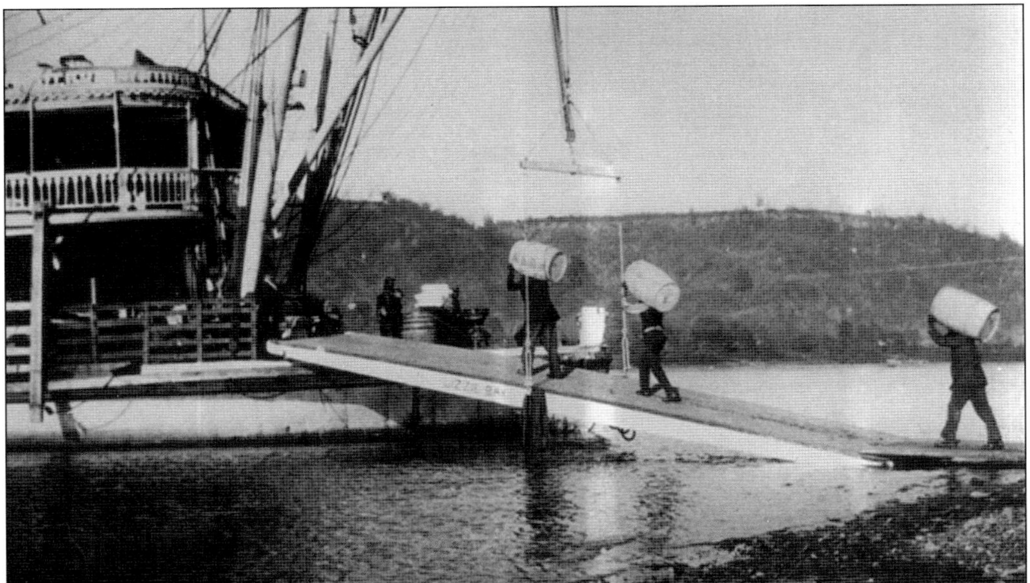

Workmen load a steamboat with barrels of whiskey produced at the Richwood Distillery outside Milton. (Courtesy of Mac and Linda Gordon.)

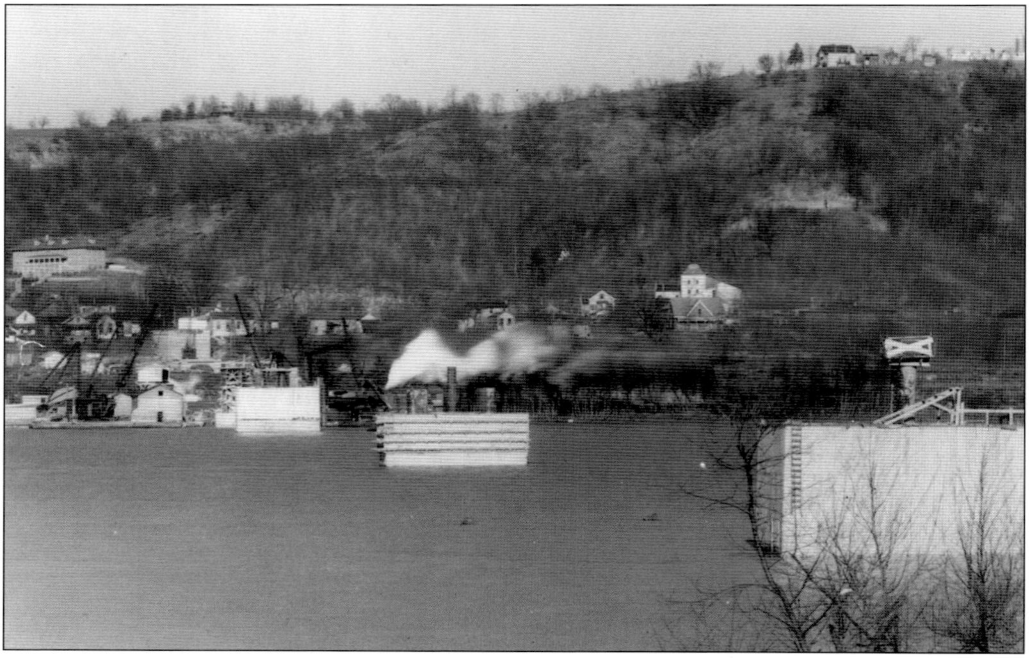

Caissons surround the construction of concrete piers for the Milton-Madison Bridge, which was completed in December 1929. The original steel-truss bridge was built for $1 million by J.G. White Engineering Corp. and operated by the National Toll Bridge Company. Until 1949, pedestrians paid 5¢ to cross the bridge and vehicles were charged 45¢. Early photographs of the Milton-Madison Bridge appear in postcards like the one below. An iconic landmark, it is the only Ohio River span between Markland Dam, 26 miles upriver, and Louisville, Kentucky, 42 miles downriver. After the original 20-foot-wide bridge was demolished and the piers reinforced, the main truss of the new 40-foot-wide span, built on temporary piers, was slid into place in 2014 using hydraulic jacks. It is the longest truss in the world to have been moved into place using this process. (Above, courtesy of Darrell Henderson; below, author's collection.)

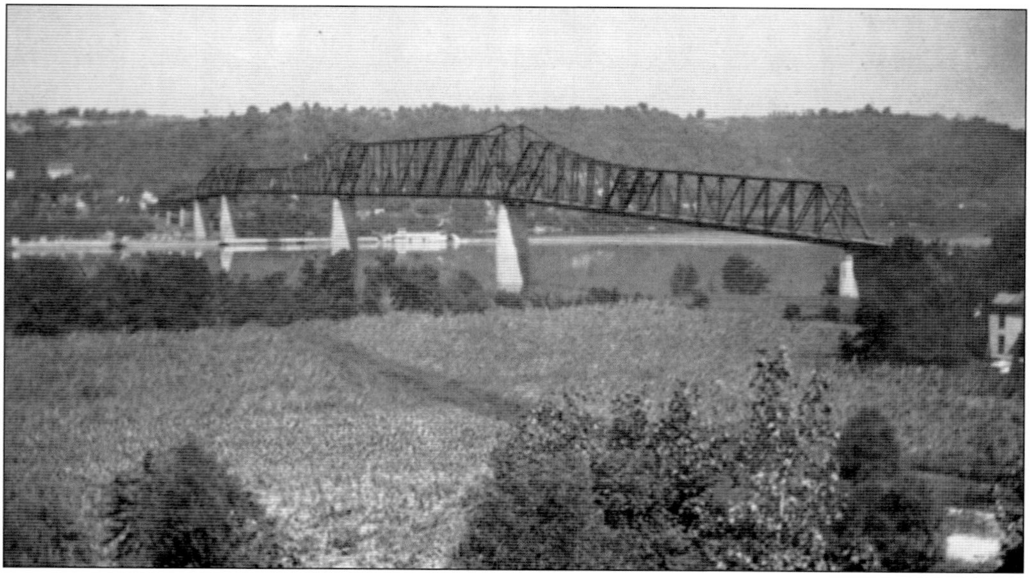

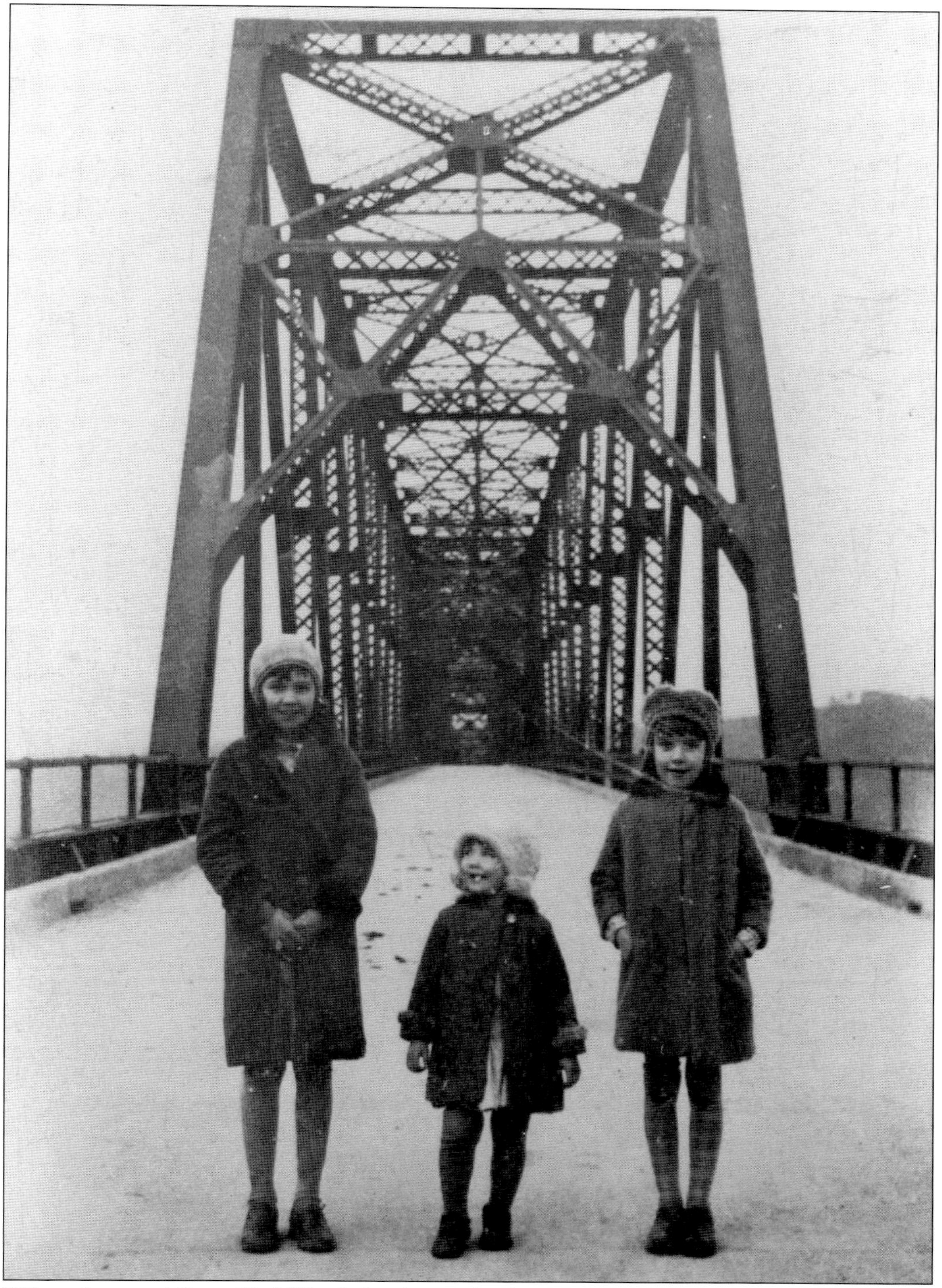

Wilma, Jean, and Doris "Sis" Wood, daughters of Milton undertaker Wilbur Wood, stand on the Milton side of the bridge shortly after it was completed. Wilma, who later married Vincent Oakley, still operates the Wood-Oakley Funeral Home. Their son, Donald "Donnie" Oakley, operated the funeral home and was Trimble County's deputy coroner. He was Milton's mayor for 12 years until his death at age 53 in 2009. (Courtesy of Gary Rowlett.)

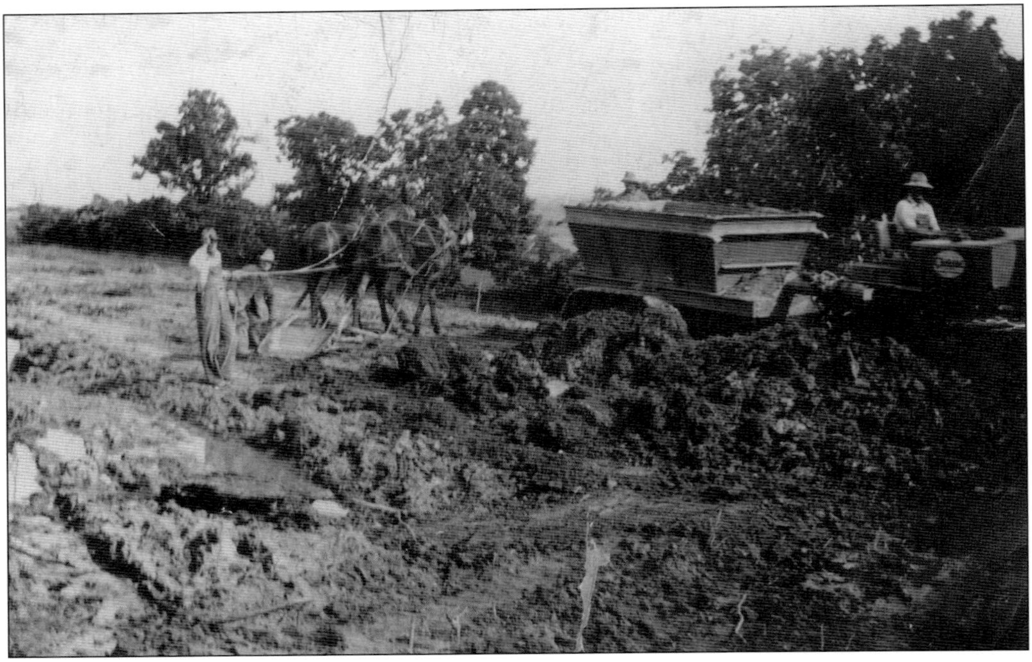

Above, work crews clear land to build Kentucky Highway 37, now US 421, which runs south from Milton to Bedford and then on to Campbellsburg in Henry County. Below, a steam shovel is used to remove a portion of Milton Hill for the new highway, which takes travelers across the Milton-Madison Bridge into Indiana. (Above, courtesy of Gary Rowlett; below, courtesy of Madison Jefferson Public Library.)

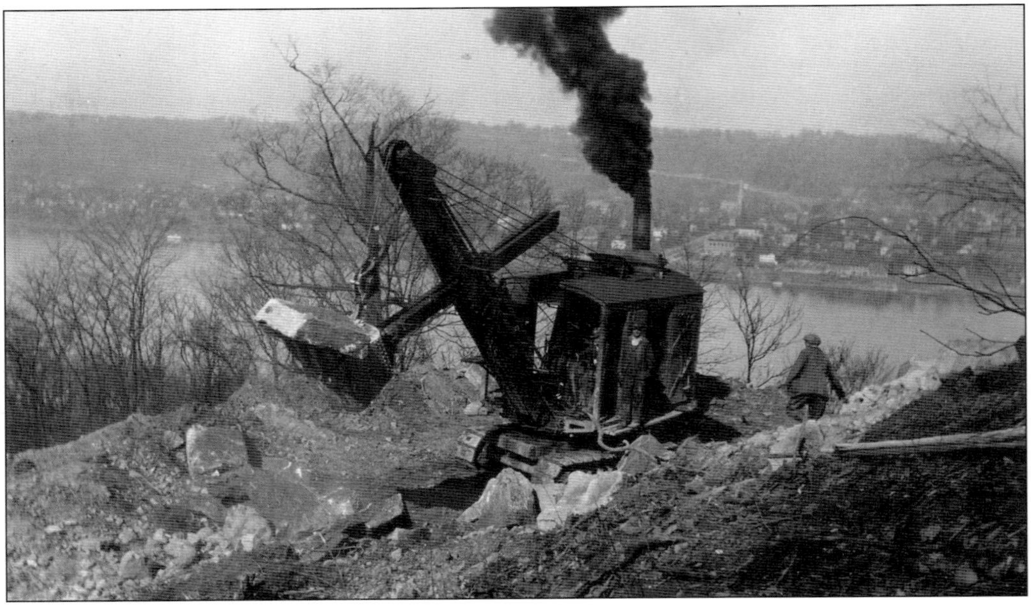

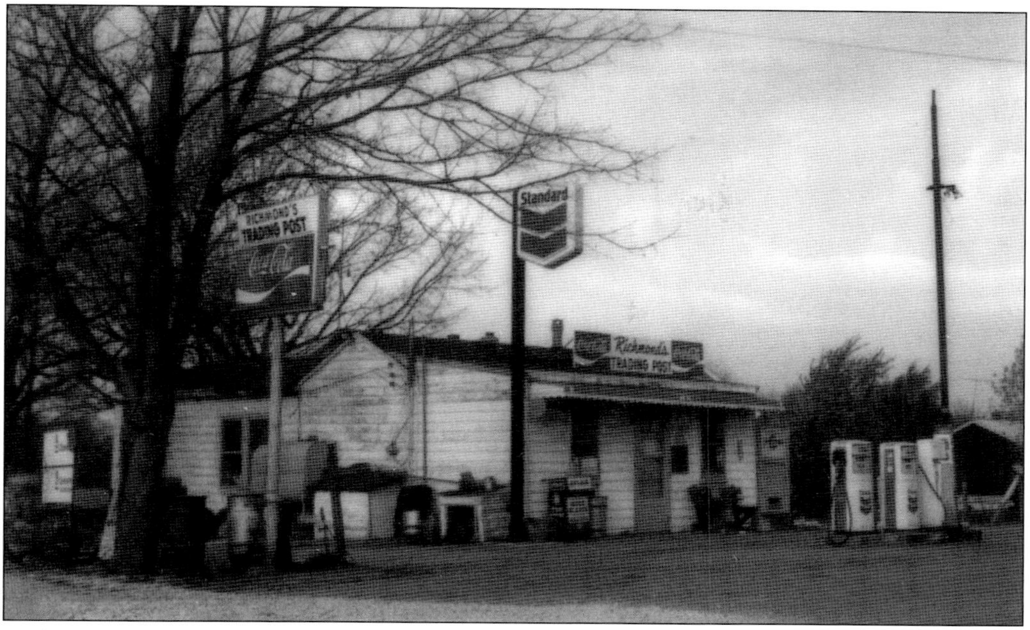

Richwood's Trading Post, a grocery store and gas station, was a popular stop for travelers along the new highway halfway between Milton and Bedford. The building still remains, but the business relocated next door. (Courtesy of Gary Greenwood.)

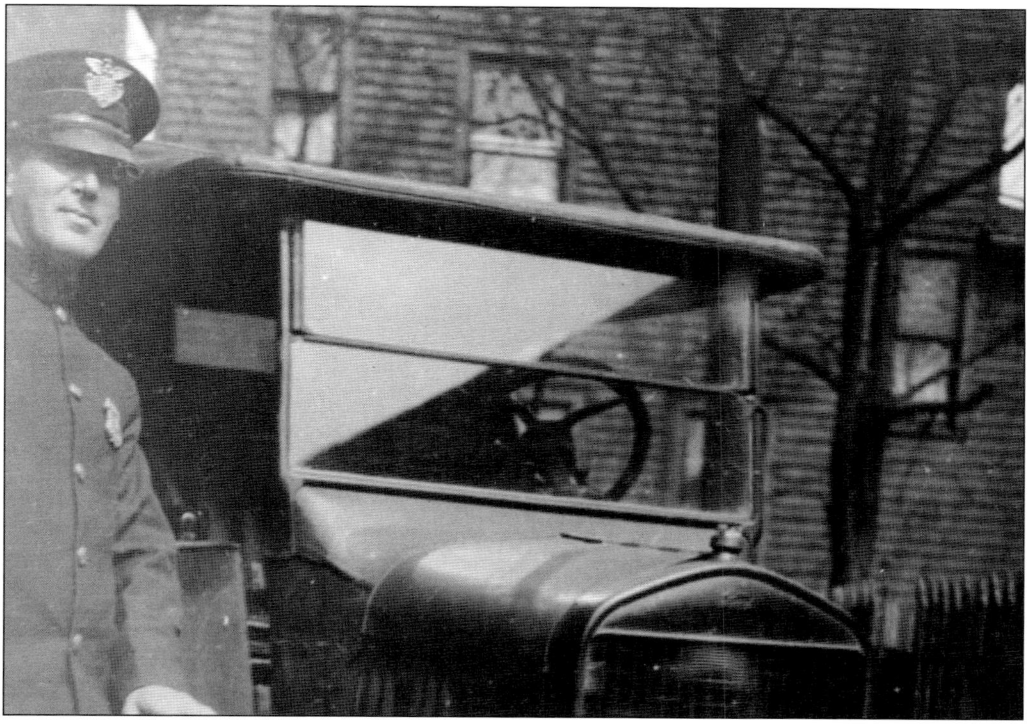

Virgil Bayne, a Milton native, poses with his Cleveland Police Department vehicle in the 1930s. He and his partner were killed in a filling station robbery on December 18, 1937. He is buried in Moffett Cemetery and his grave is marked by a memorial placed by the Cleveland Police Department. (Courtesy of Bill Henderson.)

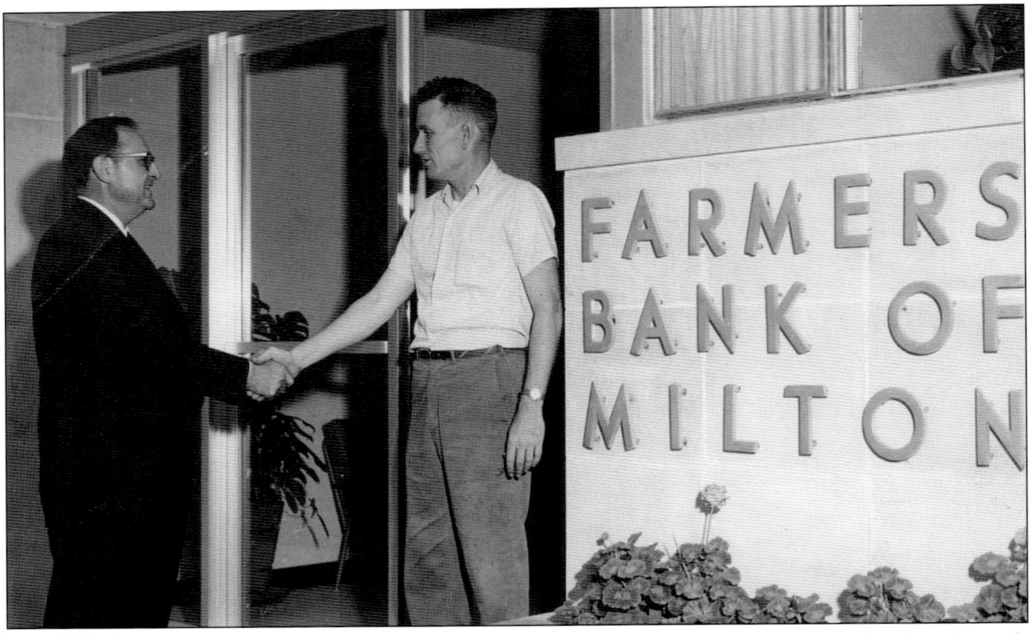

Harry Lee Waterfield, an unsuccessful candidate for governor in the 1950s, shakes hands with N.W. Henderson in this public relations photograph taken while Waterfield was campaigning. Henderson was working at the bank that evening with his son, Bill, who earned money for college as the bank's custodian. (Courtesy of Bill Henderson.)

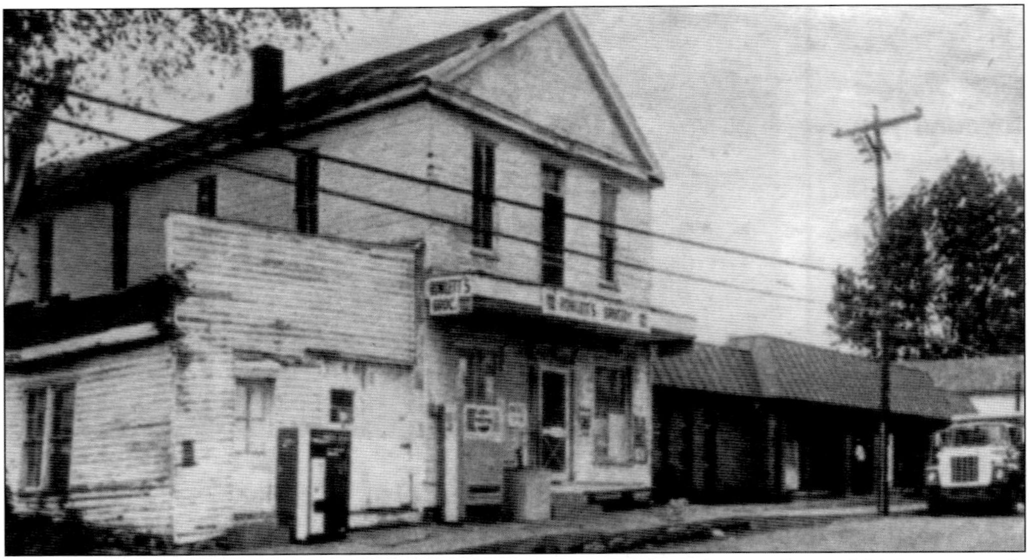

Rowlett's Grocery was one of many thriving businesses in Milton during the mid-20th century. It was located next to the modern-looking Farmers Bank building on Ferry Street. Both buildings to the left are gone, replaced by a parking lot for the bank, a private residence, and a car wash. (Courtesy of Diane Perrine Coon.)

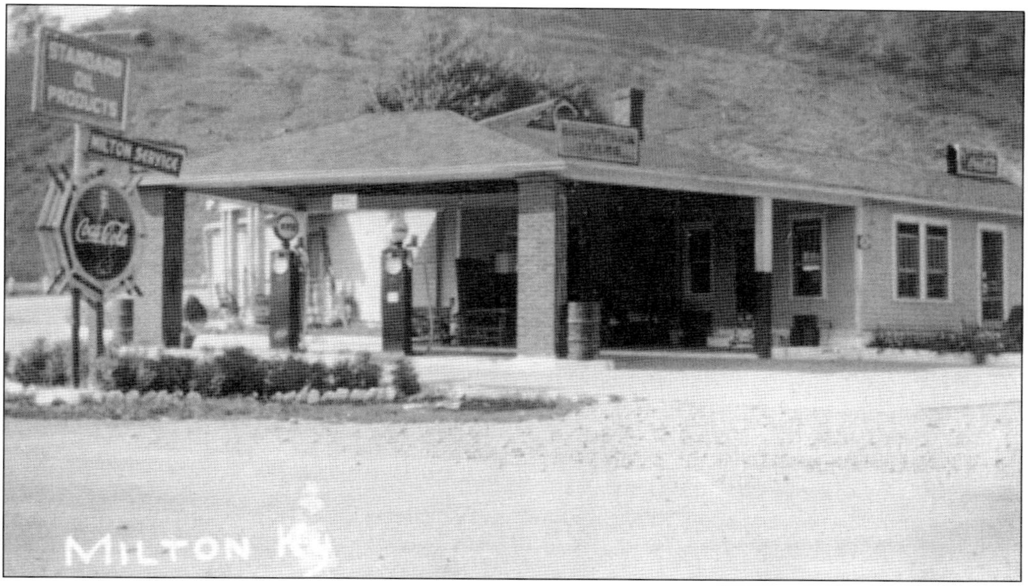

The U-Turn Inn was a service station selling Standard Oil products and Goodyear tires at the corner of Ferry Street and US 421, at the base of Milton Hill. The site is now the location of Milton's Dairy Queen. (Courtesy of Darrell Henderson.)

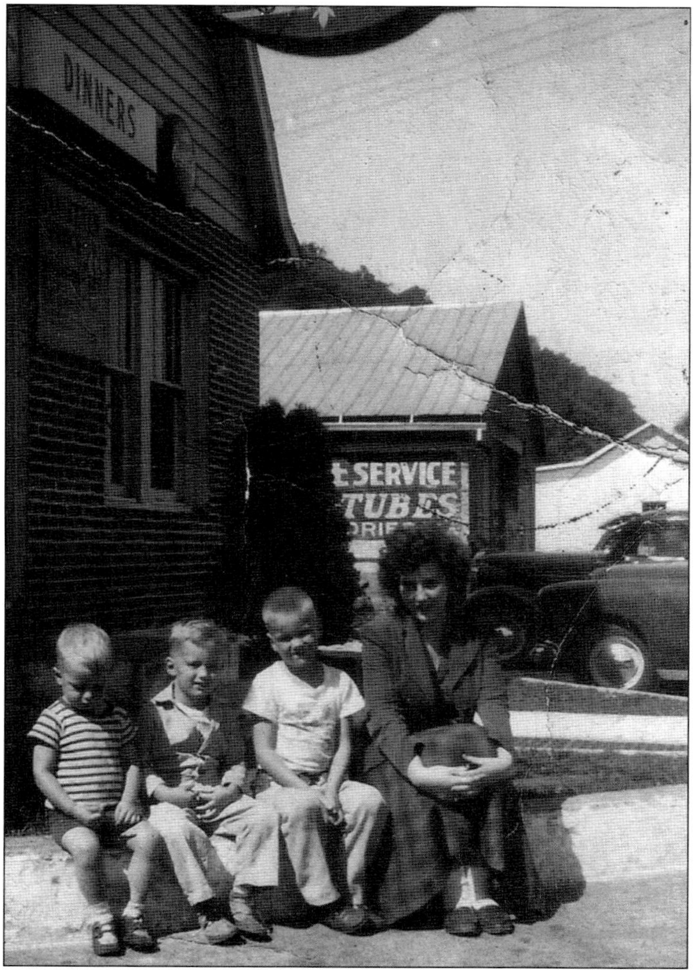

The Henderson family, owners of the U-Turn Inn, sit out front of the establishment on a sunny day. (Courtesy of Darrell Henderson.)

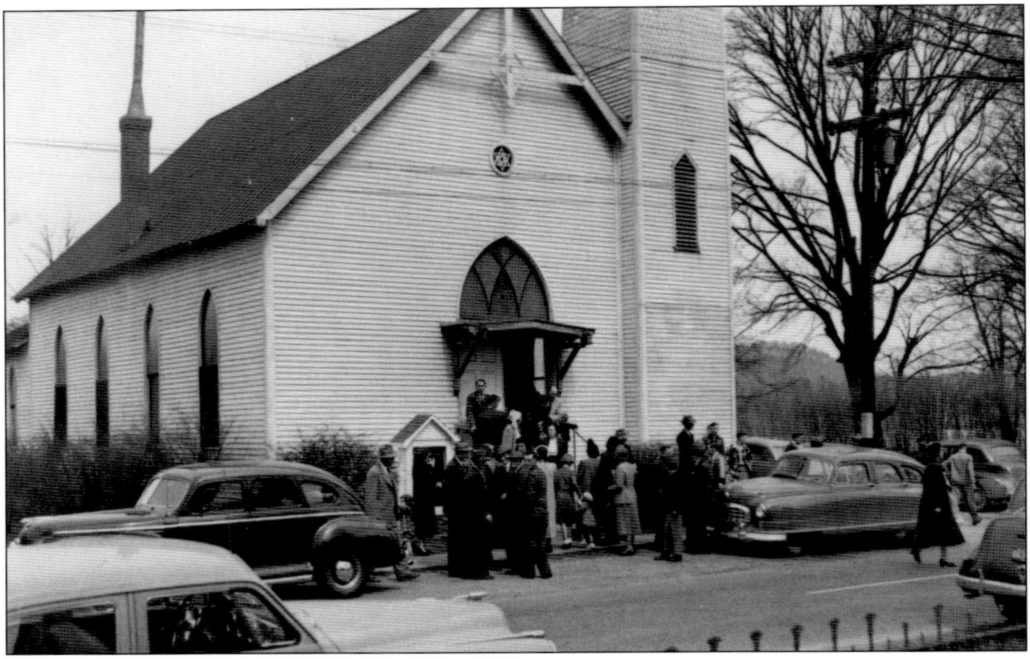

Parishioners leave the United Methodist Church, once located in downtown Milton across from what is now Milton Park. Below, church officials burn the mortgage to the building, which was eventually destroyed by floodwaters. A new church was built at the top of Milton Hill, across from Peck Pike. (Both, Courtesy of Mike Gross.)

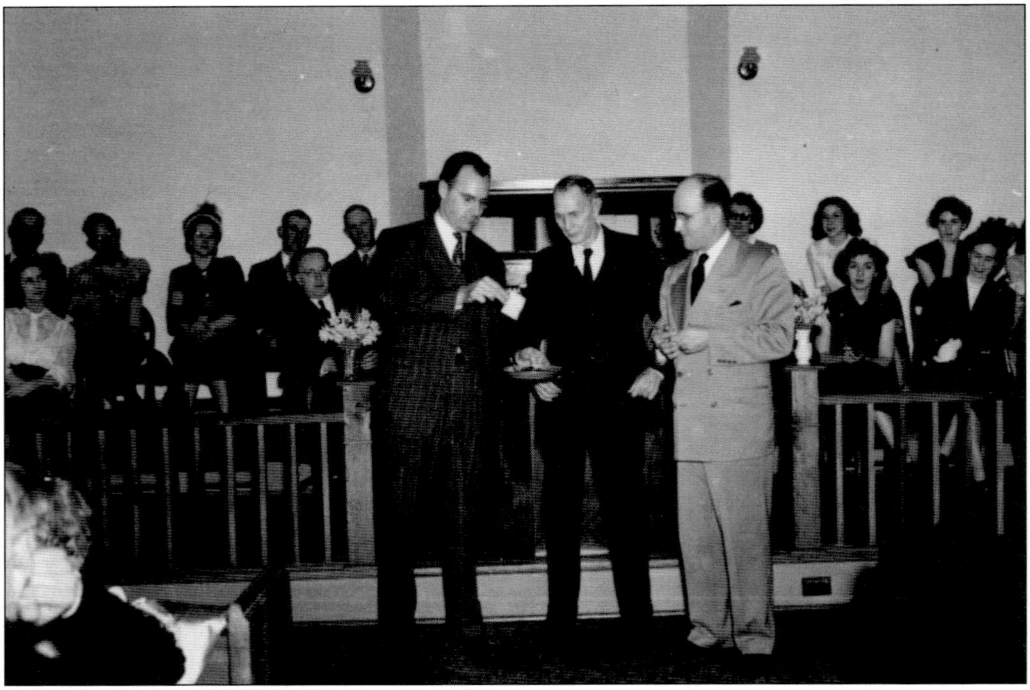

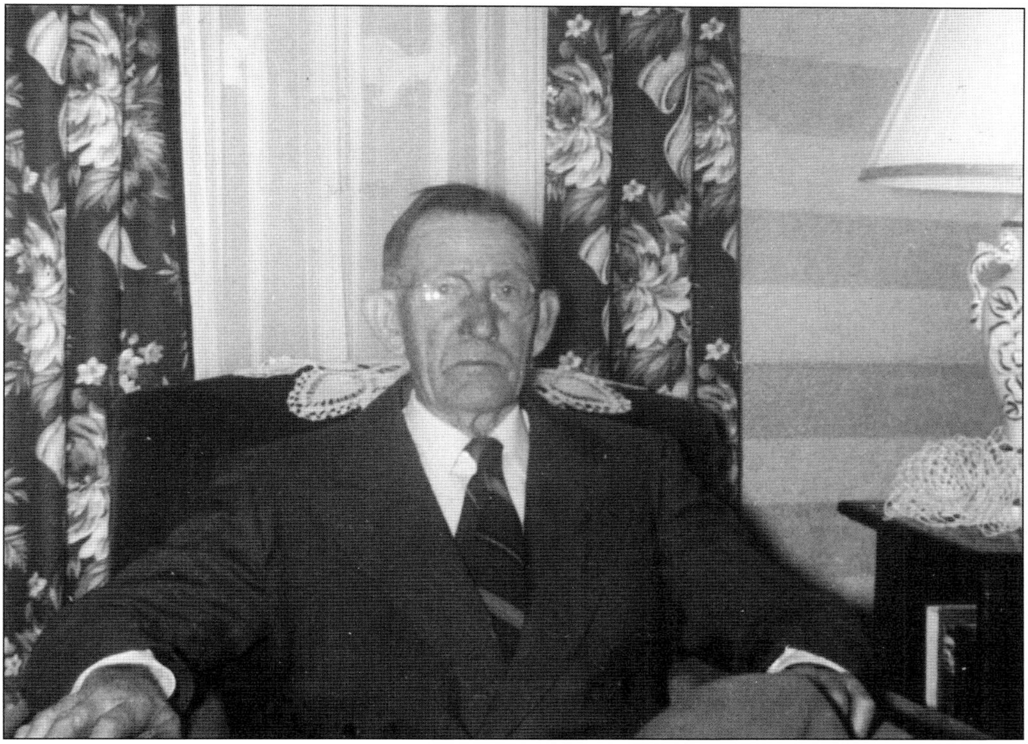

The Rev. Daniel Boone Taylor was a Methodist minister who founded the Callis Grove Tabernacle off New Hope Road in central Trimble County. (Courtesy of Ted Taylor.)

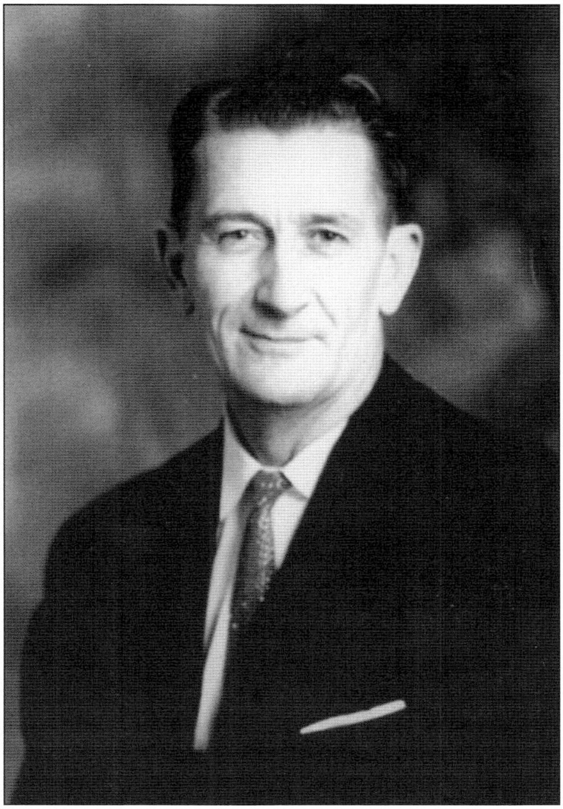

The Rev. Harry W. Wood, son of James and Giles Hancock Wood of the Carmel district, was a well-known preacher who also was very adept at fixing radios and just about anything else mechanical. During his ministry, he held 45 revival meetings in Trimble County and traveled to 48 of the 50 states to preach. He also spoke at a reunion of the Corn Creek Academy. (Courtesy of Gary Rowlett.)

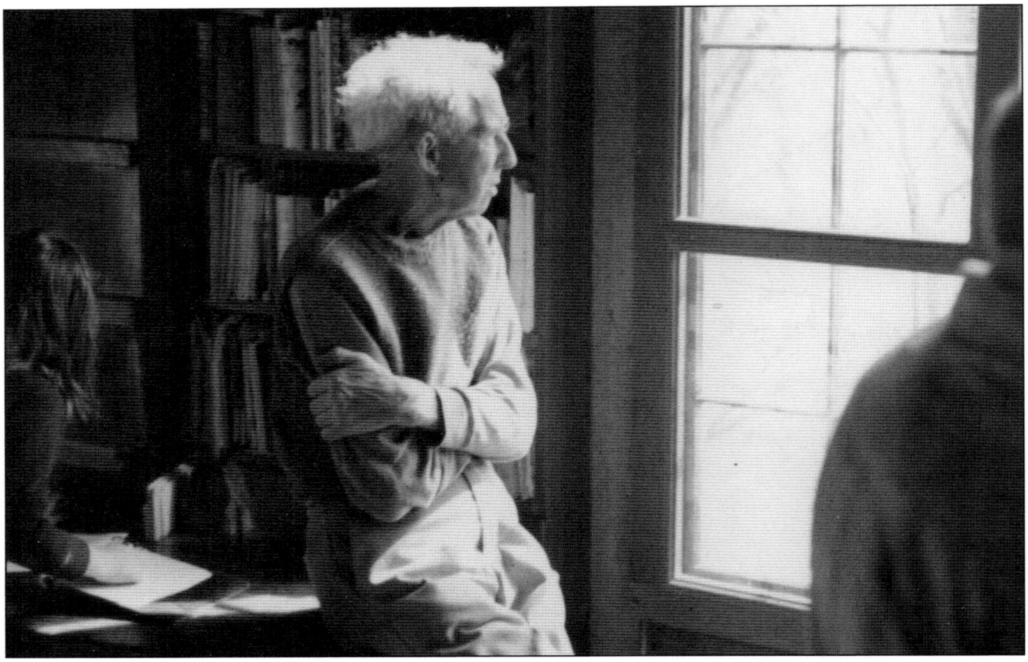

Renowned landscape painter Harlan Hubbard looks out the window of his primitive-style home in Payne Hollow, not far from where the notorious Delia Webster had her farm. After spending eight years traveling the Ohio and Mississippi Rivers on a shantyboat, an adventure recounted in his book *Shantyboat*, he and his wife, Anna, built a secluded home in the woods overlooking the Ohio River. They lived modestly, growing and canning their own food and eschewing modern conveniences, including electricity, plumbing, and running water. The couple was known for welcoming visitors, including a local church group, into their home and entertaining them with concerts—Harlan on the violin and Anna on the grand piano. (Both, courtesy of Bill Henderson.)

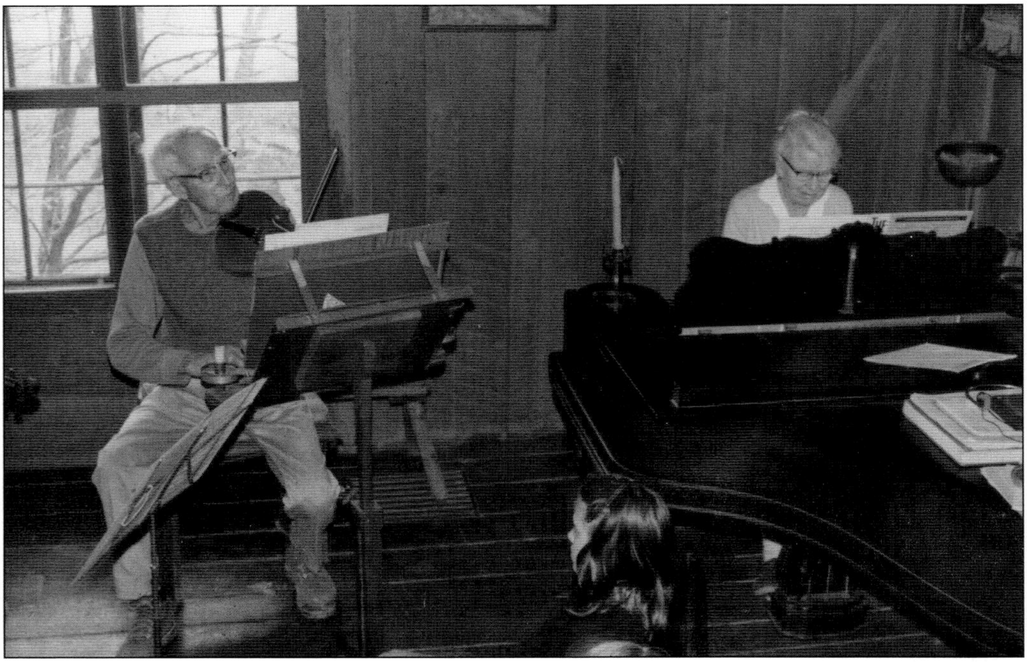

Two

Bedford

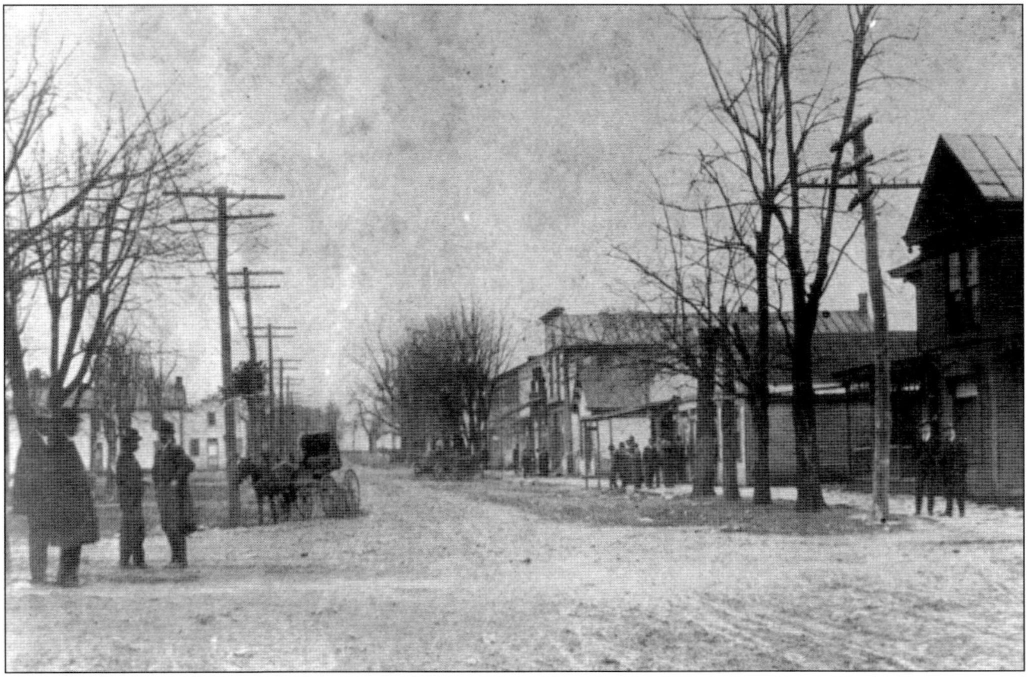

The city of Bedford was established in 1816 and became the county seat when Trimble was formed in 1837. The courthouse was built in the village square. A medicinal spring located just outside the city drew visitors from hundreds of miles away in the 1840s until an outbreak of cholera in 1851. But the town continued to thrive with several grocery stores, hardware and dry goods stores, and several restaurants, though most of the city's original buildings from the late 1800s and early 1900s have been destroyed by fire. (Courtesy of Gary Greenwood.)

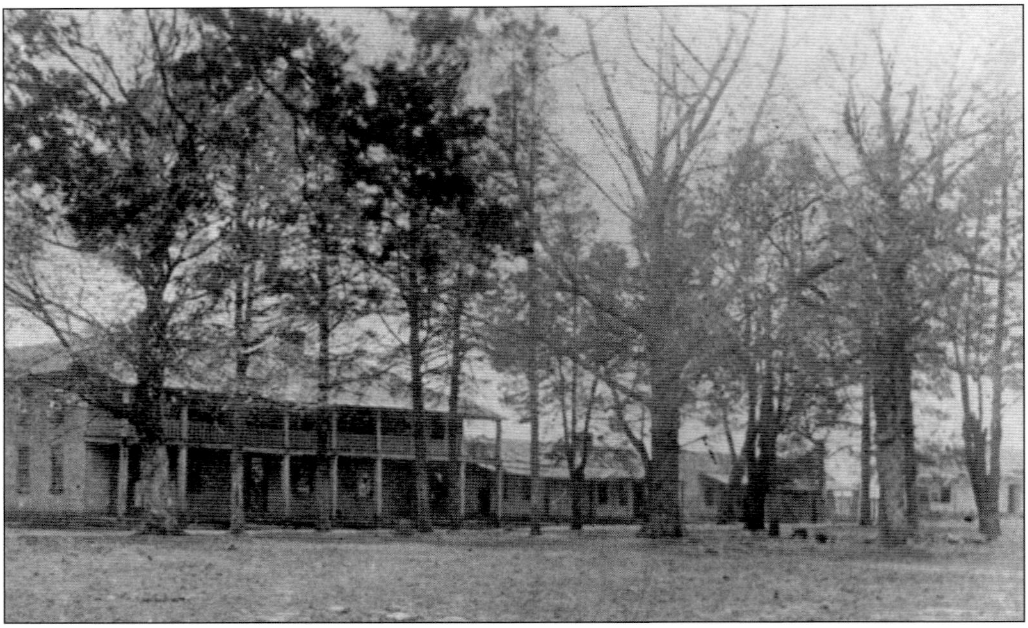

Bedford Springs Hotel was established in 1840 by Noah Parker and his wife, who discovered the mineral springs that were said to have medicinal value. The Parkers and their son, Nathan, operated the hotel. Nathan Parker later became a major in the Confederate army, serving in the 4th Kentucky Cavalry under Col. Henry Giltner. He died in May 1864 at a battle in Wytheville, Virginia, and is buried in Bedford Cemetery. The hotel burned down in 1967. (Courtesy of Gary Greenwood.)

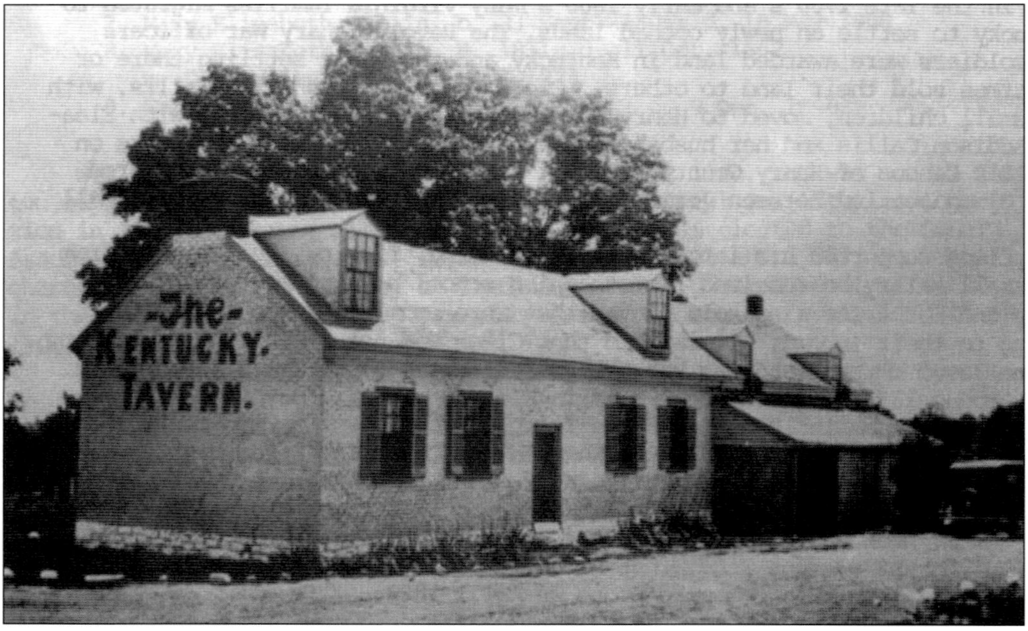

The old Kentucky Tavern, today in ruins on US 42 north of Bedford, likely was Kings Tavern, where slaveowners from Carroll, Trimble, and surrounding counties met in 1847 to draft a resolution to the state legislature to resolve the problem of fugitive slaves escaping north. The situation was one of several that led to Sen. Henry Clay's Fugitive Slave Act of 1850. (Courtesy of the *Trimble Banner.*)

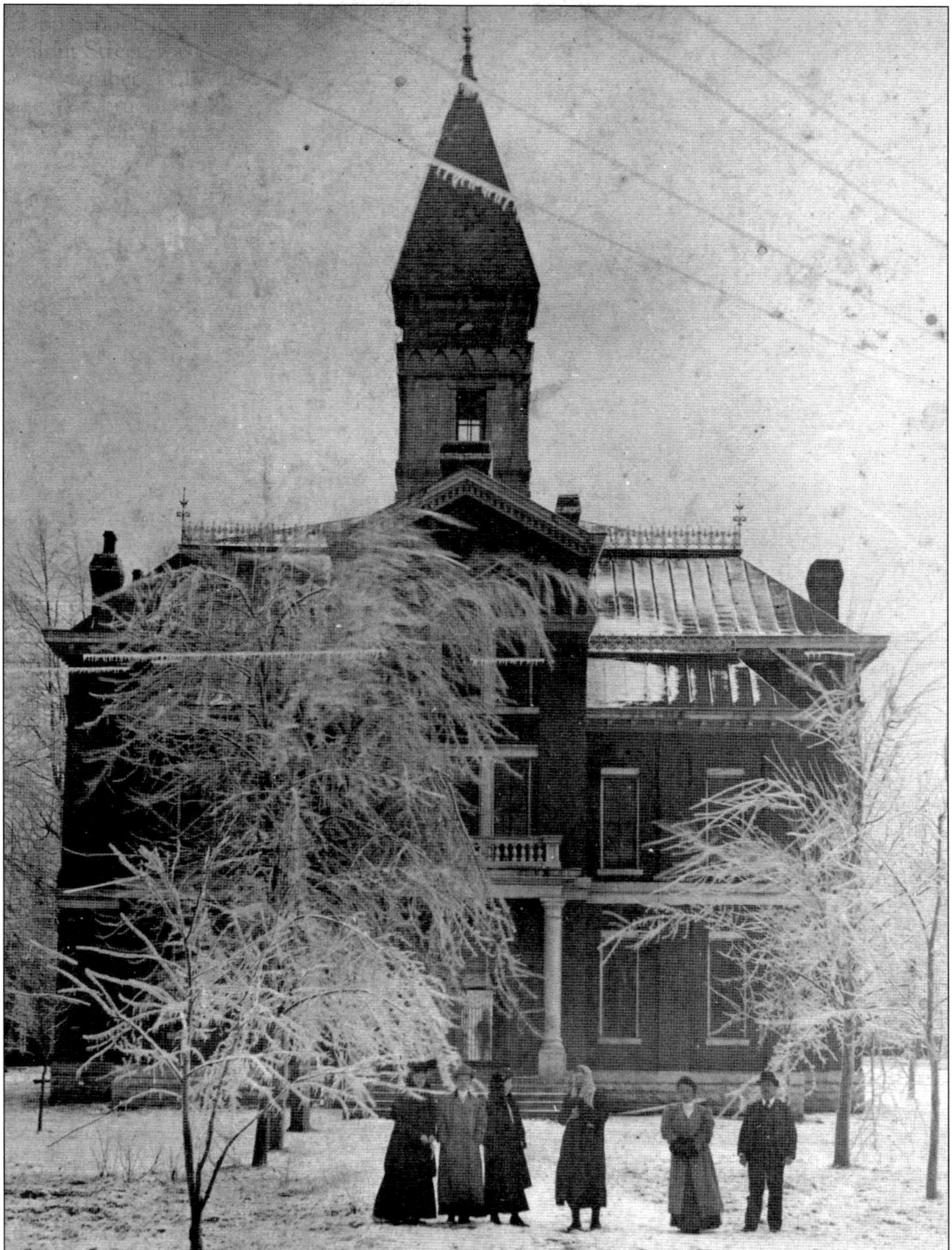

A family poses in front of the second courthouse during the aftermath of a winter storm around 1916. The Victorian building was constructed in 1884 by B.F. Fletcher Jr. of Aurora, Indiana, for about $12,500. It was gutted by fire in 1952; the existing courthouse was built using the foundation and the original walls of the first story. (Courtesy of Mildred Pardo Pruitt.)

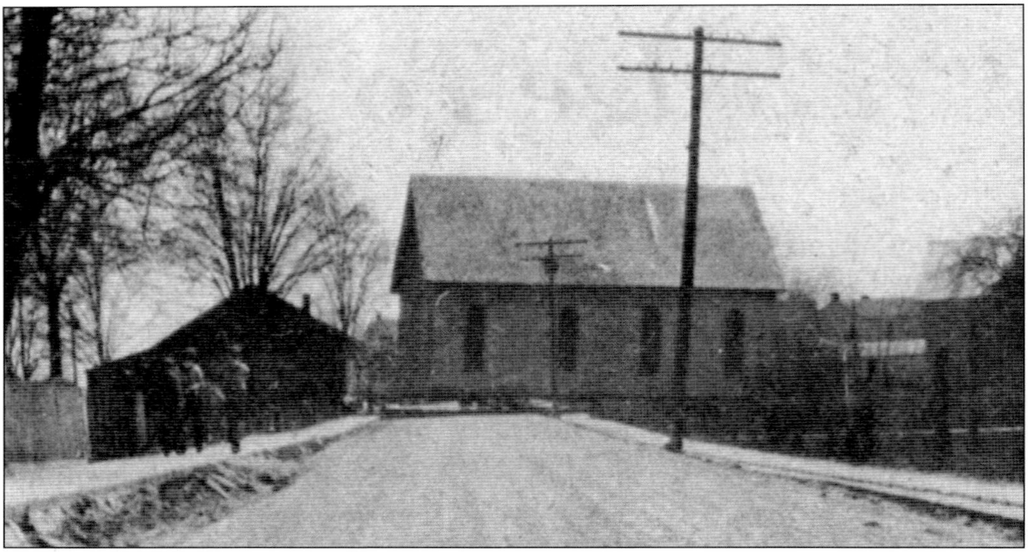

Originally Bedford's Catholic church, this building later became a movie theater when the Catholic congregation dwindled. It was first operated by A.L. Voiers as the Florence Theater and later by Keith H. Hood and Louise B. Logan for silent movies with player-piano accompaniment. It was purchased in 1930 and given to the Baptist congregation to replace its church, which burned down. (Courtesy of Hilda Parrish.)

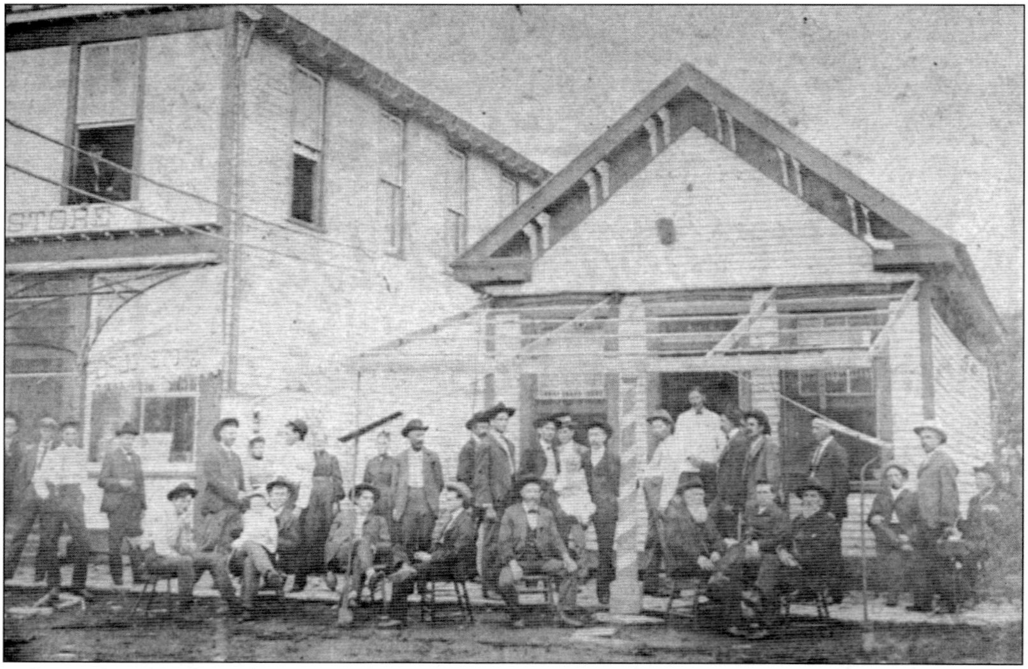

A host of Bedford residents pose in front of Alonzo Coghill's barbershop, at right, in this early 1900s photograph. Coghill stands in the doorway to his shop. Others pictured are W.C. Morgan, A.B. Clem, Eugene Mosley, E.B. McCain, D.H. Peak, W.B. Gills, Dick Stewart, Mrs. Coghill, and D.L. Bell. Looking out the upstairs window at left is Effie Mosley, switchboard operator for the Home Telephone Company. This entire block of buildings was destroyed in a 1935 fire. (Courtesy of the *Trimble Banner.*)

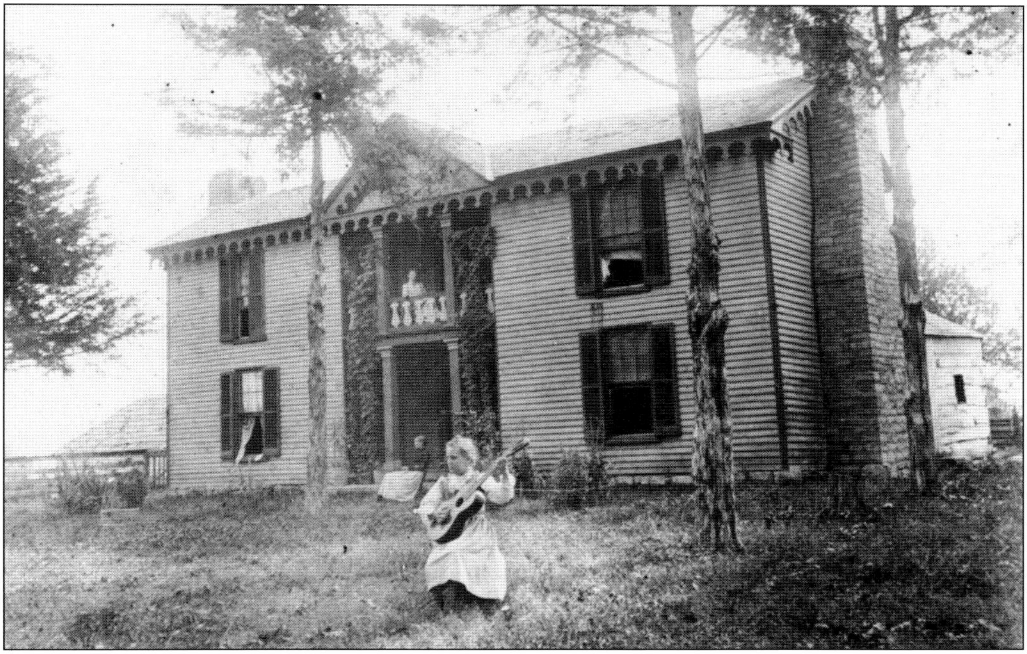

Cedar Heights was built by John W. Stewart, a Scottish immigrant who settled on a farm in the southern part of Trimble County. Portions of the farm are still owned by his descendants. In the background is his widow, Jane Williamson. On the balcony is likely daughter Arabella. The girl playing guitar may be Jane's granddaughter Lillian. (Courtesy of Robert Bruce "Bob" Stewart Jr.)

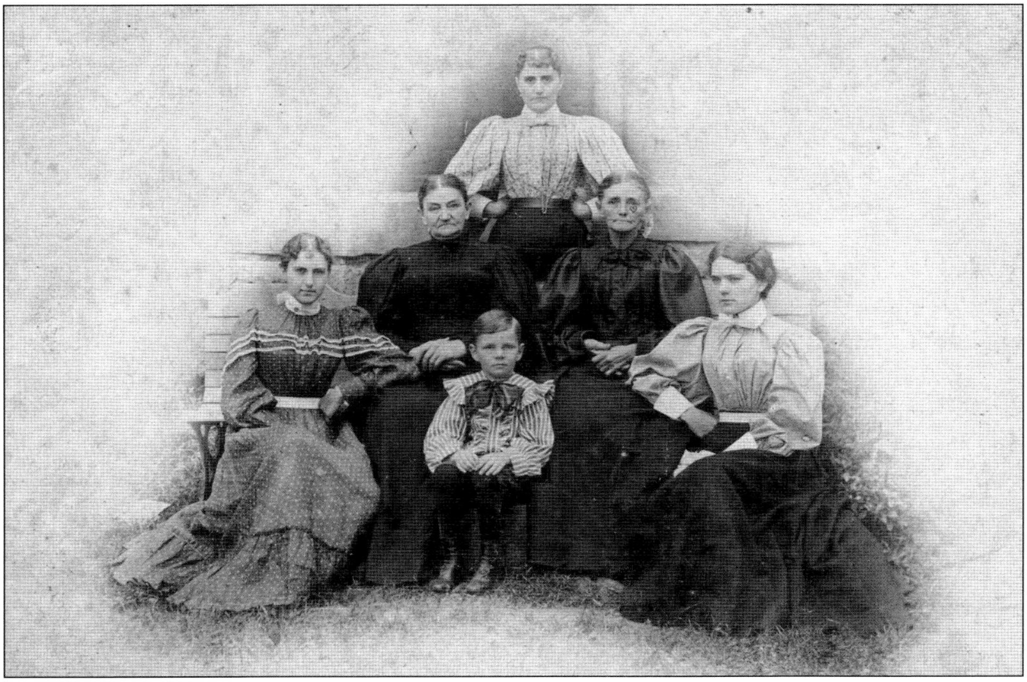

Several generations of the Sanders family pose for this portrait, probably taken in the 1870s or 1880s. (Courtesy of JoDeva Ogden.)

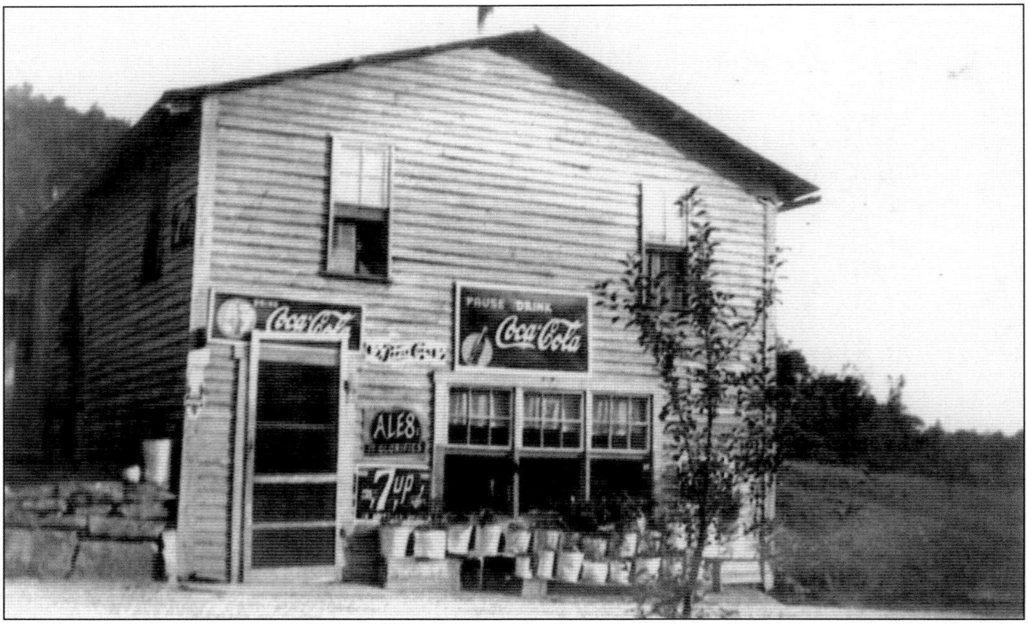

Lawrence Moore's general store was on Mount Pleasant Road across from Mount Pleasant church. Moore would travel to Louisville and Madison, Indiana, with cattle to sell for the neighborhood. A life-long Trimble County resident, he was a son of Benjamin and Mary Moore. (Courtesy of Mildred Pardo Pruitt.)

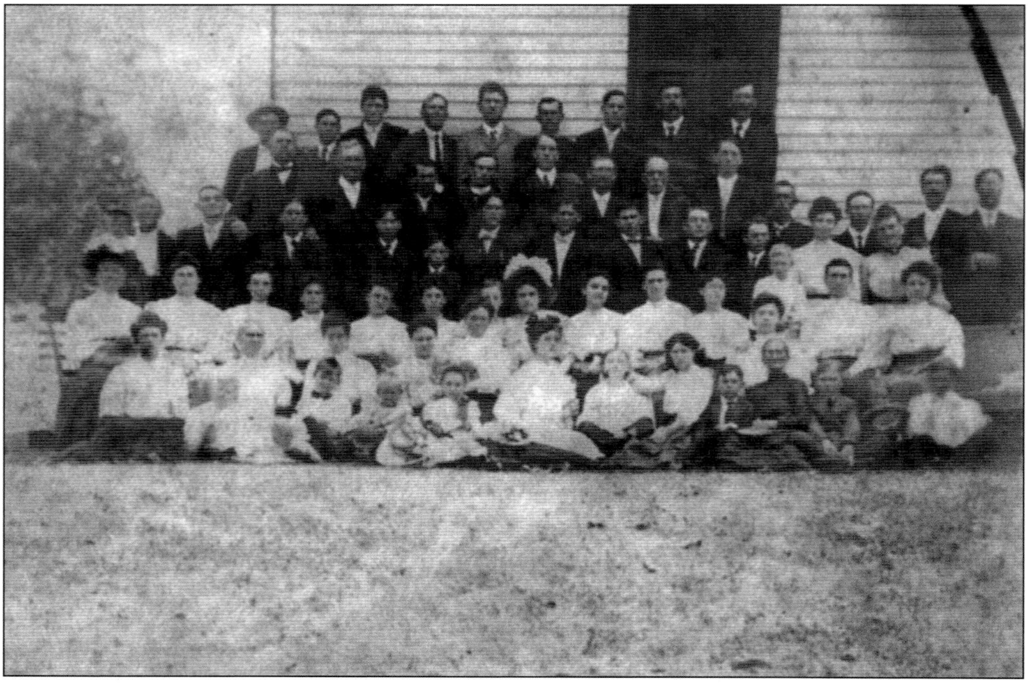

Members of Antioch Baptist Church near Ewing Ford, between Bedford and Campbellsburg on US 421, gather for an all-day meeting with dinner on the grounds around 1915. A church history states that the Baptist Church of Jesus Christ at Antioch was founded in 1866, and the existing building was completed in 1870. Its first pastor was William B. Smith. (Courtesy of Kim Vittitow.)

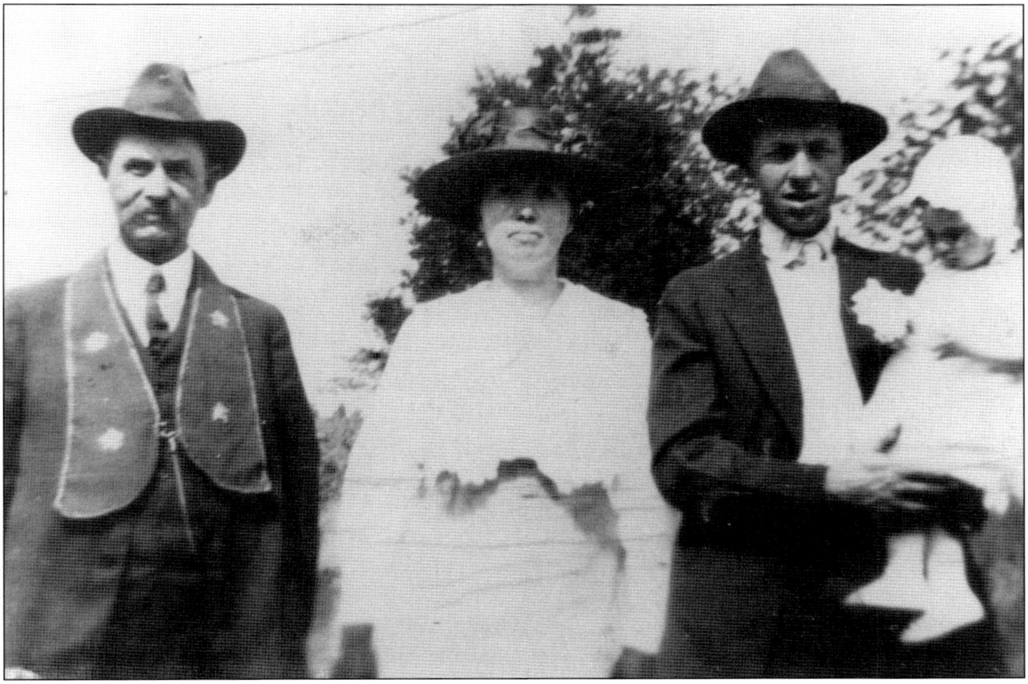

Four generations of the Williams and Ralston families posed for this photograph, taken about 1920. From left to right are William Ivan Williams (who lived in the Barebone district of Trimble County), Stella Huston (Williams) Ralston, and Elmer Ralston and his daughter, Lillia Stella Ralston. Lillia married Victor Hamilton in 1939. (Courtesy of Sue Ralston Reid.)

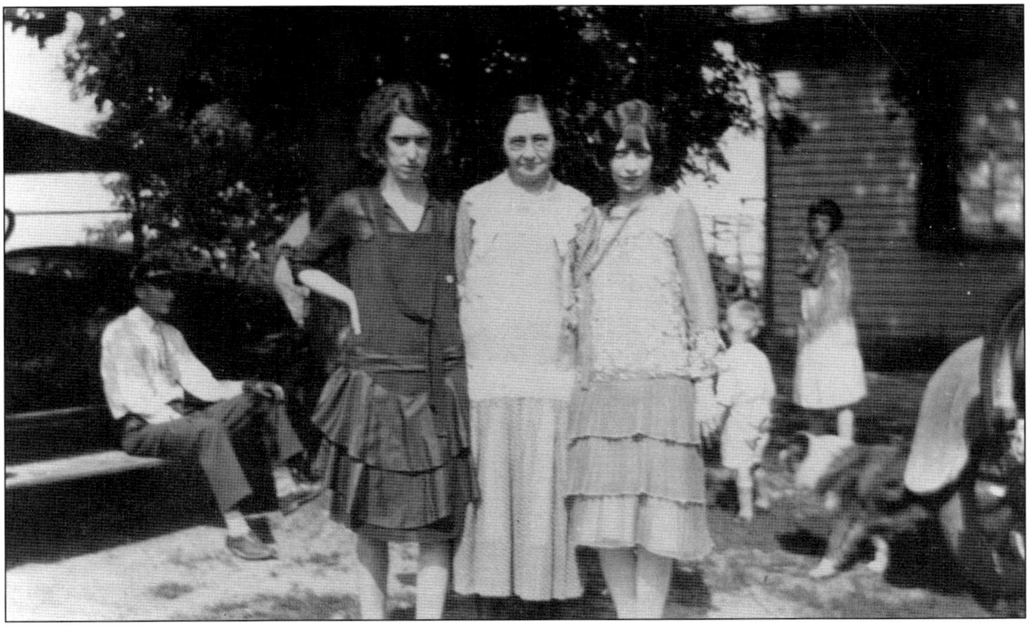

Giles Wood stands with two of her flapper daughters-in-law—Katherine (left), wife of Deward Wood, and Hallie Wood, wife of Norvel Wood. Hallie and Norvel met in Madison, Indiana, while she was staying at the Central Hotel as part of a theater troupe. Another son, Harry Wood, became a well-known Methodist minister. (Courtesy of Gary Rowlett.)

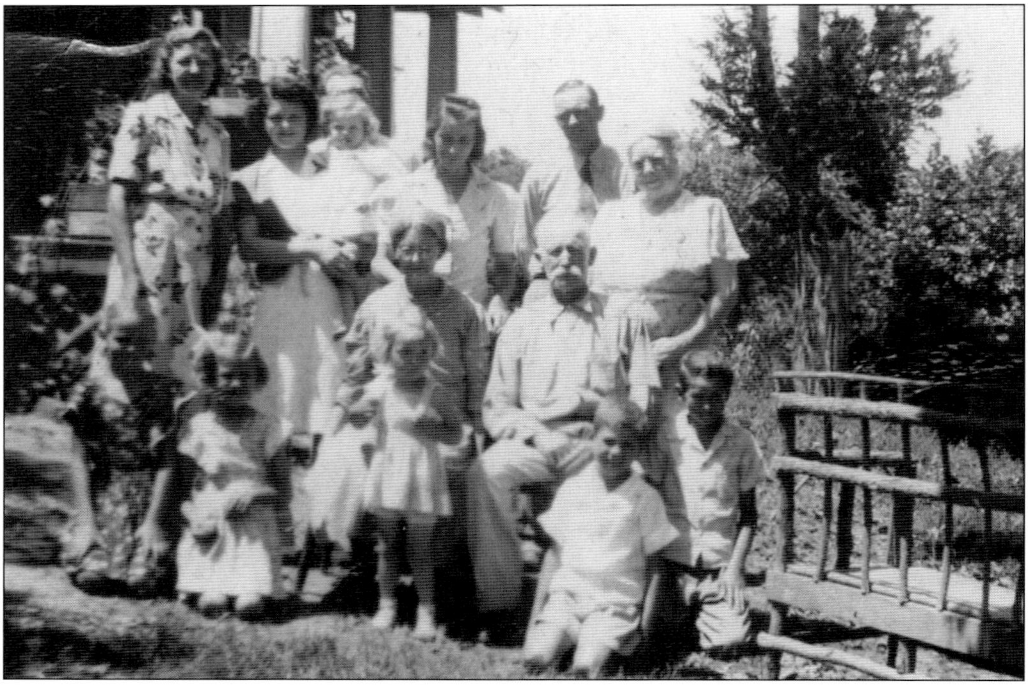

James and Frances Egerton pose with their family during a gathering at the family home outside the Bedford city limits. James "Billy" Egerton served as a deputy sheriff when his brother, Clarence, was elected Trimble County sheriff. (Courtesy of Frederica Congleton.)

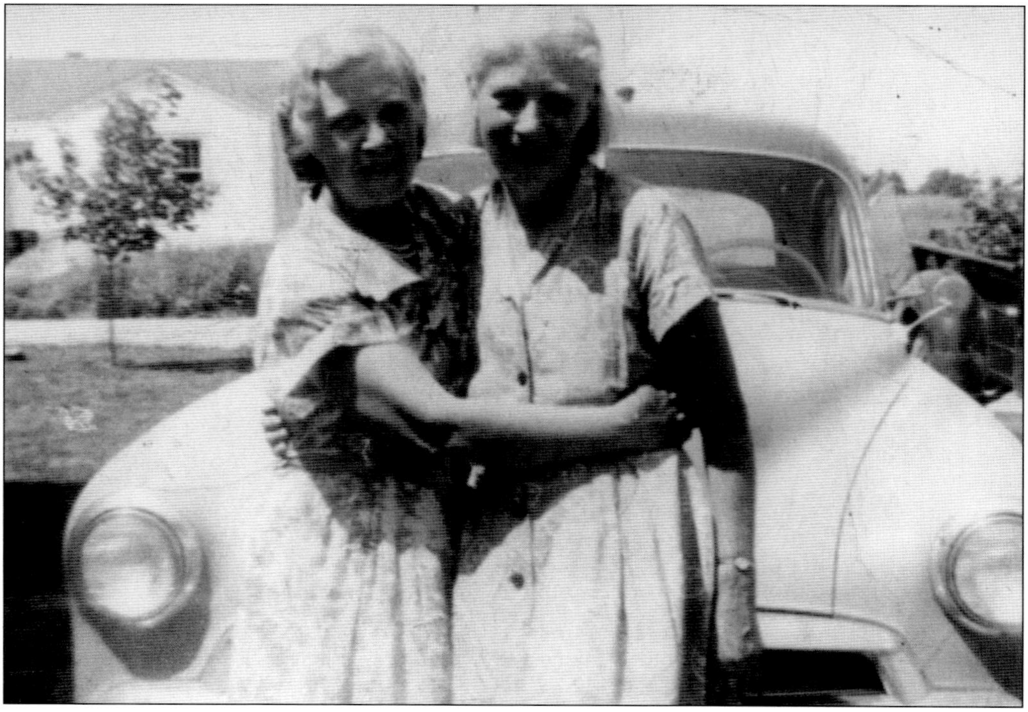

Sisters Clara Wood Boatwright and Pearl Wood Carson hug while posing in front of the Boatwrights' house on Cutshaw Lane in Bedford. (Courtesy of Charlene Boatwright Ellis.)

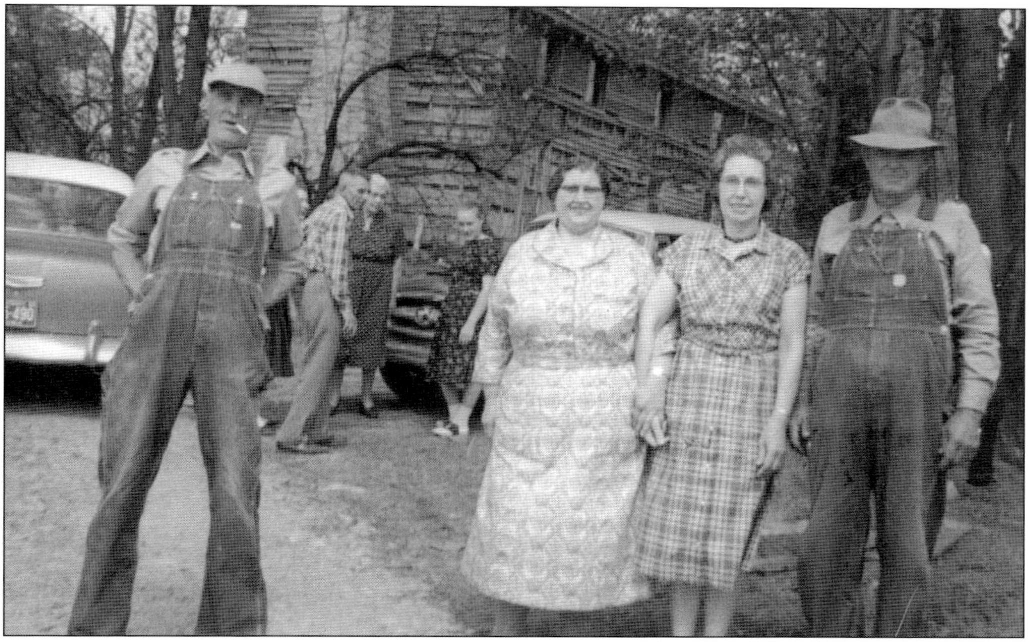

From left to right, siblings Ralph Bell, Viola McNeely, Myrtle Rowlett, and John Bell pose in front of the old Bell home, one of the oldest houses in the county that has been renovated by another family. In the back are, from left to right, Frank Wentworth, Renny Adams, and Renny Mae Bell (John Bell's daughter). Ralph's parents were William Ambrose and Lucy Ellen (Jones) Bell, daughter of Jessie and Nancy Crafton Jones. (Courtesy of Carolyn Crafton Adams.)

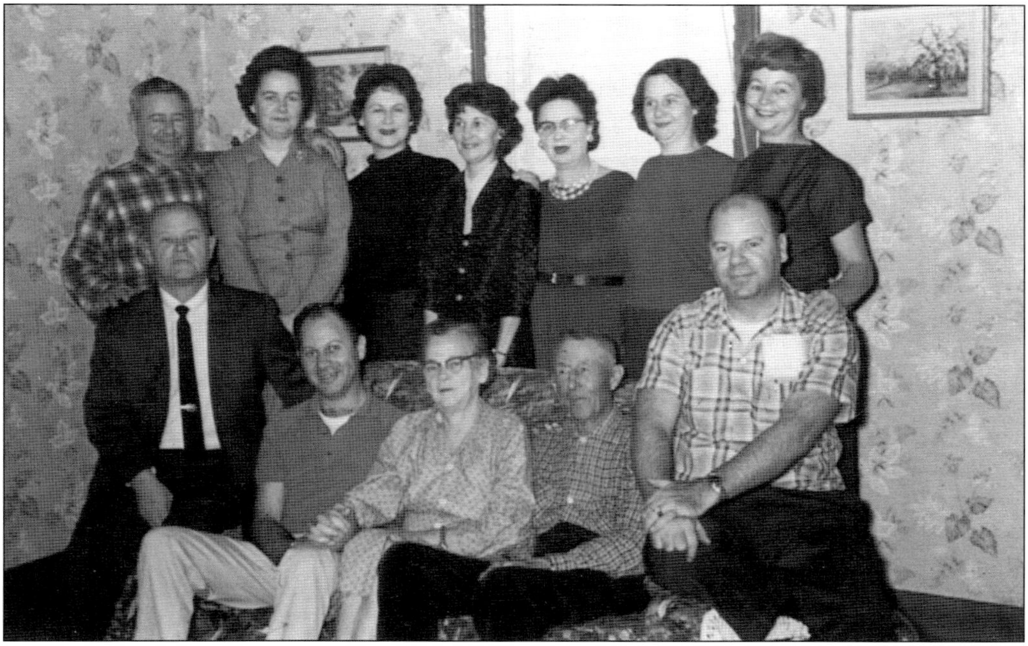

This 1961 Taylor family Thanksgiving photograph includes, from left to right, (first row) Doug, Kelly, parents Stella (Black) and Tom Taylor, and Asa; (second row) Morgan, Maxine, Lida, Alyne, Evalena, Wanda, and Zilpah. This was taken on Thanksgiving Day 1961, before Mrs. Taylor died on Christmas Eve. (Courtesy of Wanda Cook.)

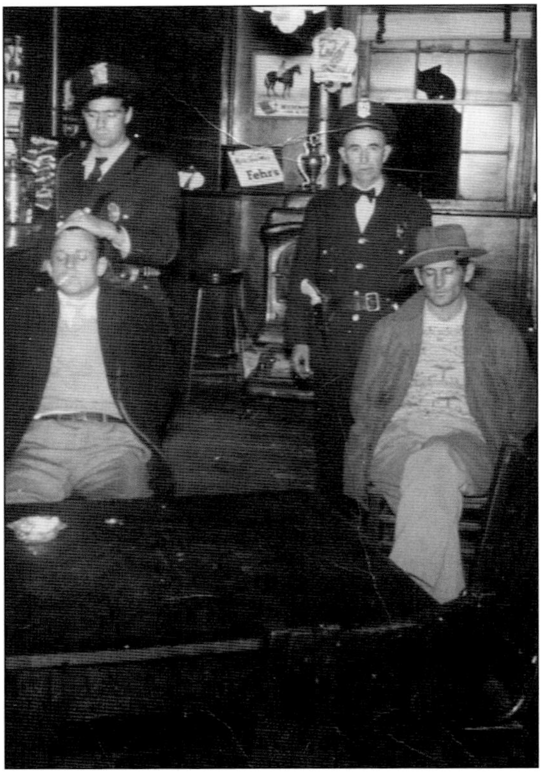

Harry Webster, in uniform at right, was Bedford's town marshal for many years in the mid-20th century. He had a reputation for being tough on crime. In this photograph, Webster and a Kentucky state trooper pose in a Bedford establishment with two men who appear to be handcuffed. (Courtesy of Lucy Webster Smith.)

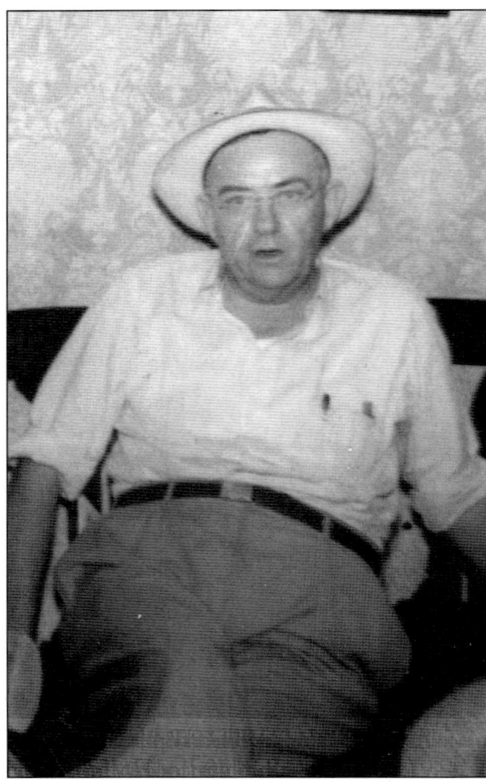

Carroll Miles, who served one term as Trimble County sheriff from 1938 to 1941, is pictured during a visit to John Rand's insurance office in Bedford, across from the courthouse. (Courtesy of Reggie Rand.)

Pearl Mahoney Williams served as Trimble County jailer from 1927 to 1934, taking over after her husband, James Rollie Williams, was shot and killed in the courtyard while trying to make an arrest. At the time, she was pregnant with their 10th child. She fulfilled the remainder of her husband's term and was reelected twice. The first prisoner she tended was the man who shot and killed her husband. (Courtesy of Trimble County fiscal court.)

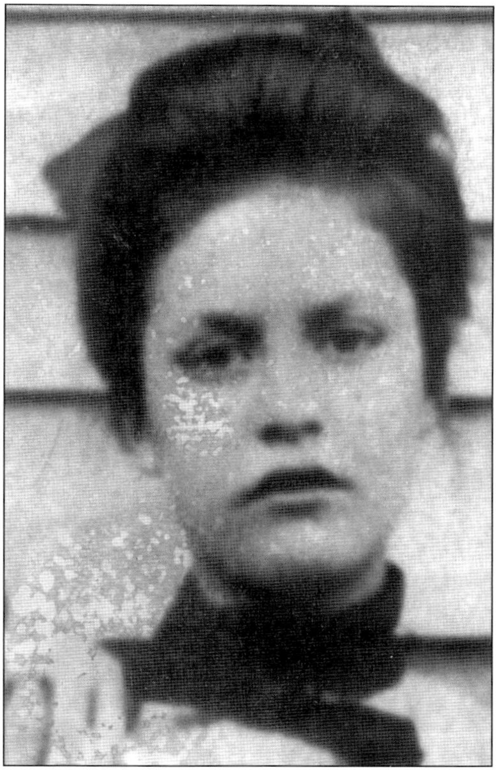

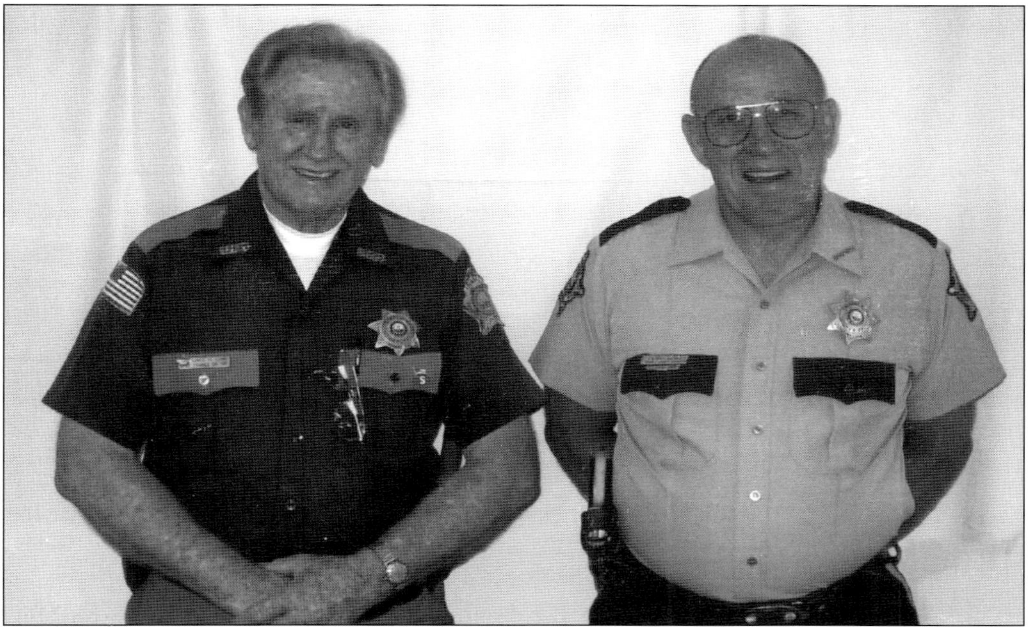

Brothers Howard and Denny Long both served terms as Trimble's sheriff and deputy sheriff. Howard Long was elected sheriff three times, the first time in 1966, serving under County Judge Clyde "Jack" Greenwood. He was sheriff a total of 16 years; his last term ended in 1993. He also served as chief deputy when his brother, Denny, was elected sheriff in 1994. Both men retired from law enforcement in 2002. (Courtesy of Trimble County fiscal court.)

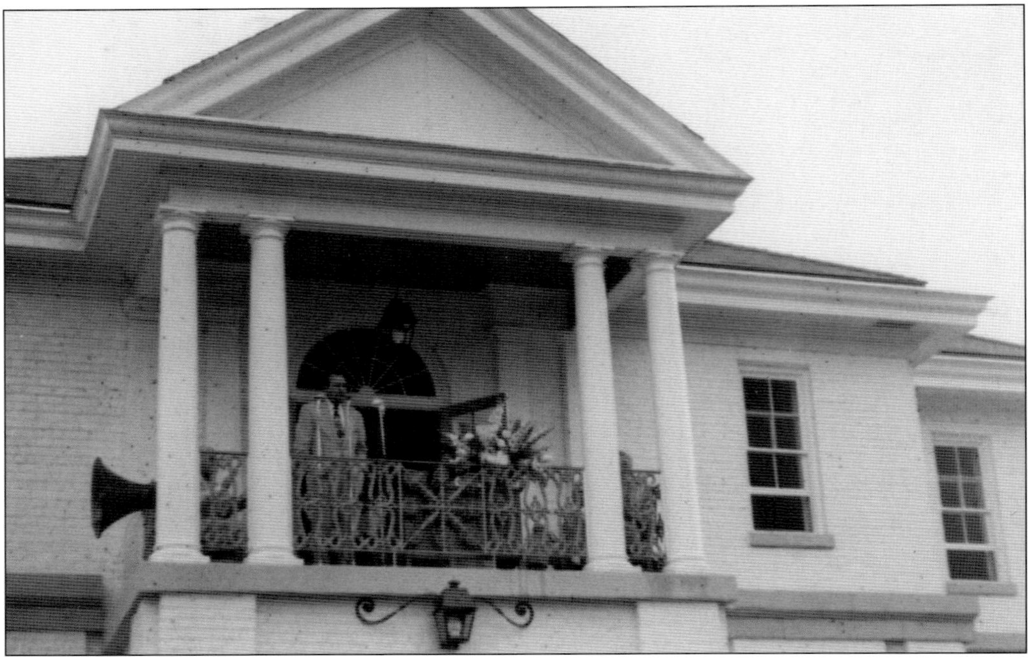

The newly rebuilt Trimble County courthouse was dedicated in 1954 during a public ceremony on the courthouse lawn. The foundation and walls of the first floor were salvaged after fire ravaged the building in the early morning hours of March 5, 1953. The new building was designed by architect Carl D. Russell and built by contractors W.W. Burgess and J.D. Frost of the Barnett Lumber Company. The project was completed under County Judge L.C. Yager and Magistrates W.S. Garriott, Elgin Ogden, Ralph Clem, and Ovia Callis. (Both, courtesy of Reggie Rand.)

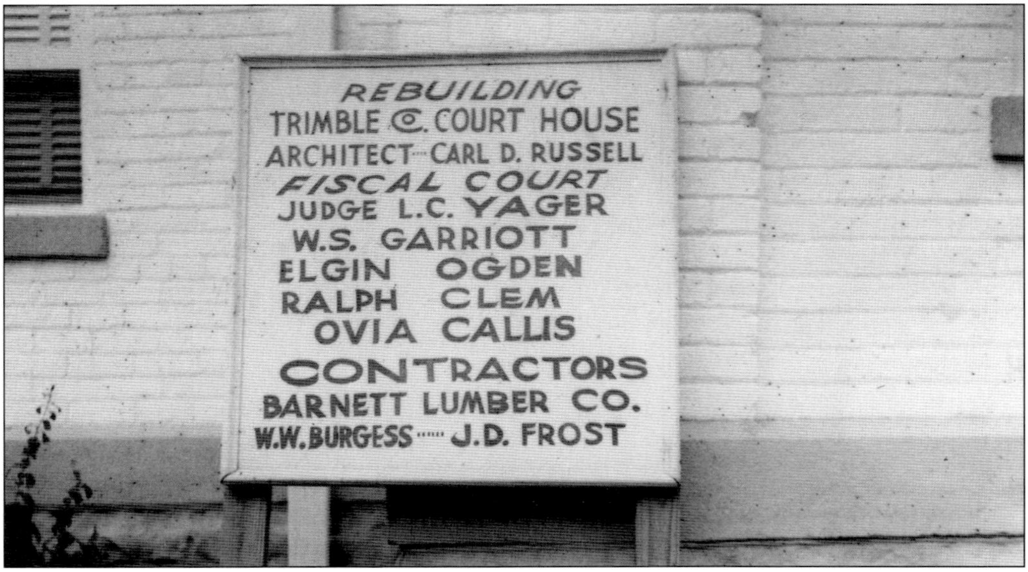

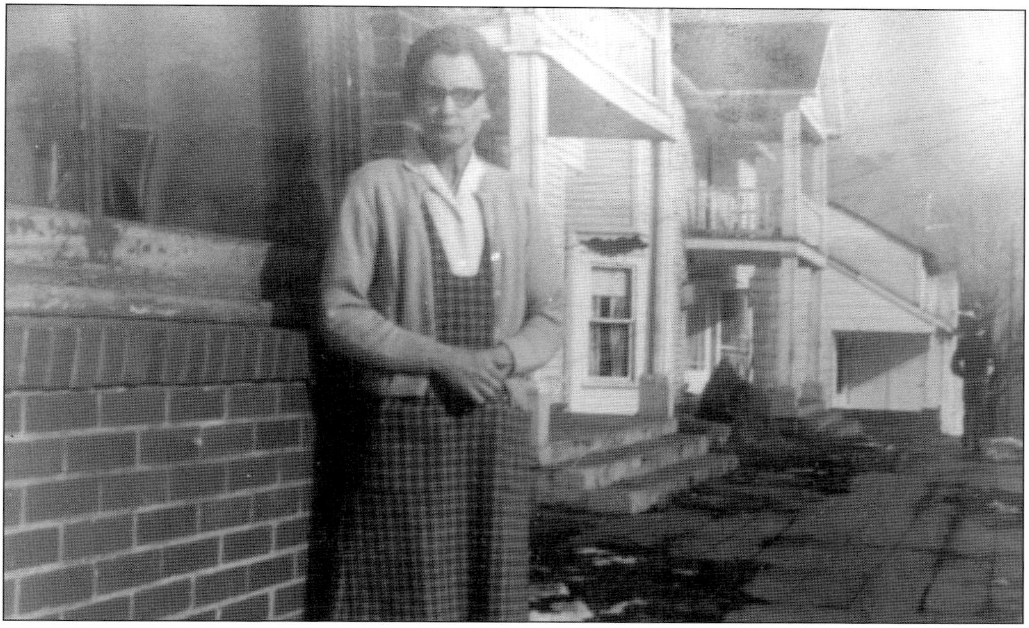

Ora Eckert, a longtime teacher in Trimble County schools, stands outside the Community Store. (Courtesy of Frederica Congleton.)

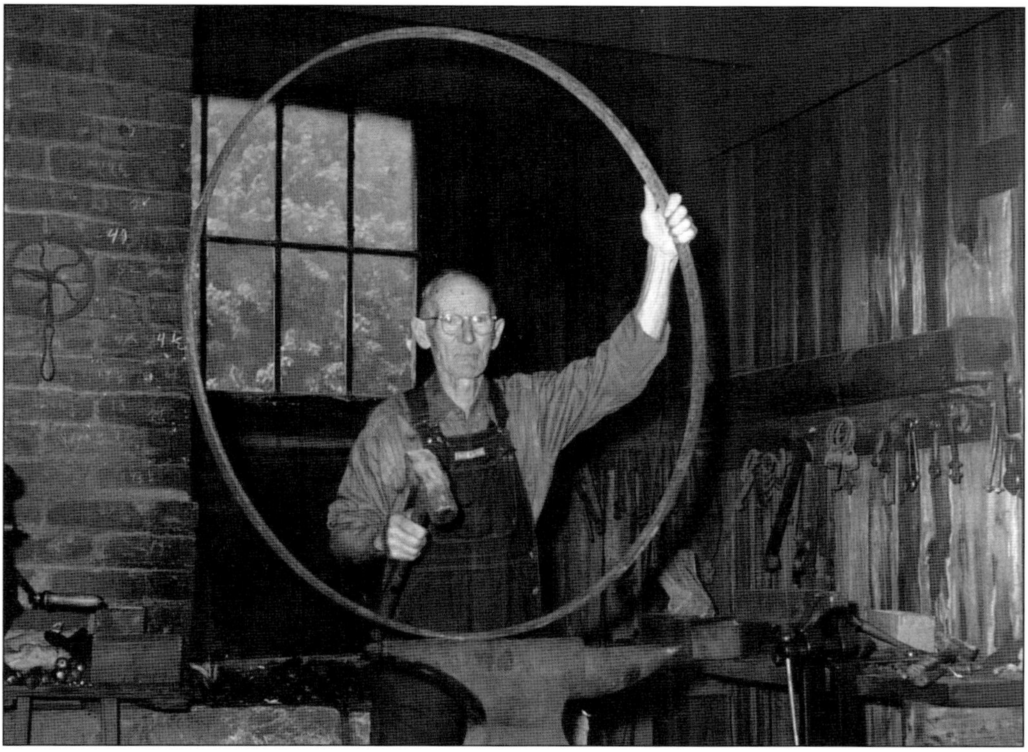

Clem Beach shapes a wagon tire at the anvil in his blacksmith shop located at the corner of Victory Drive and Church Street in Bedford. Beach served as the village smithy for more than a half century, moving his shop to West Street near his home as motor vehicles began to replace horses as the primary mode of transportation. (Courtesy of Trimble County Public Library.)

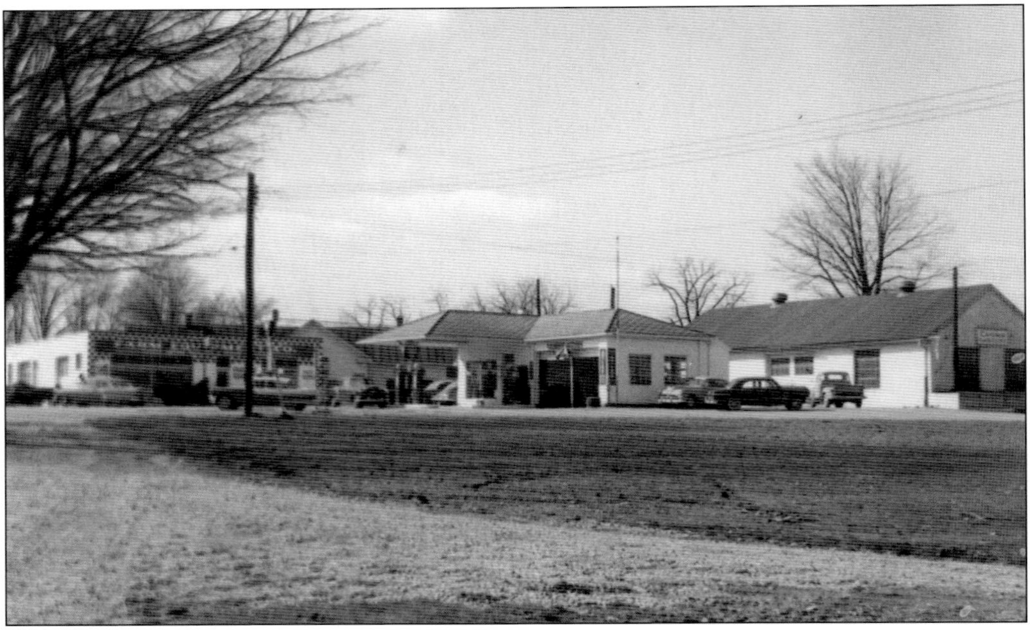

The triangle-shaped lot at the junction of US 421, which goes to Milton, and US 42, which goes to Carrollton, has long been the location of various gas and service stations. Here is a photograph of the intersection before the Little Town and Country restaurant obscured the view of the Ransdell home. A farm equipment store was on the other side of 421, now the location of Bedford Hardware. (Courtesy of Frederica Congleton.)

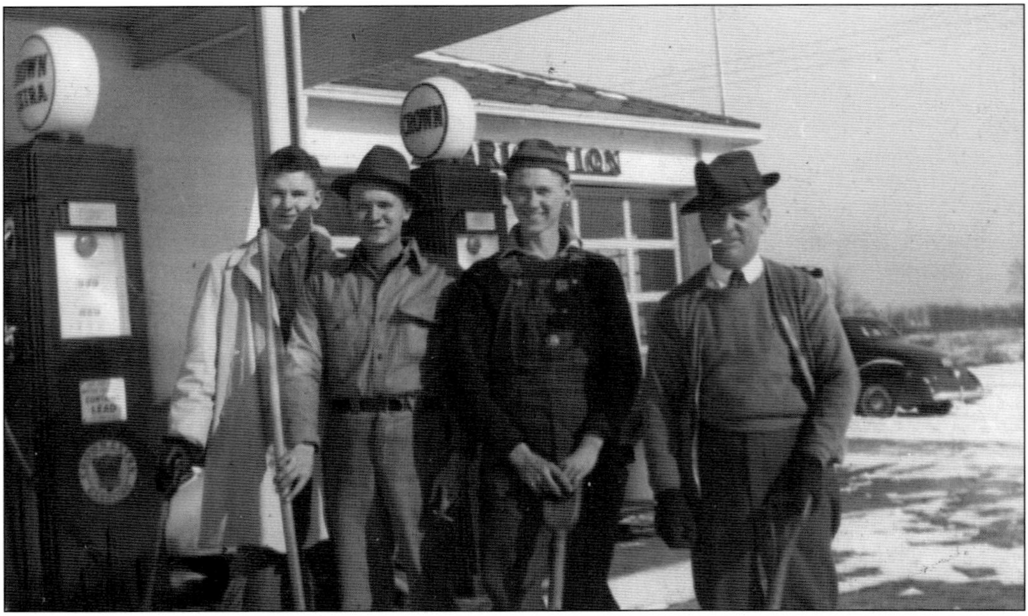

Breathit Hutcherson, far right, stands with his employees, Kenneth and Ollie Melvin (center, left to right), and an unidentified man in front of the gas pumps at the Bedford Garage and service station. The location today is home to the Stop-n-Go Marathon station and convenience store. (Courtesy of Mildred Pardo Pruitt.)

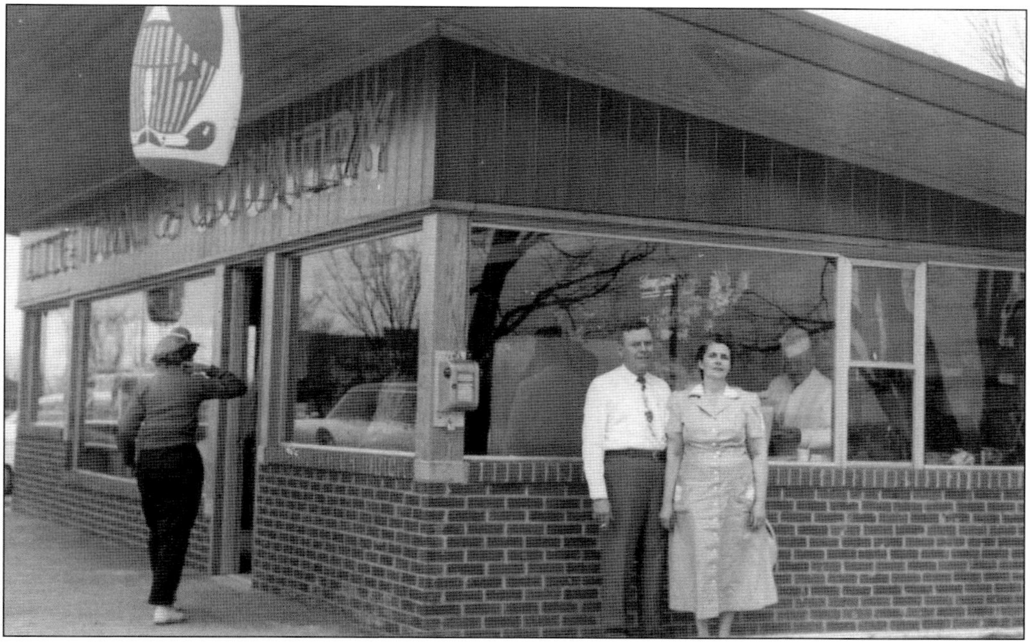

As a carhop heads inside to place an order, Charlie and Gladys Ransdell pose in front of their restaurant, Little Town and Country, a local landmark complete with an original neon sign. Still in operation, the diner-style restaurant remains a favorite of local residents and tourists, some famous, whose pictures can be seen hanging inside. The establishment began as a drive-in but later was expanded to allow for indoor seating as well as seating at the bar, shown below. Ransdell owned several restaurants, including the Belle of Carrollton, Churchill's in Carrollton and Shelbyville, and the Moon River in Warsaw, Kentucky. (Both, courtesy of Frederica Congleton.)

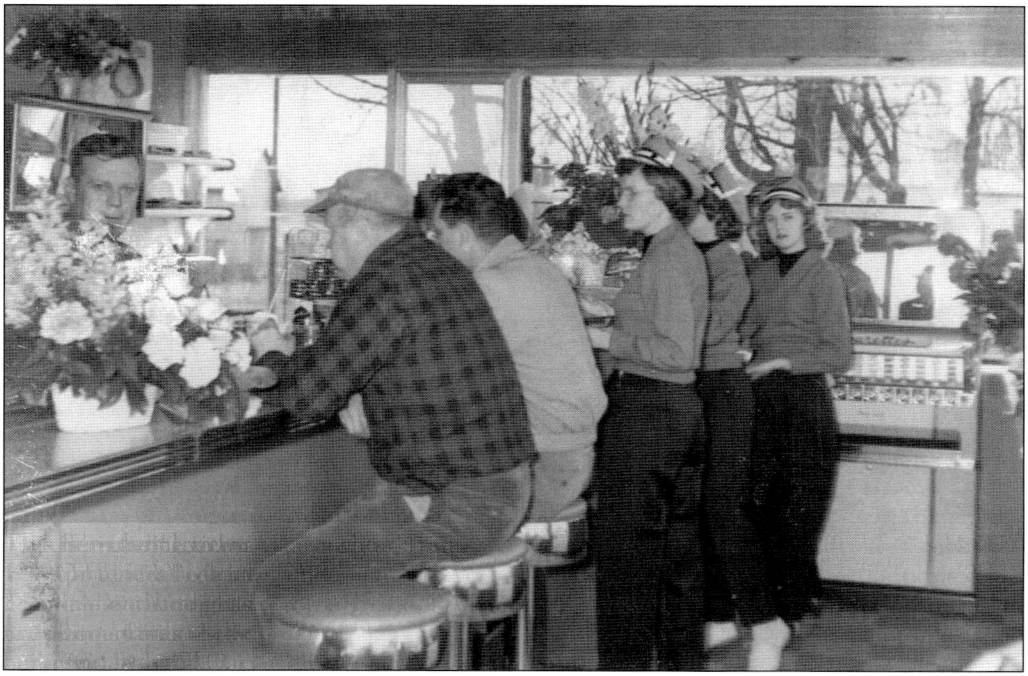

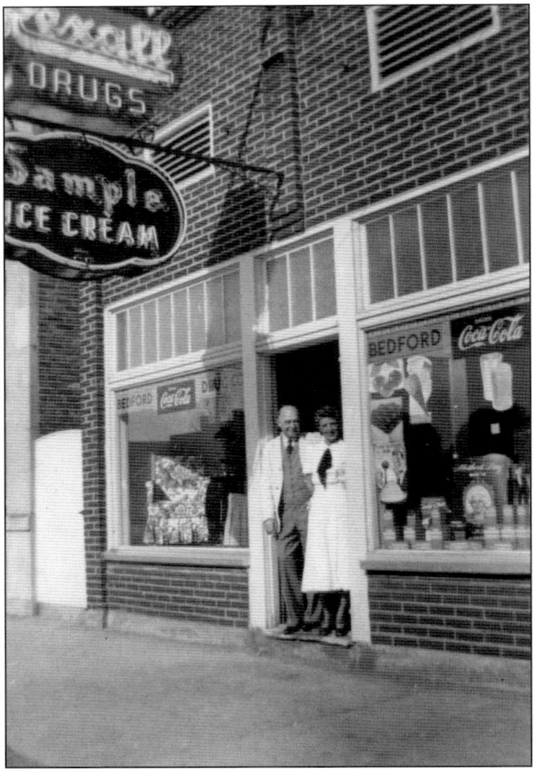

Pictured is one of several drugstores in Bedford during the mid-20th century. This shop was known as the Bedford Drug Company. The town's main drugstore eventually would be Morgan's, which was located between Little Town and Country and the Bedford Post Office. (Courtesy of Robert Bruce "Bob" Stewart Jr.)

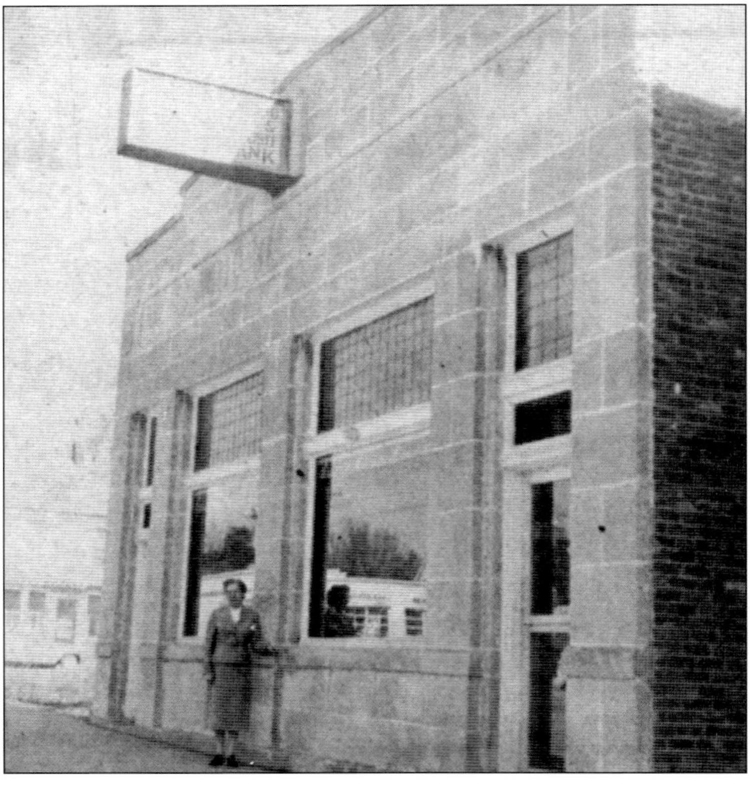

Louise B. Logan worked for the Bedford Loan and Deposit Bank for 64 years, starting as a clerk in 1910 and later serving as vice president and director. This was the second location, which began as a two-story building. A fire in 1935 damaged the second floor, which was removed when the building, located on Main Street, was restored. It was again remodeled during an expansion in 1970. (Courtesy of the *Trimble Banner*.)

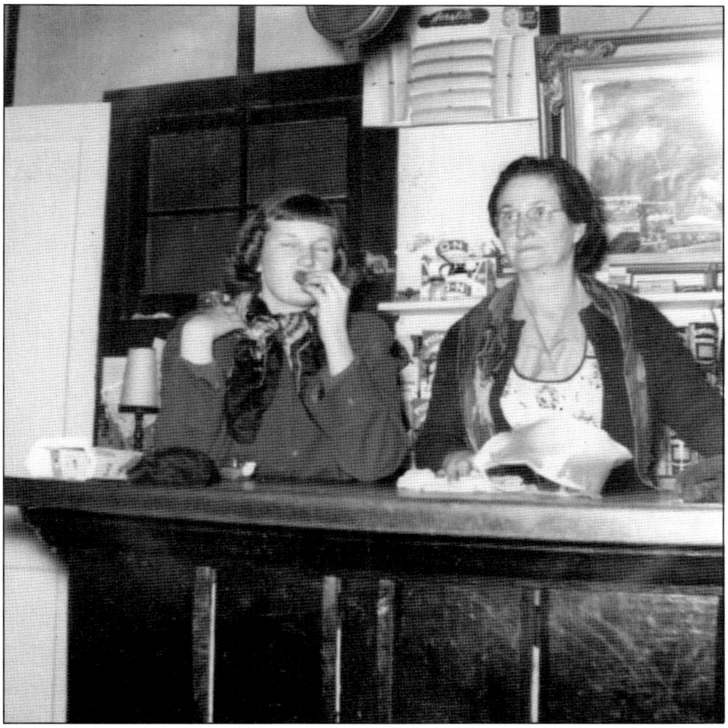

Joanne Callis (left) stands behind the counter at White Tavern with Mary Alice "Mom" (Wright) Berry, who owned the establishment at the corner of New Hope Road and US 421 with her husband, Oswald. The tavern operated from the 1930s to the 1950s. Both Mr. and Mrs. Berry died in 1964. (Courtesy of JoDeva Ogden.)

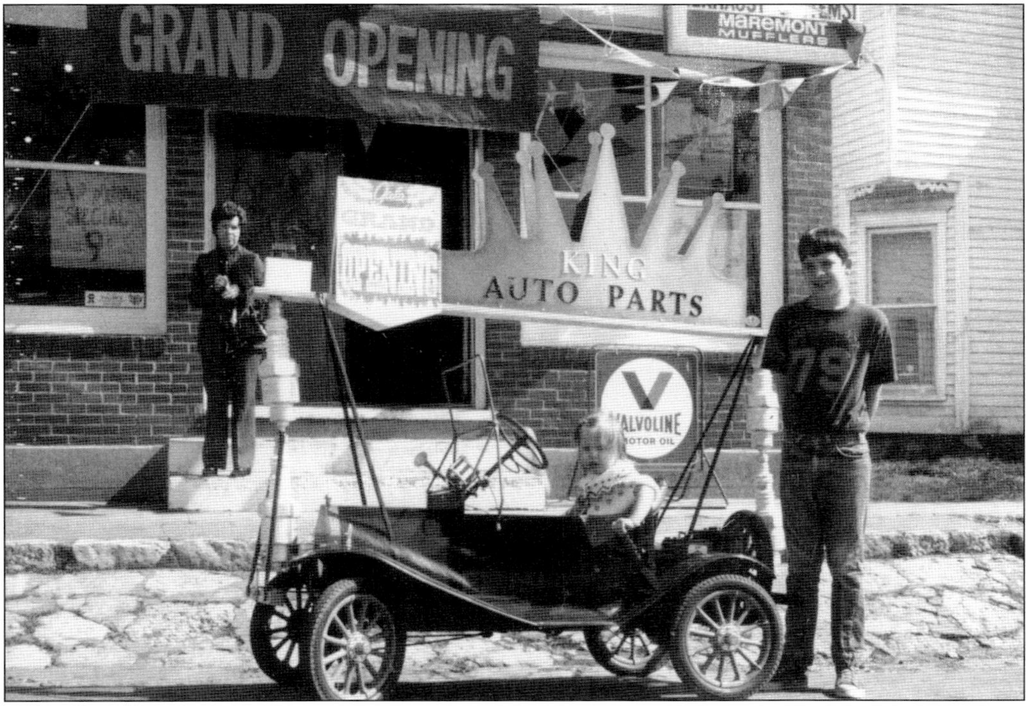

Betty Ransdell brought her daughter, Frederica, and son, Charles, to the grand opening of the King Auto Parts store in Bedford. Owner Paul Perry, who at one time owned locations in Carrollton, Owenton, Eminence, and LaGrange, was a devout Christian who named the stores to honor his beliefs. (Courtesy of Frederica Congleton.)

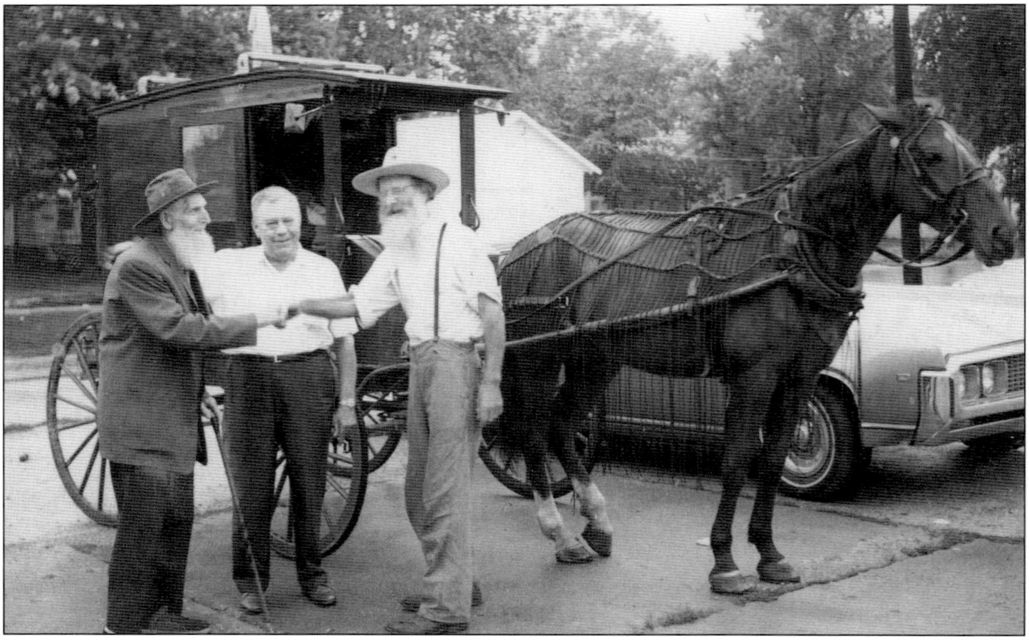

Charlie Randsdell, center, and Delth Estes, left, welcome a man traveling through town in a horse and wagon in the 1970s. Estes, who was a farmer on Sulphur Pike, was known for his trademark white beard, from which he would magically pull coins to the delight of local children. (Courtesy of Frederica Congleton.)

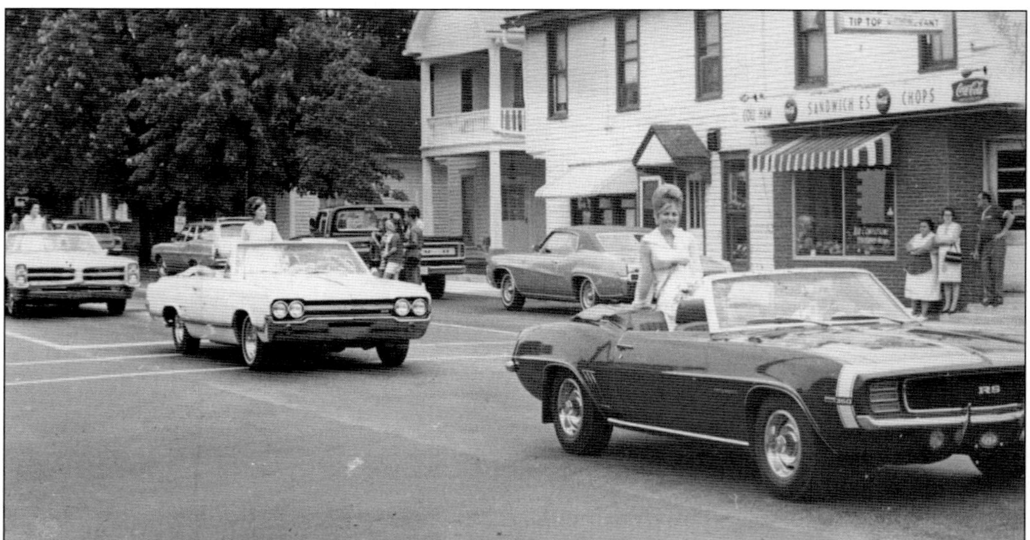

A parade of Trimble County pageant royalty travels down Main Street past the Tip Top Restaurant. The sign touts "Country Ham, Sandwiches, Chops" and, of course, Coca-Cola in an air-conditioned atmosphere. (Courtesy of Hilda Parrish.)

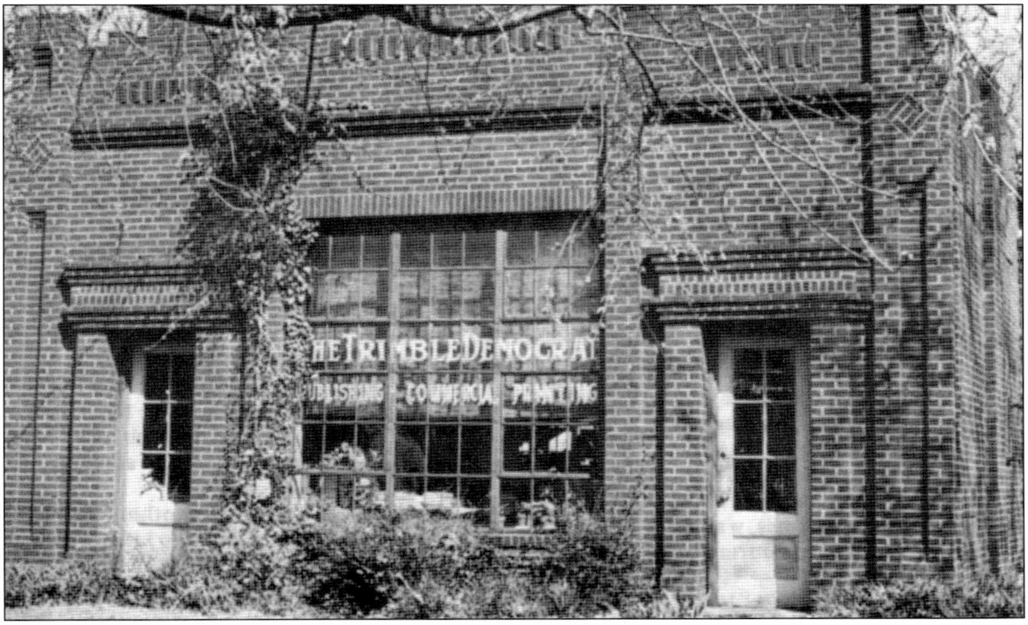

The *Trimble Democrat*—also known as the *Trimble Banner Democrat* and now simply the *Trimble Banner*—once was housed in this building on Church Street facing the courthouse square. The weekly newspaper has been keeping tabs on Trimble County news since February 1879. The *Milton News* merged with the Bedford-based newspaper in 1913. The publication was purchased by Landmark Community Newspapers in 1995. (Courtesy of Gary Greenwood.)

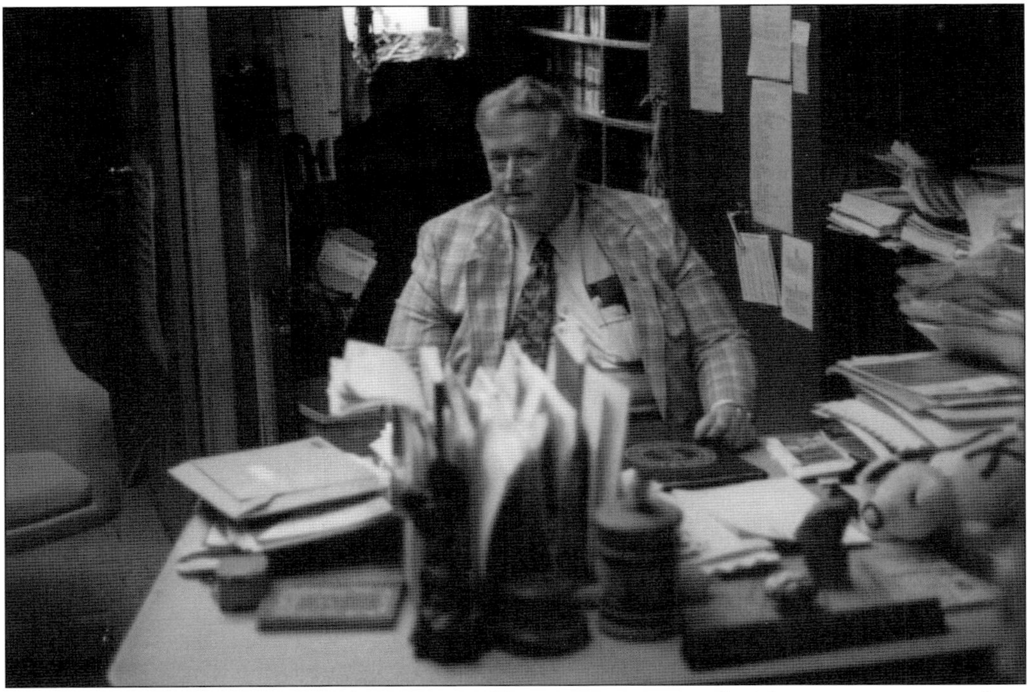

Clyde "Jack" Greenwood worked for the *Trimble Banner Democrat* for 32 years, serving as editor until his retirement in 1982. Greenwood also served as Trimble County judge in the 1960s, remaining editor of the newspaper throughout his term. (Courtesy of Gary Greenwood.)

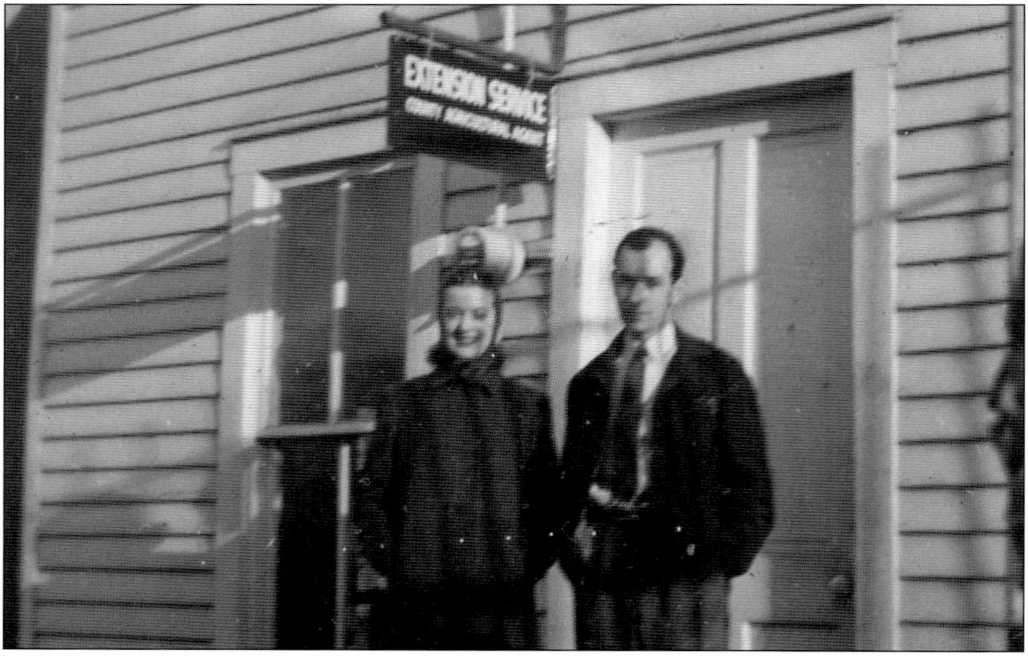

Trimble County extension agent J.D. Tolbert and his wife, Geraldine, pose in front of the Bedford office. The office, once located above what is now Rand Insurance, was damaged by fire in the 1940s and moved to the building that now is the judge-executive's office and the fiscal court meeting room. Former extension clerk Mildred Pardo Pruitt said the building was heated with a woodstove. (Courtesy of Robert Bruce "Bob" Stewart Jr.)

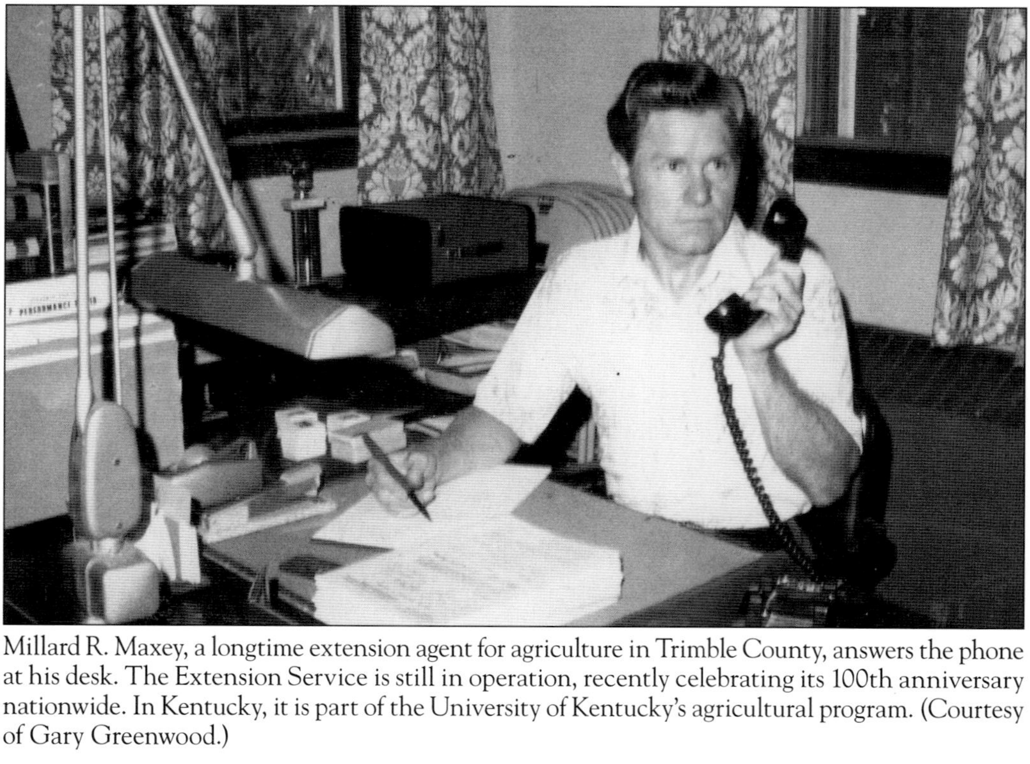

Millard R. Maxey, a longtime extension agent for agriculture in Trimble County, answers the phone at his desk. The Extension Service is still in operation, recently celebrating its 100th anniversary nationwide. In Kentucky, it is part of the University of Kentucky's agricultural program. (Courtesy of Gary Greenwood.)

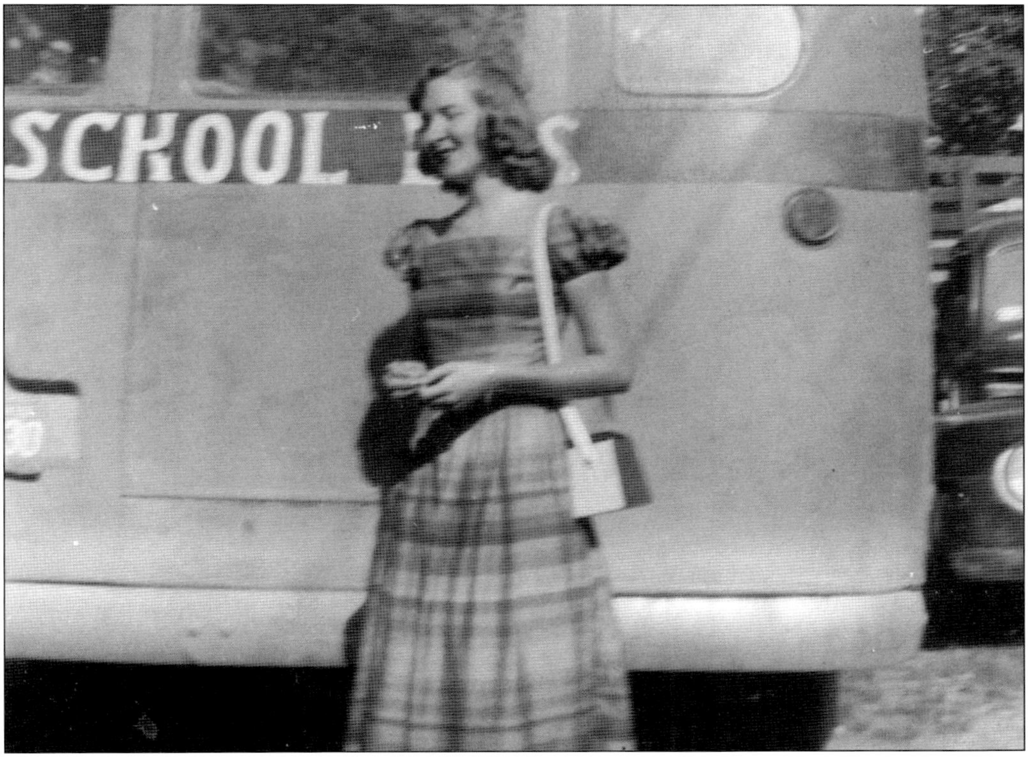

Mary Helen Hargrove Land served as Trimble County's second home demonstration agent at Trimble County extension office. (Courtesy of Kay Sachleben Barnes.)

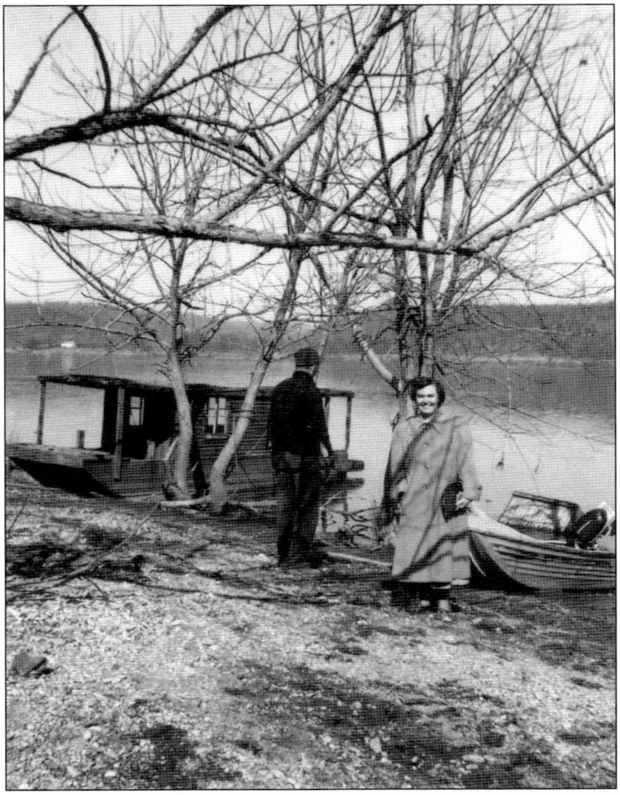

Joy Venters arranges a trip across the Ohio River at Wise's Landing in 1948. Venters was an English teacher at Trimble County High School. She also was an accomplished artist who donated paintings that were sold through advertisements in *Architectural Digest* magazine and raised $43,000 for charity. (Courtesy of Robert Bruce "Bob" Stewart Jr.)

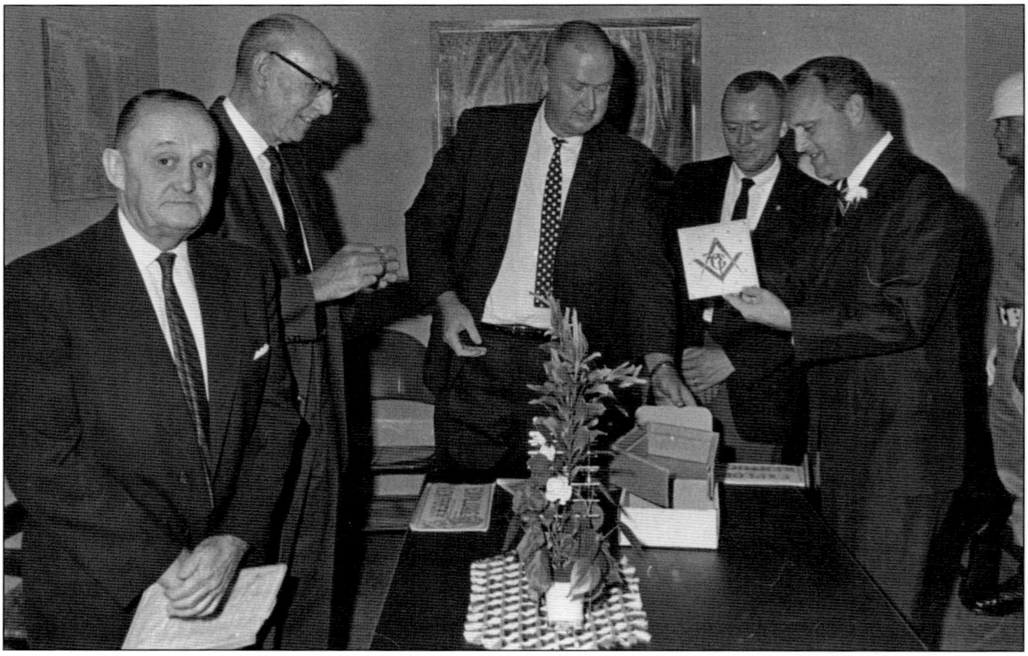

Local politicians meet with Kentucky's 51st governor, Edward Thompson "Ned" Breathitt, during a visit to Trimble County. From left to right are John William Rand, county clerk and Bedford Bank president Wallace Wright, County Judge Clyde "Jack" Greenwood, Jim Pirtle, and Breathitt, who served as governor from 1963 to 1967. (Courtesy of Gary Greenwood.)

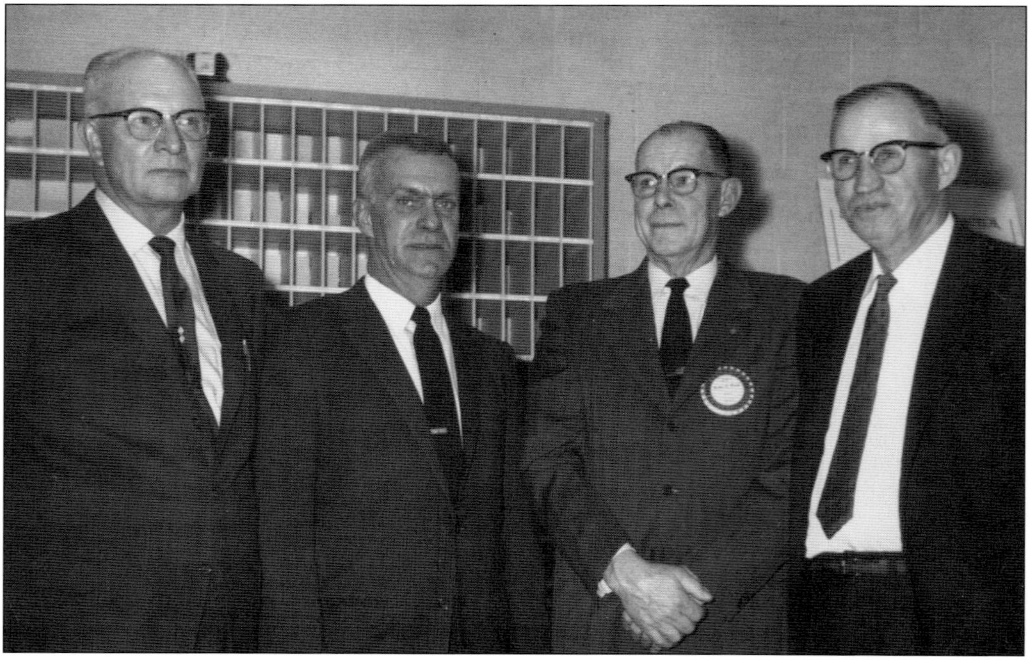

The Bedford post office on Main Street was dedicated in a ceremony on December 5, 1959, which included its rural mail carriers, from left to right, Wilbur Abbott, Harold Bryan, Keith H. Hood, and Flournoy Callis. The property is still rented to the US government by the Bedford Christian Church, next door, which benefits from the income. (Courtesy of Jean Rand.)

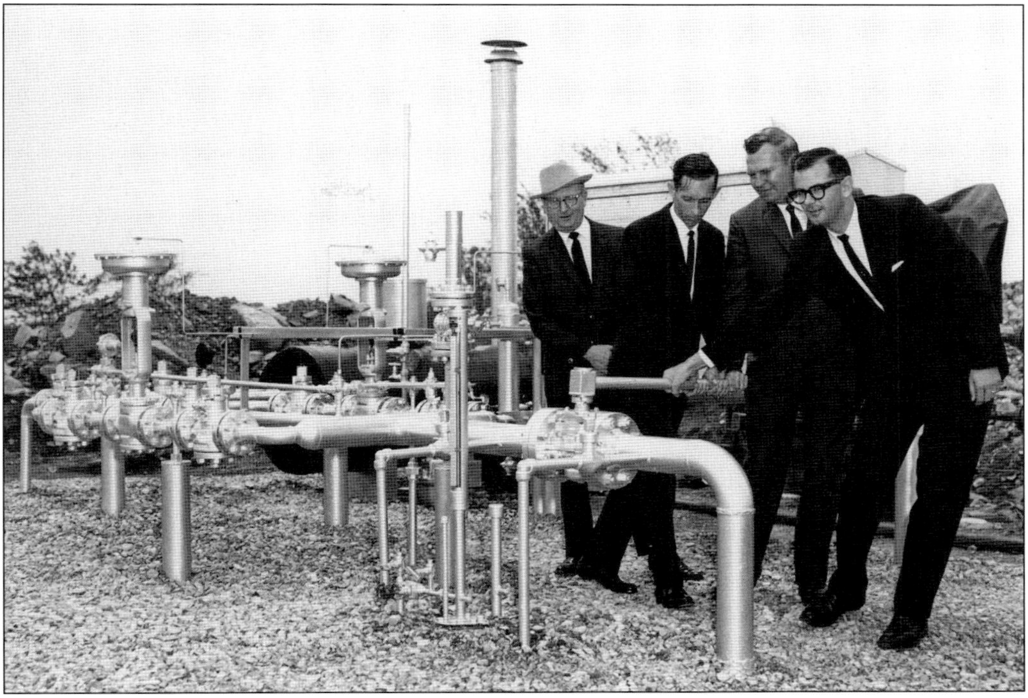

William Ransdell and others turn the valve in a ceremony dedicating the county's new natural gas service. (Courtesy of Frederica Congleton.)

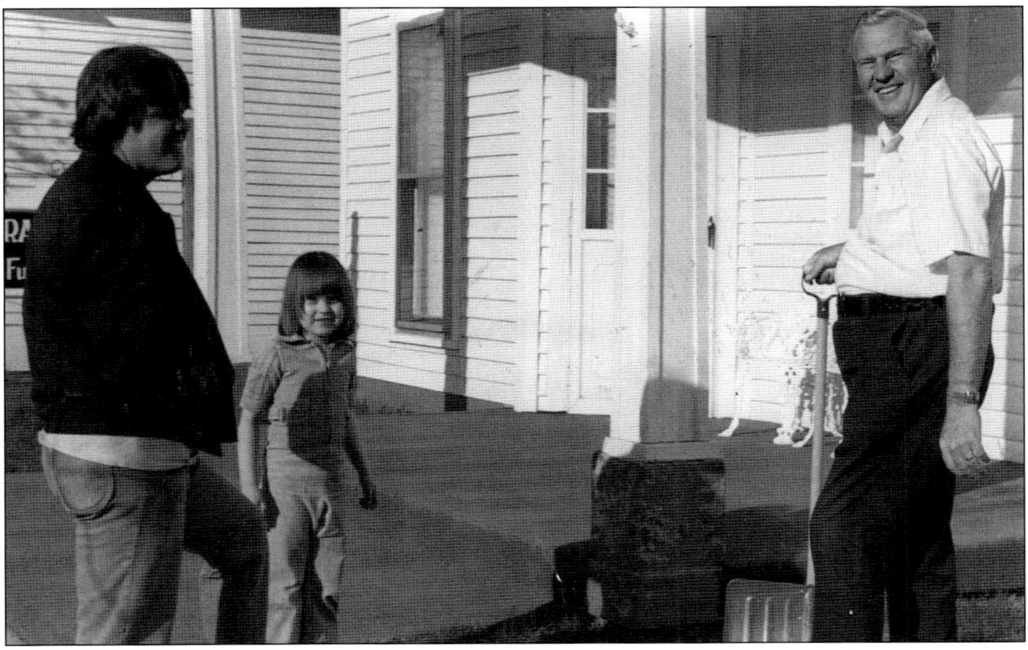

William Ransdell, right, stands in front of the first location of Ransdell Funeral Home on Main Street with his daughter, Frederica, and apprentice, Gary Ginn. Frederica and her husband, Lee Congleton, own the funeral home, now located in what once was the Wagon Wheel Inn near the outskirts of town. She also became Trimble County coroner after her father's death in 2008. Ginn was elected Fayette County coroner in 2002. (Courtesy of Frederica Congleton.)

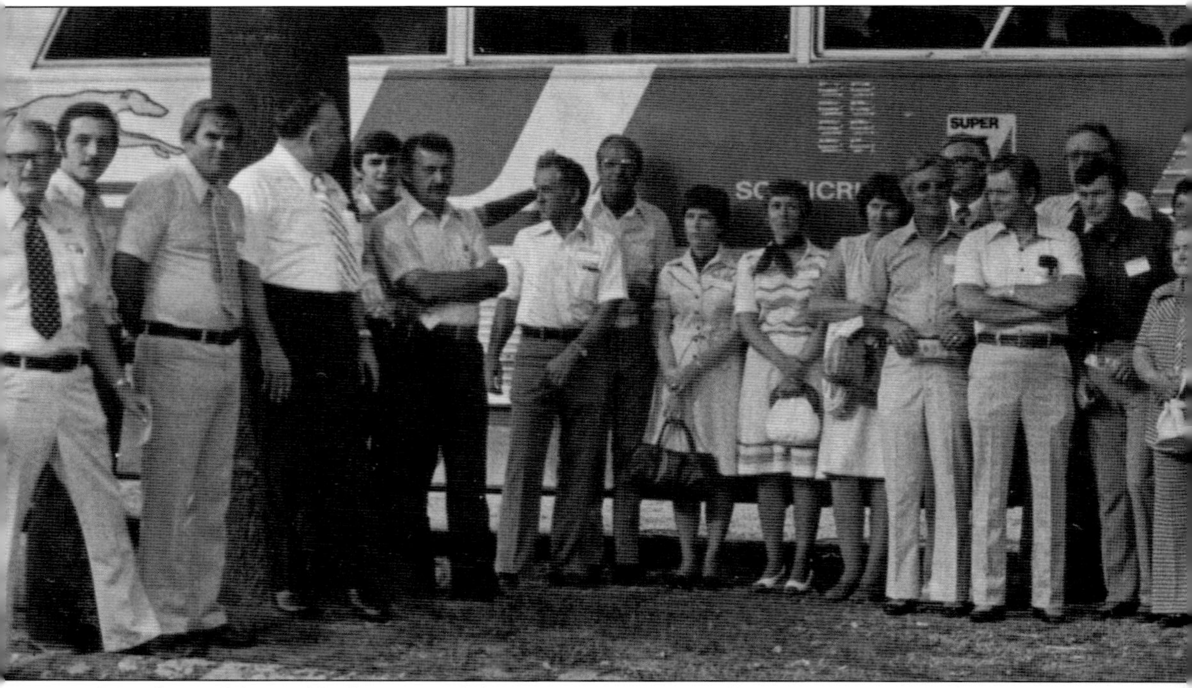

Members of the Bedford Rotary Club were guests of Louisville Gas & Electric for a tour of its Mill Creek generating facility in the 1980s to see what LG&E's proposed plant for Trimble County would look like. LG&E built the coal-fired Wise's Landing Generating Station, located on the

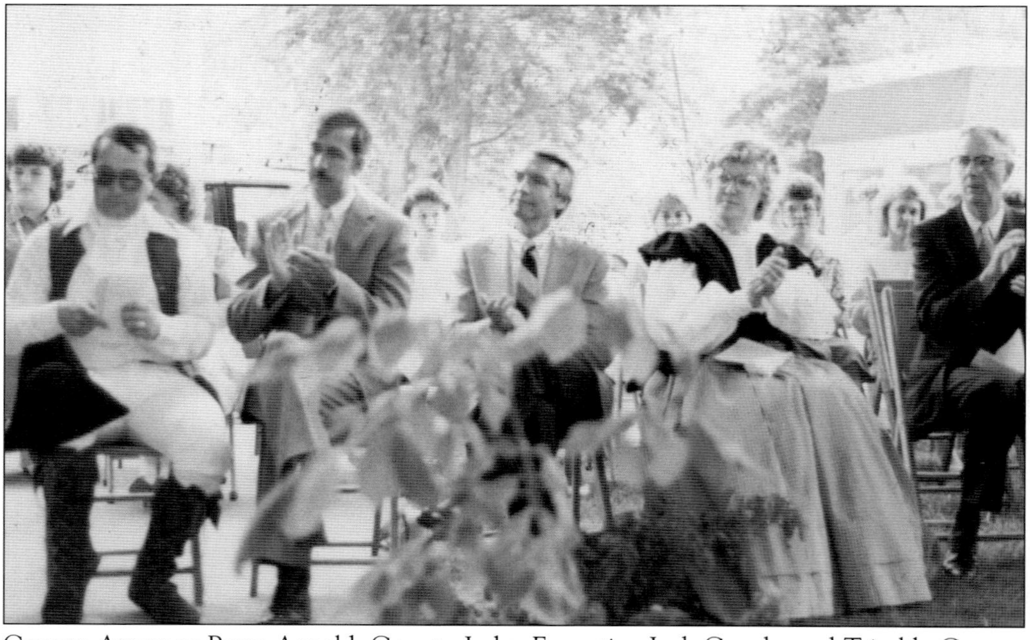

County Attorney Perry Arnold, County Judge-Executive Jack Couch, and Trimble County historian Donna Stark Thompson pose (some dressed in period costume) during the county's 1987 sesquicentennial celebration. Seated between Couch and Stark is Lt. Gov. Steve Beshear, who served under Gov. Martha Layne Collins. Beshear has served as governor since his election in 2007. (Courtesy of Hilda Parrish.)

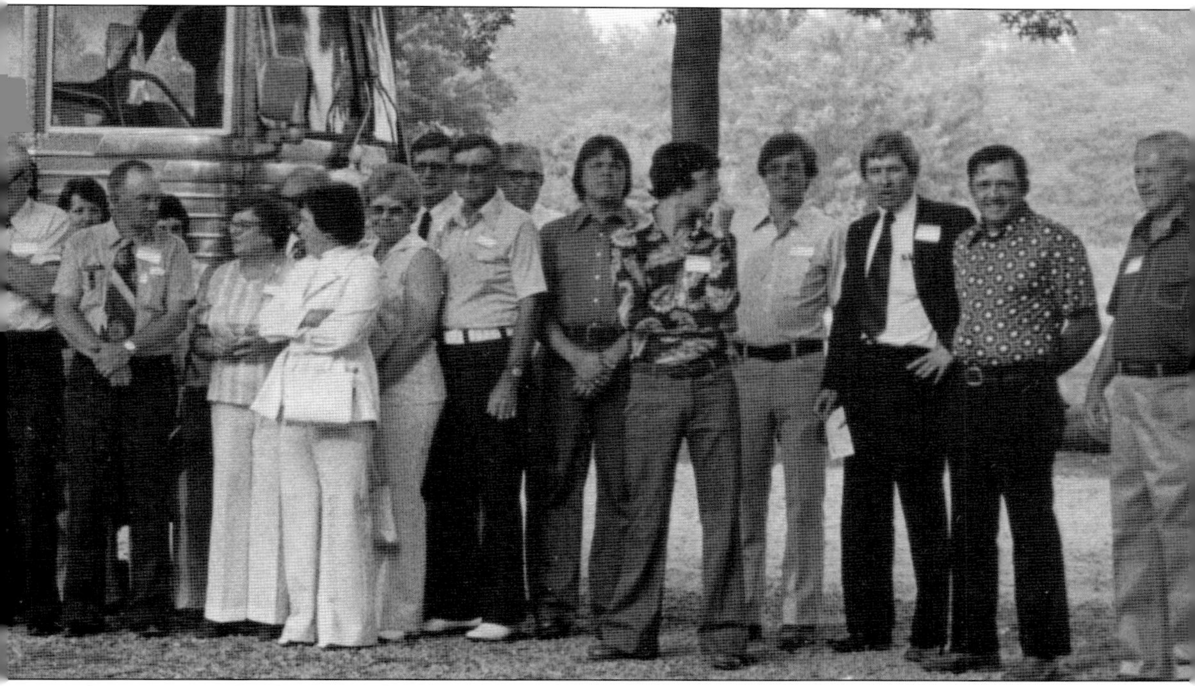

Ohio River on the far west side of the county, in the late 1980s. The plant went online in 1990. (Courtesy of Frederica Congleton.)

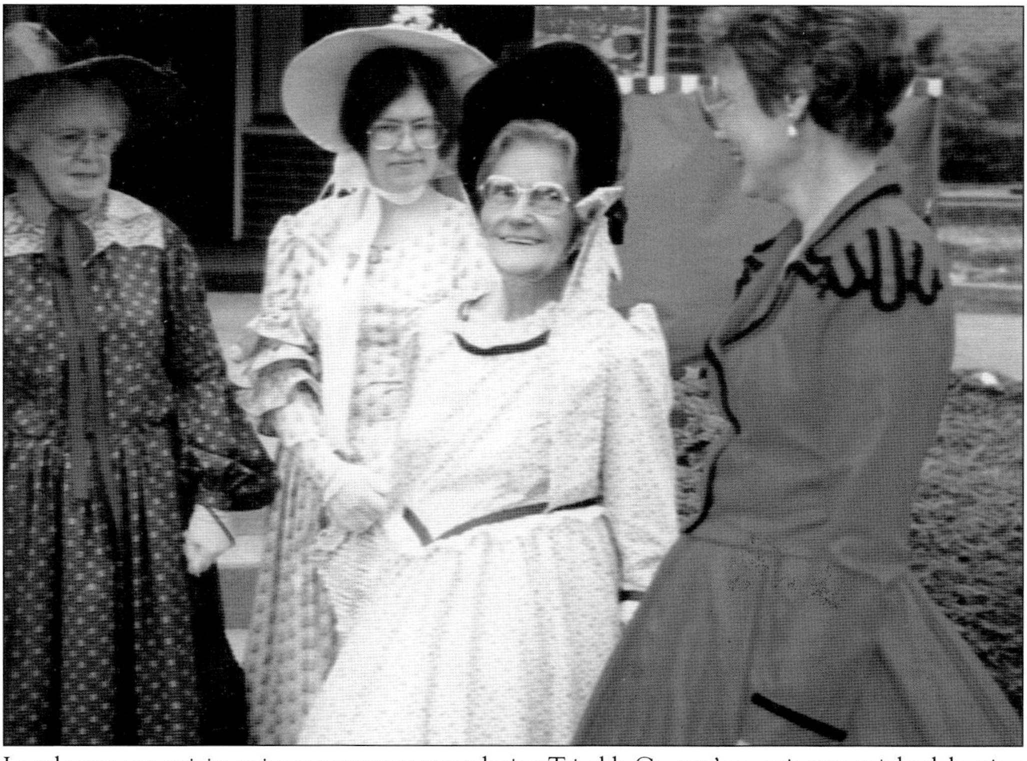

Local women participate in a costume contest during Trimble County's sesquicentennial celebration in 1987. (Courtesy of Frederica Congleton.)

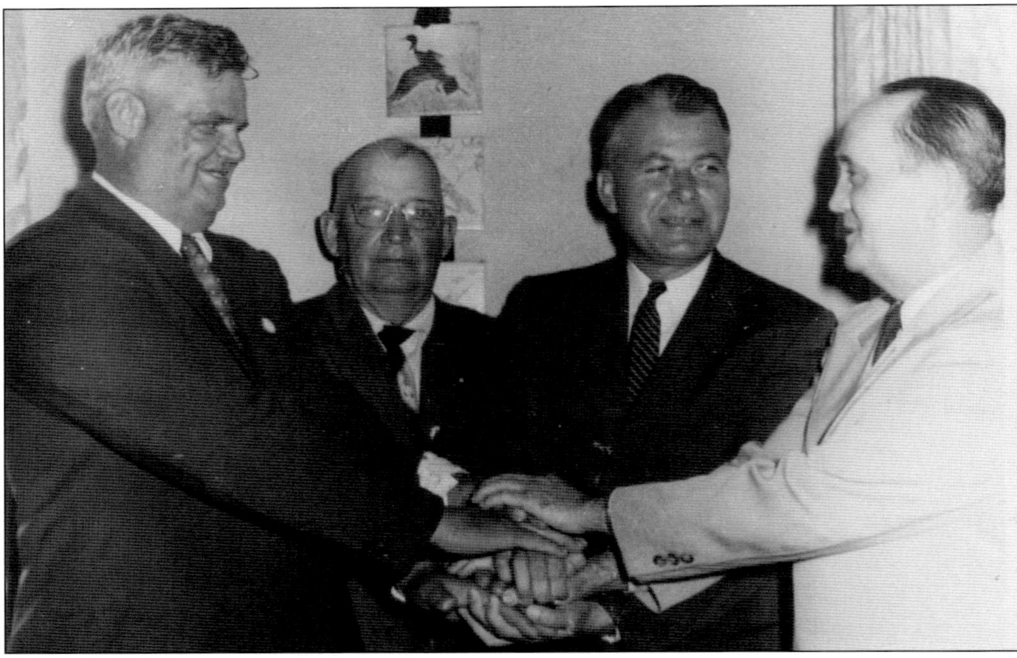

In an uncommon show of solidarity, Trimble County Republican and Democratic Party leaders shake hands after the 1959 election of Gov. Bert Coombs, who succeeded Gov. Albert B. "Happy" Chandler. From left to right are Republican Chester Ward; Republican Chairman Goode; Kentucky governor Burt Coombs, a Republican; and Democratic Chairman John Rand. (Courtesy of Reggie Rand.)

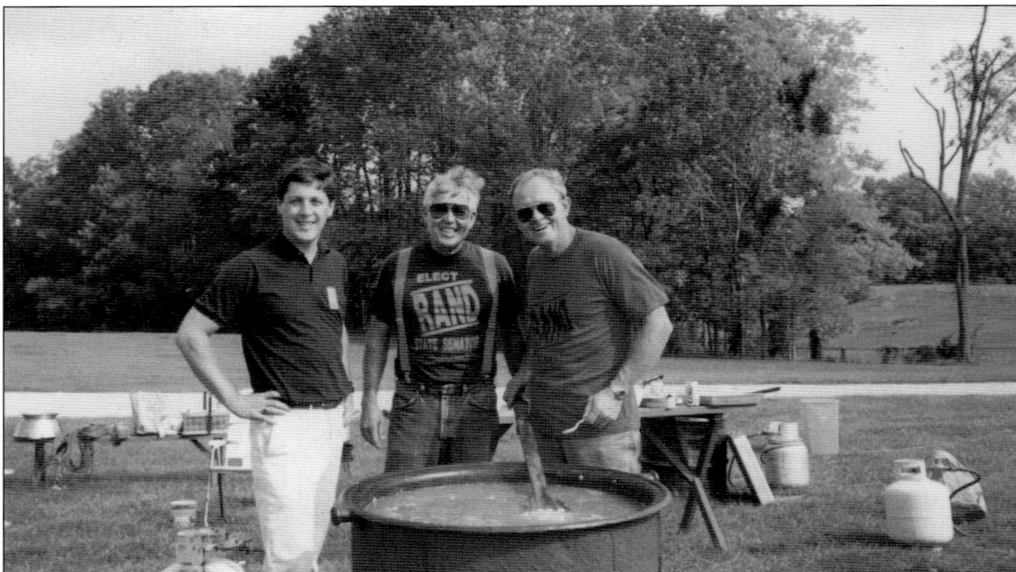

From left to right, Rick Rand, Reggie Rand, and Jim Pirtle cook up a pot of burgoo during the younger Rand's run for senator for the 26th District in 1990. Rand won that election but lost a bid for reelection in 1994. He reentered state politics in 2002, when he was elected to the House of Representative, serving the state's 47th District. He is chairman of the House Appropriations and Review Committee. (Courtesy of Reggie Rand.)

Three

Gone to War

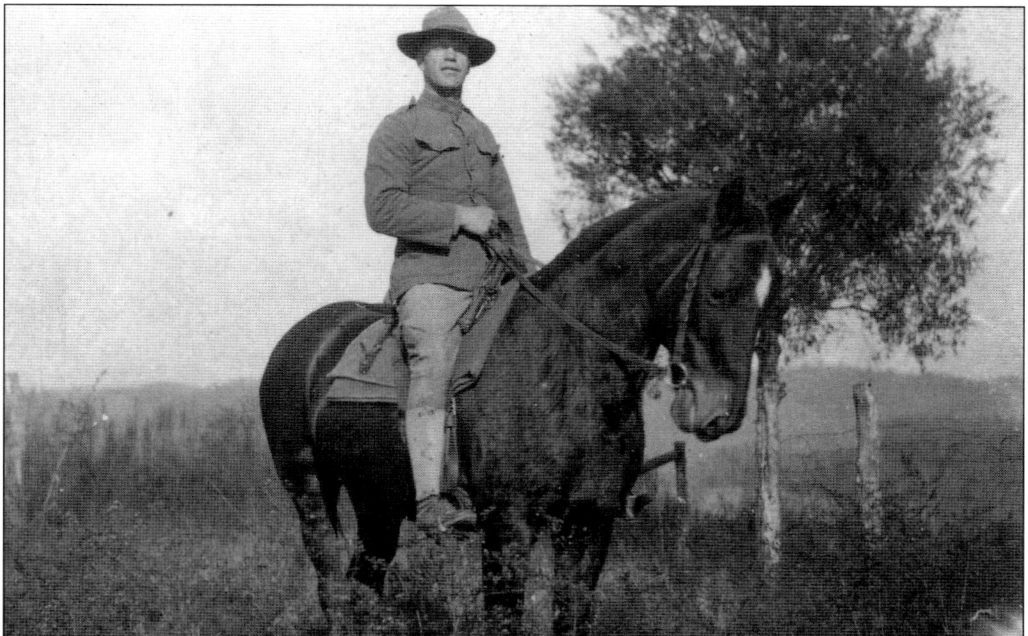

Perry Frances "Frank" Bates served in the cavalry during World War I. The son of Perry Richard and Florence Jobson Bates, he married Marguerite Green. He was a longtime farmer in the New Hope area north of Bedford. He also was known as an auctioneer and a correspondent for the *Trimble Democrat*. (Courtesy of Ted Taylor.)

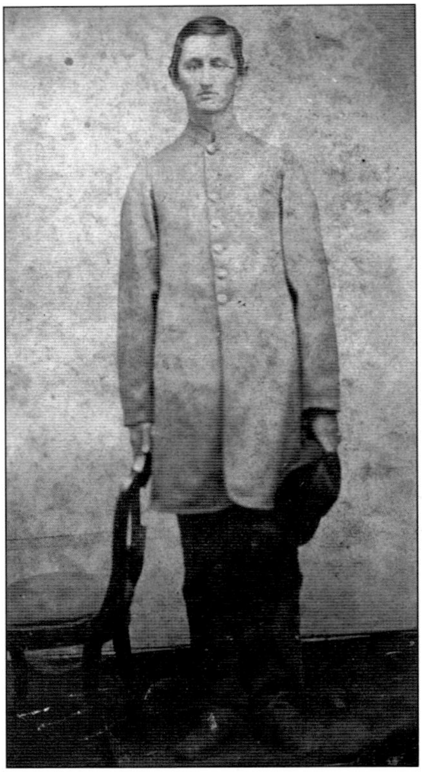

This Trimble County Confederate soldier is possibly William Rowan Jackson from the Young family. Jackson reportedly served with Gen. George Pickett and was buried in the Bedford Independent Order of Odd Fellows cemetery in his Civil War uniform. About 280 Trimble County men joined the CSA's 4th Kentucky Cavalry under Maj. Nathan Parker, with at least 18 lost in battle. (Courtesy of JoDeva Ogden.)

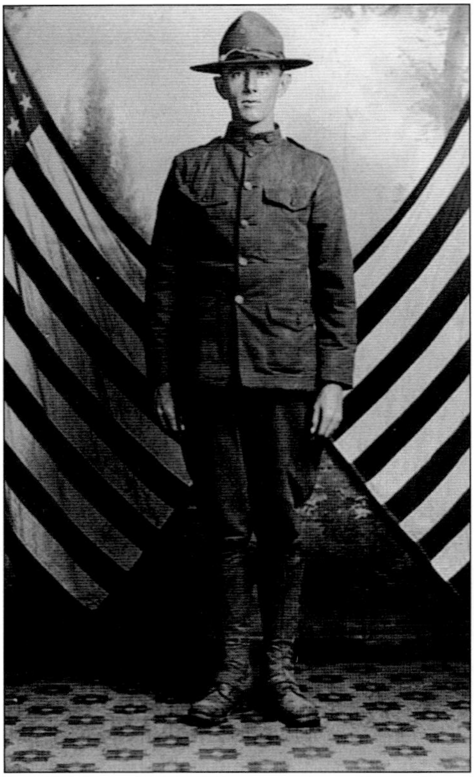

Robert Bruce Stewart Sr. spent three months of World War I at Camp Buell in Lexington after being called to report for duty on September 19, 1918. He apparently never made it to the battlefield, as Germany surrendered on November 11, less than two months later. He was honorably discharged on December 14 and sent home. (Courtesy of Robert Bruce "Bob" Stewart Jr.)

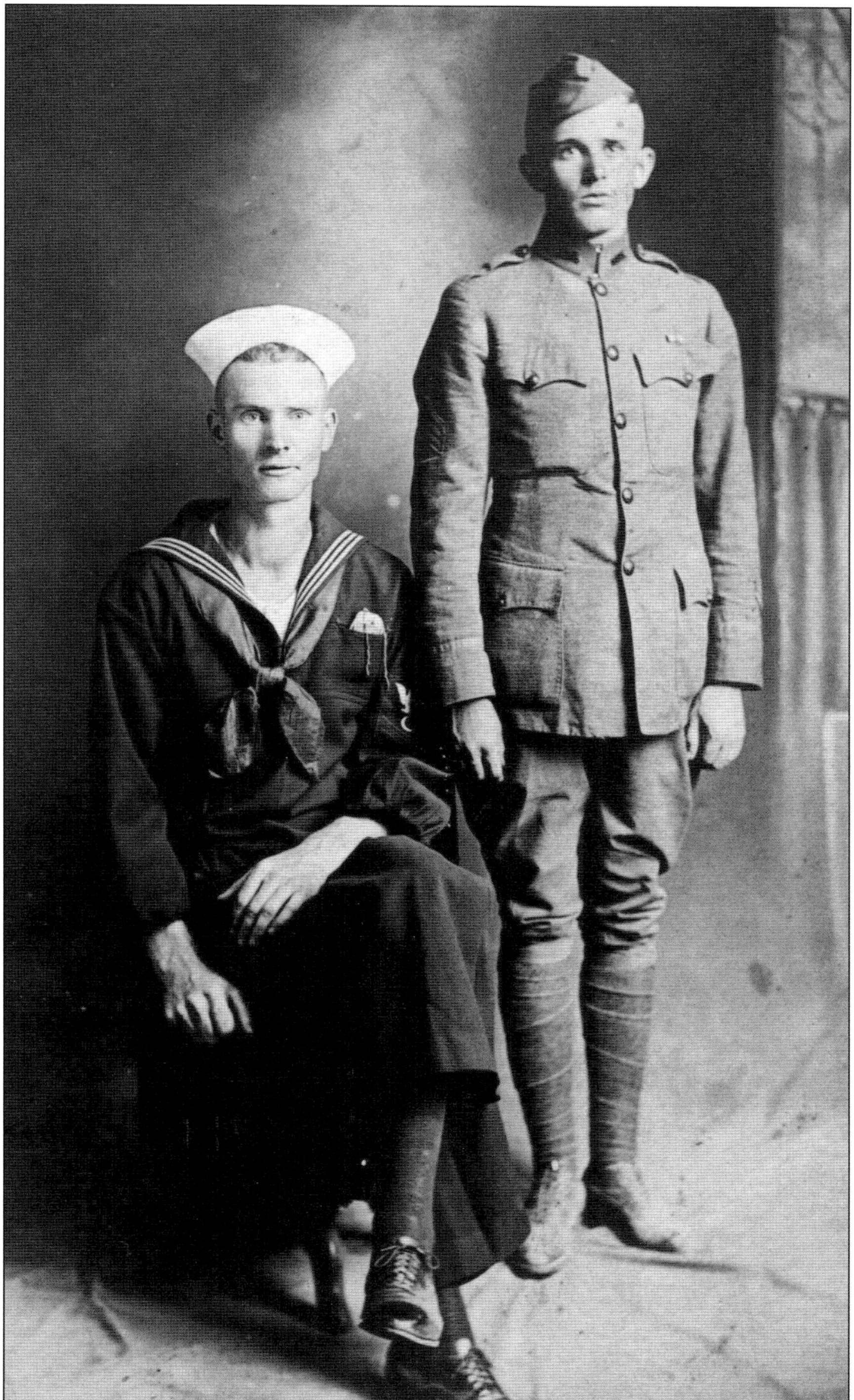

Jennings Bryan Greenwood (seated) was a son of William and Nora (McMahon) Greenwood. Named for famed orator and presidential candidate William Jennings Bryan, he served in the US Navy during World War I. His cousin William Bryan Moore (standing) also served in the US Army during the Great War. (Courtesy of Gary Greenwood.)

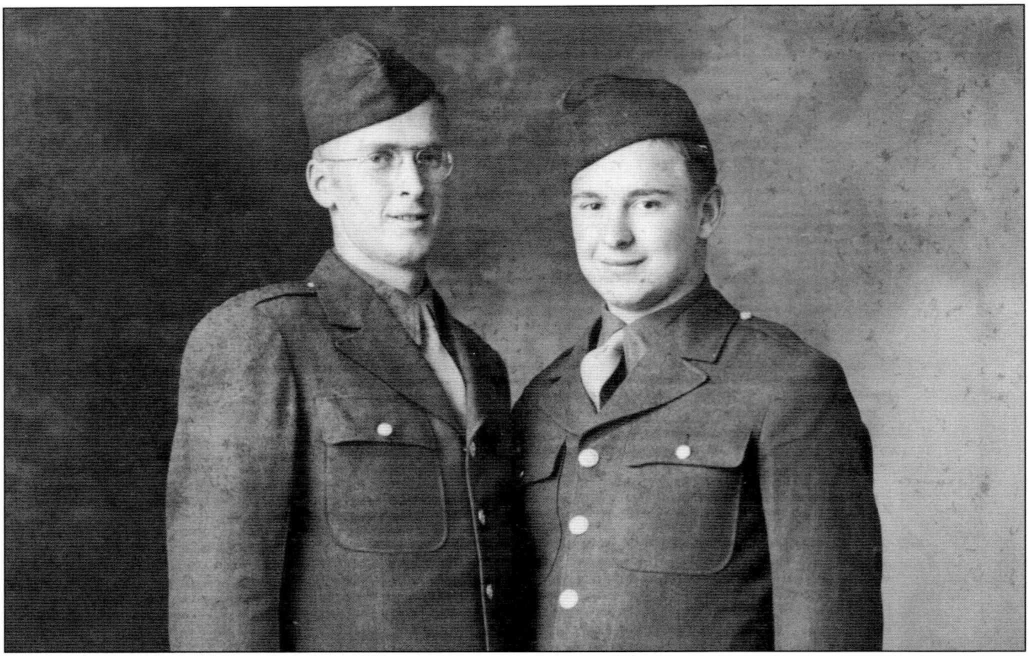

Pictured are Vernon Craig (left) and Clyde E. "Jack" Greenwood. Greenwood served as a radio operator in the HQ Battery of the 435th Field Artillery Battalion in the Pacific theater. Craig served as an automotive parts clerk and saw four major battles in Italy, earning him four Bronze Stars. (Courtesy of Gary Greenwood.)

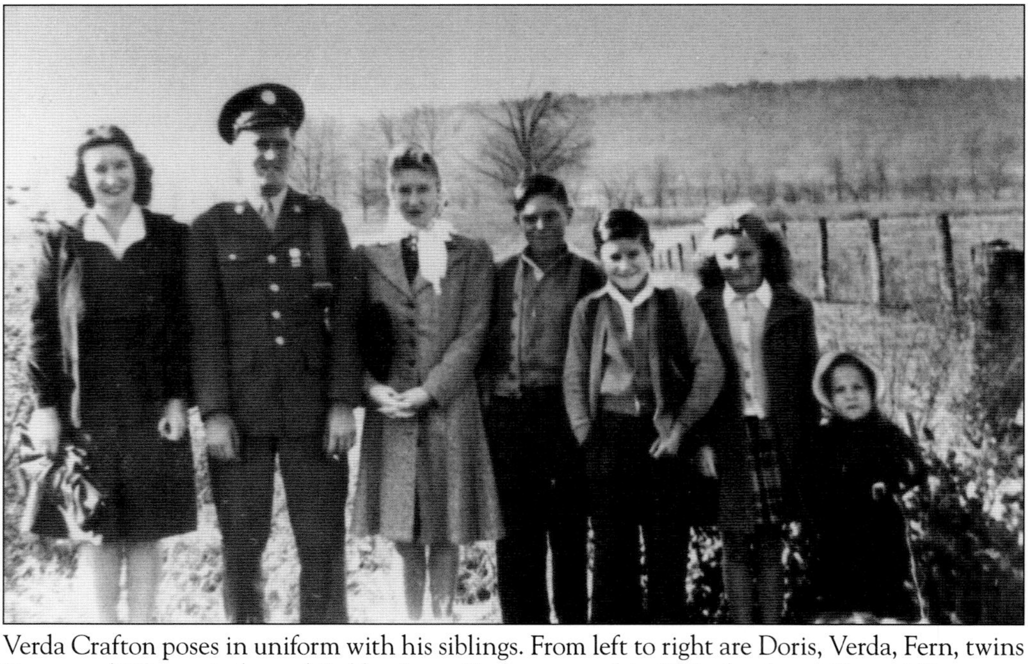

Verda Crafton poses in uniform with his siblings. From left to right are Doris, Verda, Fern, twins Payne and Wayne, Judy, and Bobby Ann. Crafton served in Rhineland and Central Europe as a crewman in the 556th Automatic Weapons Battalion, Coast Artillery Corps, earning the American Theater Ribbon, EAME Theater Ribbon, two Bronze Stars, and World War II Victory medal, as well as a good conduct medal. (Courtesy of Carolyn Crafton Adams.)

John Rand served in the Army during World War II. After leaving the service, he went into the insurance business and became very active in the Democratic Party, serving as president of the party's county organization. His grandson Rick Rand followed in his footsteps and operates Rand Insurance and serves as a representative in the Kentucky General Assembly. (Courtesy of Reggie Rand.)

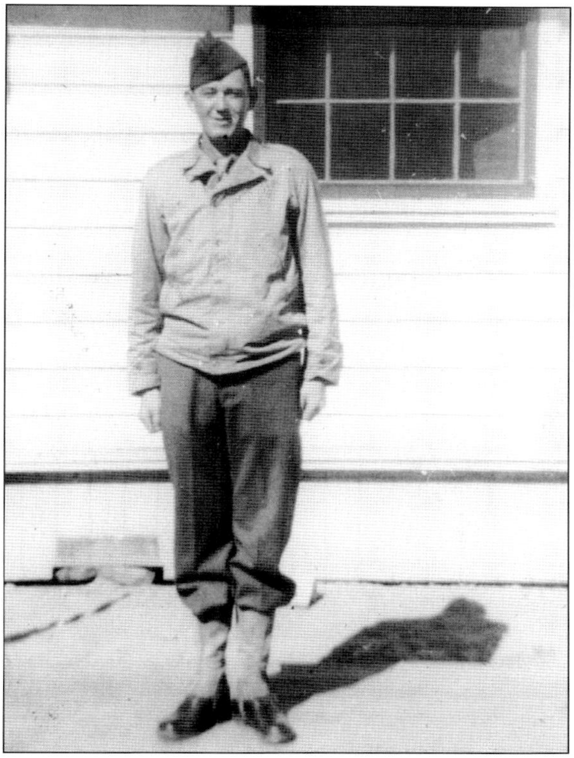

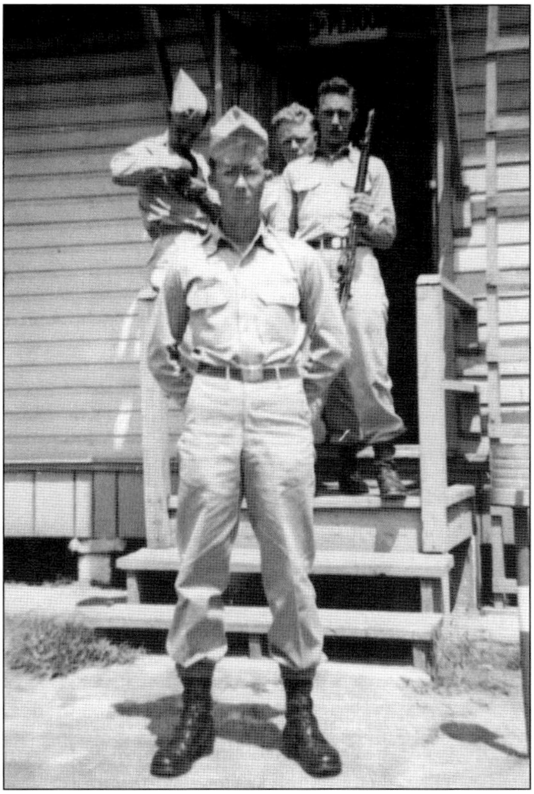

Harold Dean Ralston served in the Army at Fort Knox. After leaving the military, he worked at the Pabst Blue Ribbon brewery in Louisville and later as a mail carrier. (Courtesy of Sue Ralston Reid.)

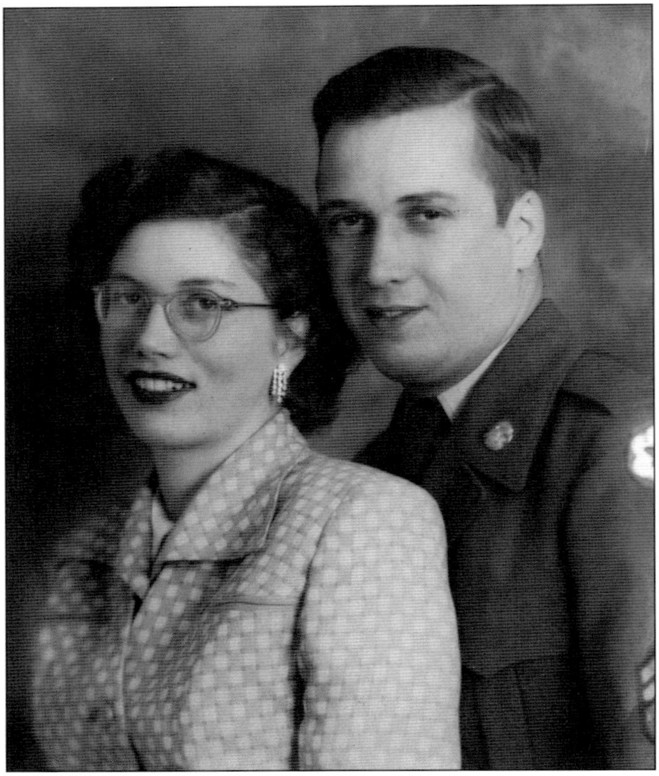

Neilen Boatwright poses in uniform with his sister, Charlene. Boatwright made a career in the Army, serving for 27 years. He later taught Reserved Officer Training Corps classes in Georgia. (Courtesy of Charlene Boatwright Ellis.)

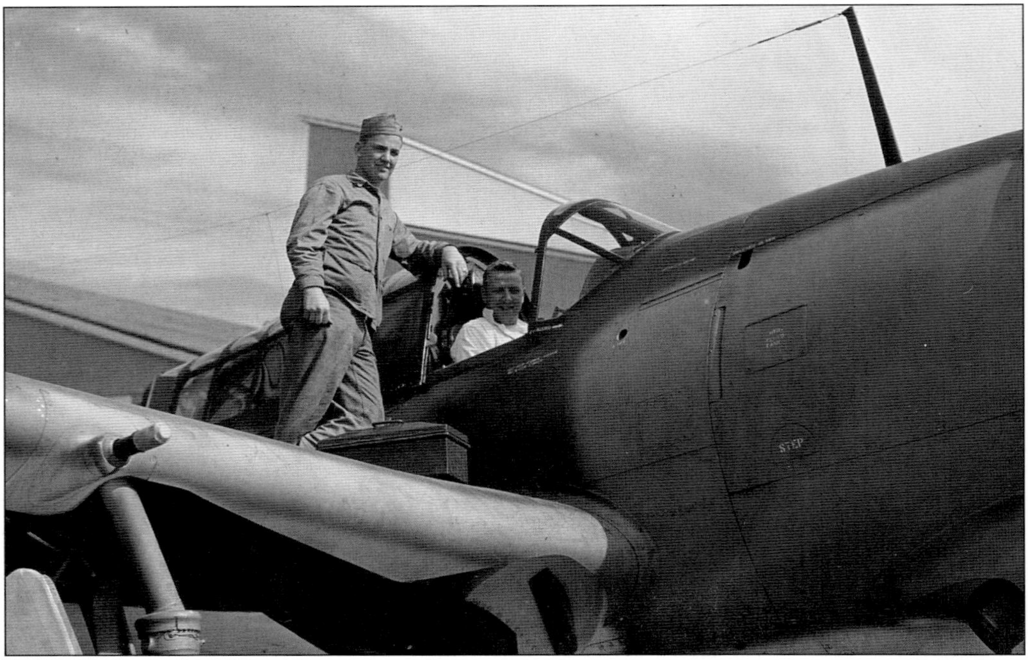

Carroll Merlin Ewing stands on the wing of a fighter during his first military stint in World War II. He also served in Korea. He settled in northern Kentucky and was mayor of Florence from 1961 to 1981. He is credited with creating the iconic "Florence Y'All" sign on the water tower next to Florence Mall. (Courtesy of Mildred Pardo Pruitt.)

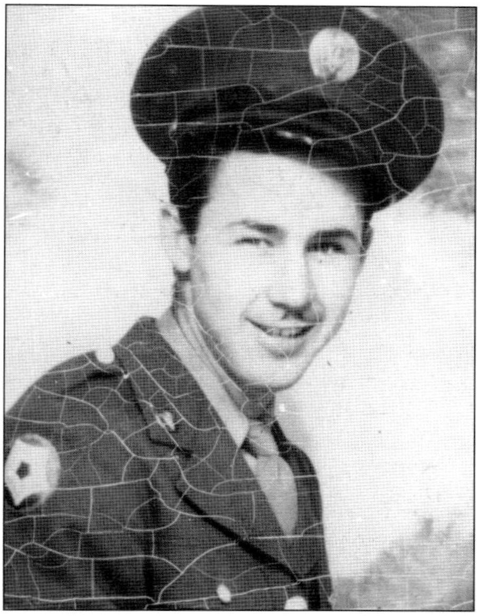

Cecil Hubert Ralston served in the Army during World War II. He started in the infantry but was reassigned as an ambulance driver when officials realized his left eye was a glass eye. He'd saved up money for the surgery when he was a teenager by selling his own paintings. After the war, he became an artist who worked on commission. (Courtesy of Sue Ralston Reid.)

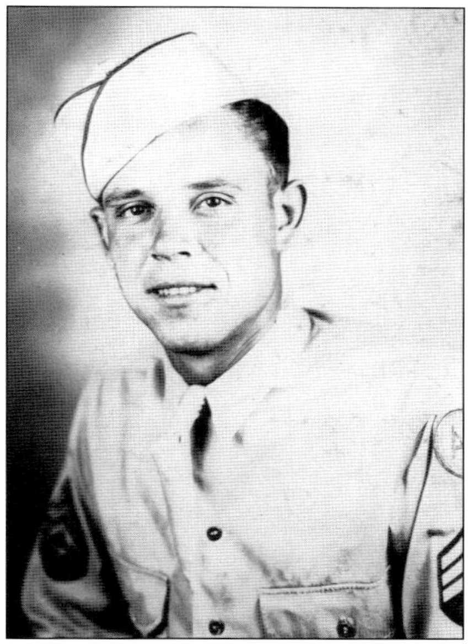

James "Billy" Wingham also served in the Army during World War II. He enlisted in January 1941 in Louisville as a warrant officer. (Courtesy of Ted Taylor.)

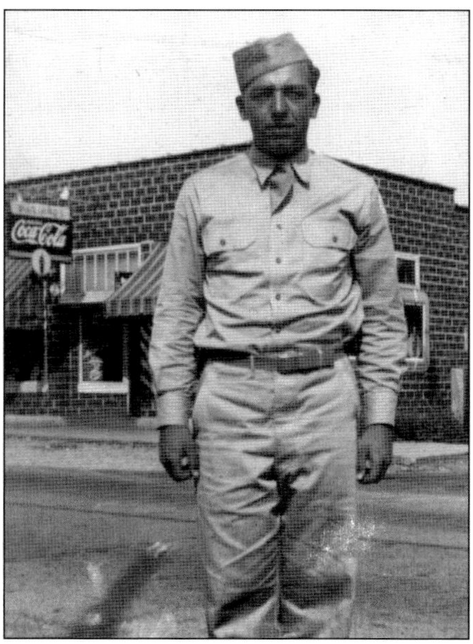

Hayward Tingle served in the 177th General Hospital, reaching the rank of corporal. He served on the US 117th General Hospital, which was stationed in Frenchay, Bristol, England, in 1944. (Courtesy of the Trimble County Public Library.)

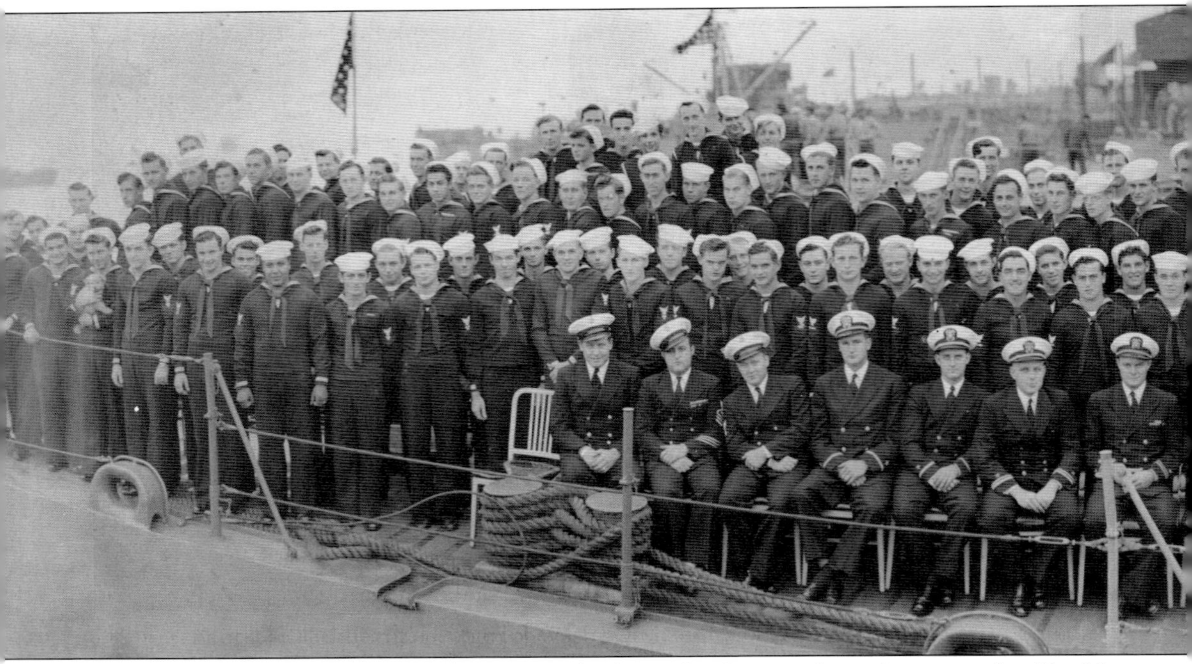

The naval unit of Arthur "Buck" Ellis is pictured. Also in the photograph is at least one other Trimble

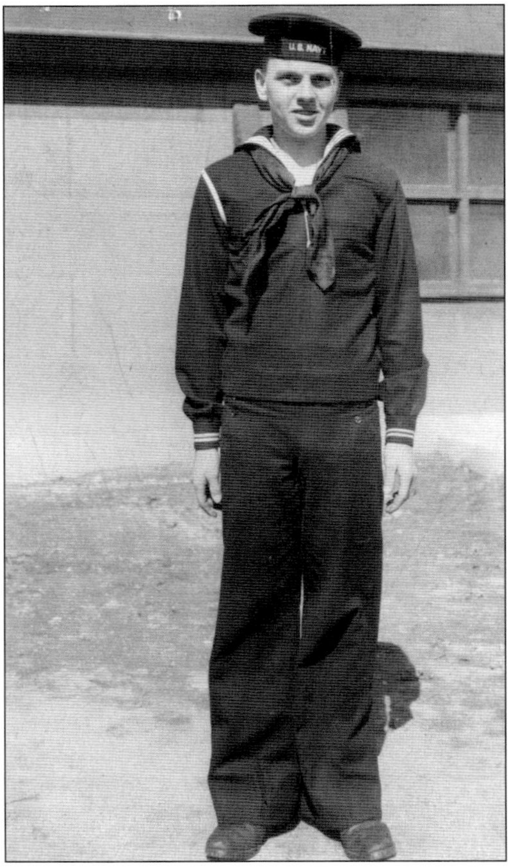

Arthur "Buck" Ellis served in the Navy during World War II. Though he was born and raised in Carroll County, he married Josie Charlene Boatwright and moved to Milton, where they raised their family. (Courtesy of Charlene Boatwright Ellis.)

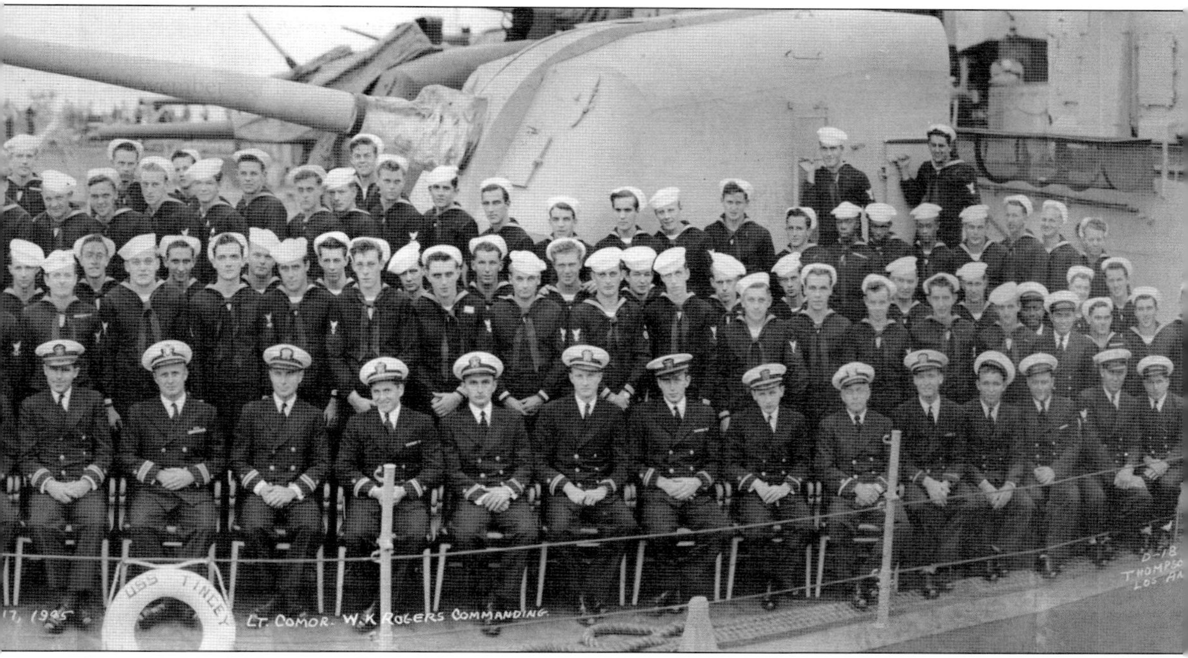

Countian, Gale P. Young, who enlisted with Ellis. (Courtesy of Charlene Boatwright Ellis.)

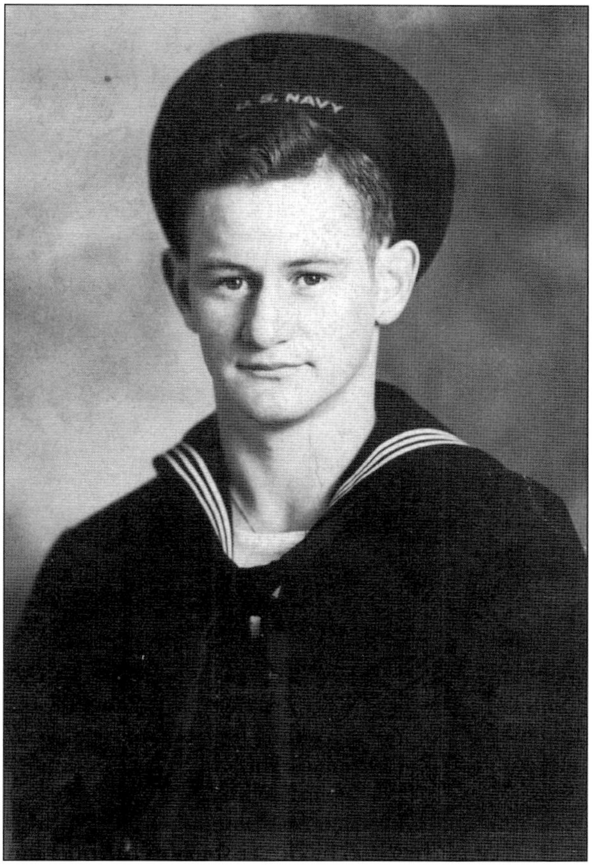

James Douglas Black served as a pharmacist's mate in Michigan, California, and the South Pacific, including Samoa and Melanesia. After returning home, he worked at the Jefferson Proving Grounds in Madison, Indiana. He was mayor of Bedford for 18 years and became the county's first emergency medical technician. (Courtesy of Eunice Black.)

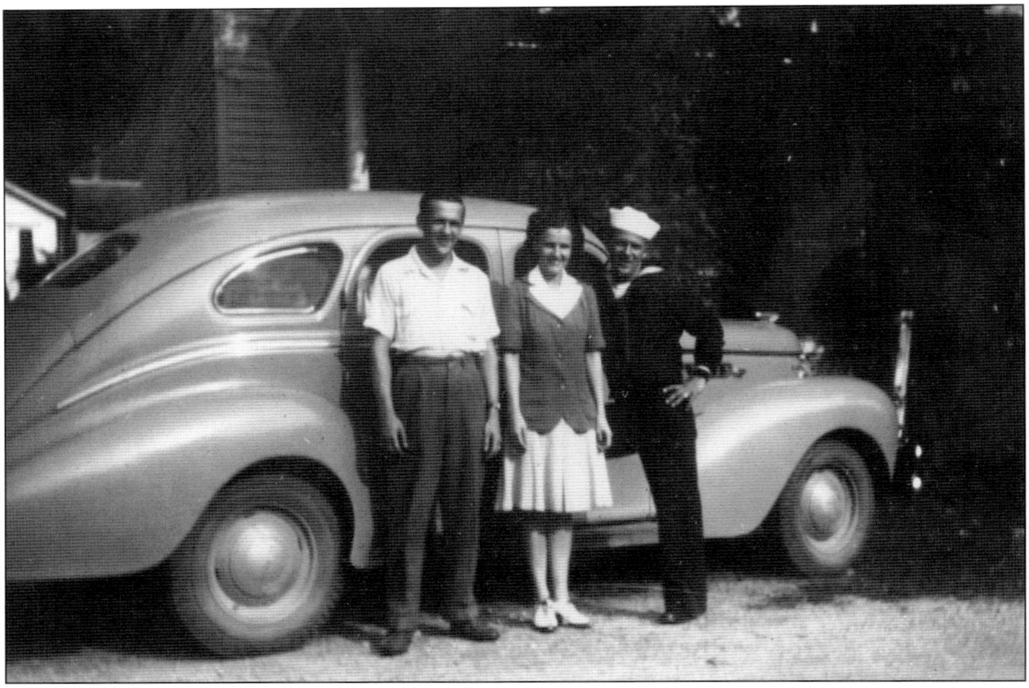

Glenford and Gladys Carder pose next to their father's 1939 DeSoto with brother Darrell Carder, who served as an electrician's mate first class in the Navy during World War II. He served on the PC-490, a submarine chaser, in the Caribbean and South Atlantic. (Courtesy of Bill Henderson.)

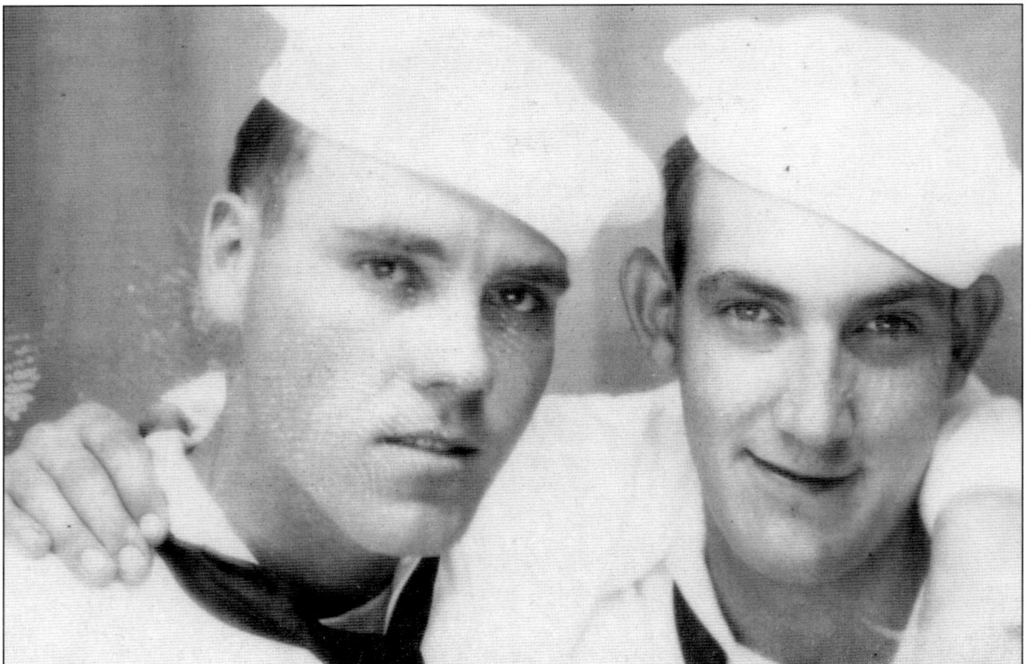

Brothers Harry Leroy "Roy" and Orba Lee Boldery pose in their Navy uniforms. Both brothers served on the LST-606, a landing ship, in the Philippines and Okinawa, Japan. (Courtesy of Trimble County Public Library.)

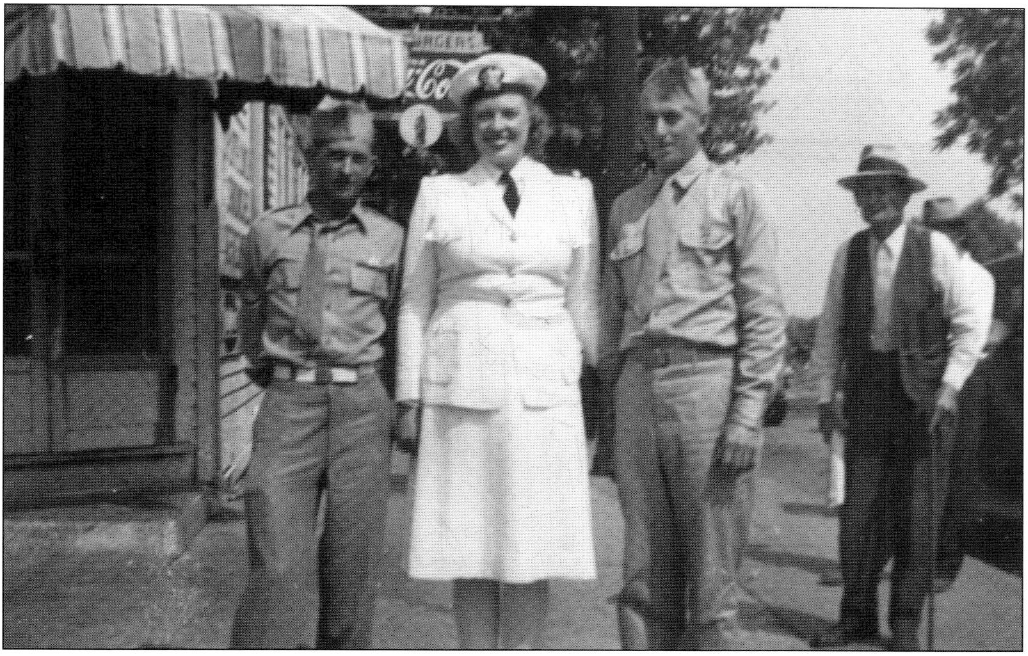

Alfred Jones, left, and Evelyn Tingle pose in uniform with another inductee named Bryan in downtown Bedford. Jones was trained as a sharpshooter but served as a cook in the 12th Battalion Armored Replacement Training Center. Tingle served in the Navy. (Courtesy of Trimble County Historical Society.)

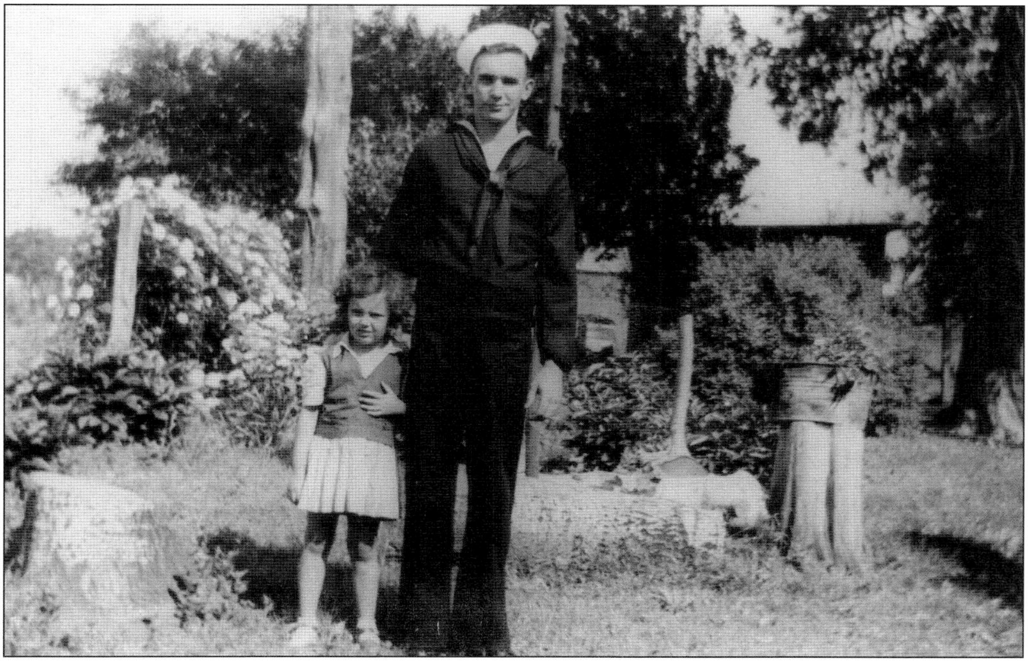

Allen Sanders poses with his cousin Alma Doris Ogden in Bedford. Allen and his brother Richard both were captured and spent time as prisoners of war in Europe during World War II. (Courtesy of JoDeva Ogden.)

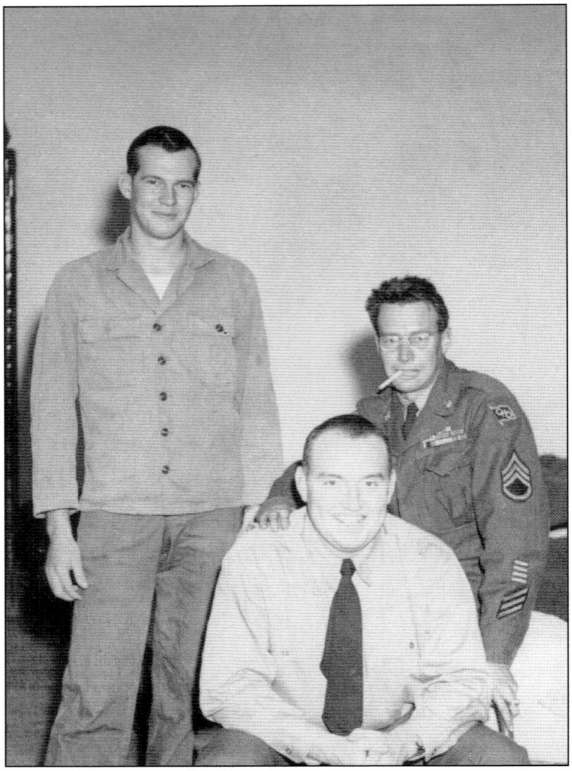

William Ransdell, standing, served in the graves registration unit in Japan during the Korean War. Ransdell returned to Bedford and open the Ransdell Funeral Home. He also served as Trimble County coroner for many years. (Courtesy of Frederica Congleton.)

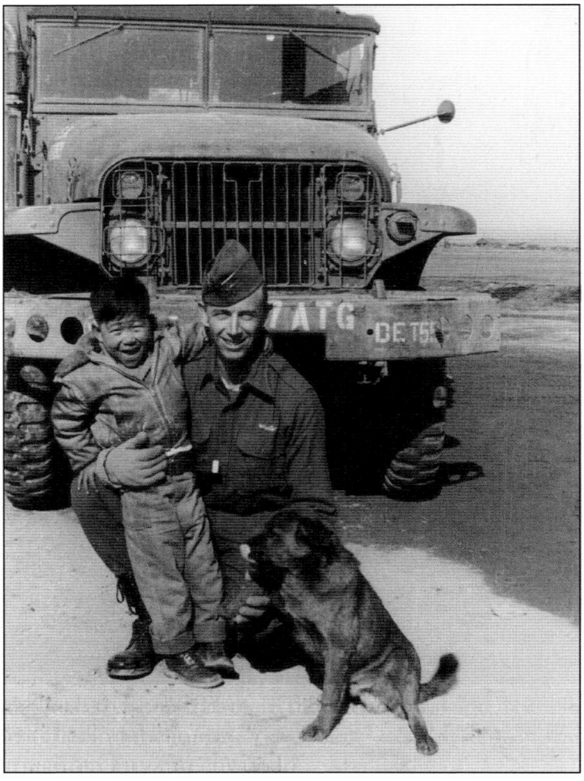

Robert Bruce "Bob" Stewart Jr. poses with a young friend in Kimpo, South Korea, in 1954. Stewart, whose father served in the Army during World War II, served in the US Air Force and, at this time, was assigned to the 11th Tactical Reconnaissance Squadron, 5th Air Force, at K-14. He retired at the rank of lieutenant colonel in 1975, serving during the Cuban Missile Crisis and later during the Vietnam War. (Courtesy of Robert Bruce "Bob" Stewart Jr.)

Maj. Gen. Benjamin J. Butler was a highly decorated combat veteran of World War II. During the war, he saw 400 days of front-line combat in Africa and Italy. In 1964, he became a commander of the 100th Division, US Army Reserve. He retired in 1970 but returned in 1973 to resume command of the division. He retired again in 1976, having earned the Distinguished Service Medal, the Silver Star, the Legion of Merit, the Bronze Star, and the Purple Heart. (Courtesy of the Trimble County courthouse.)

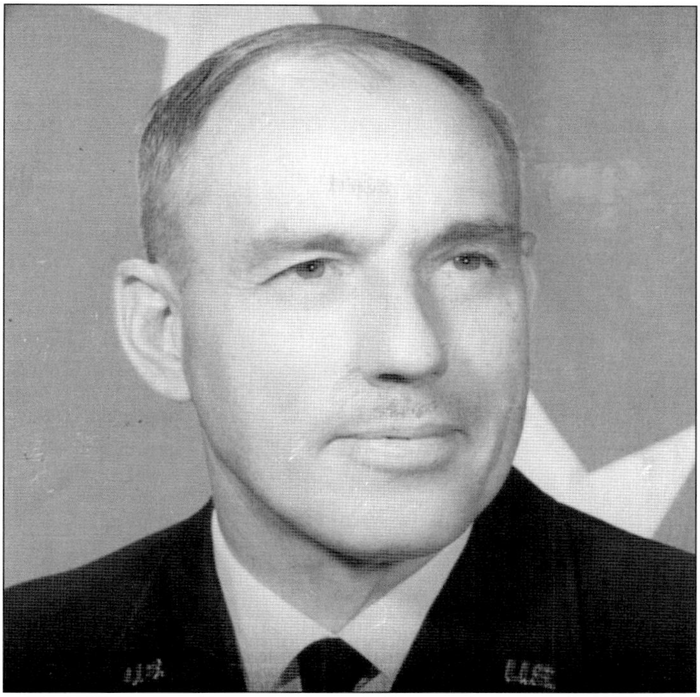

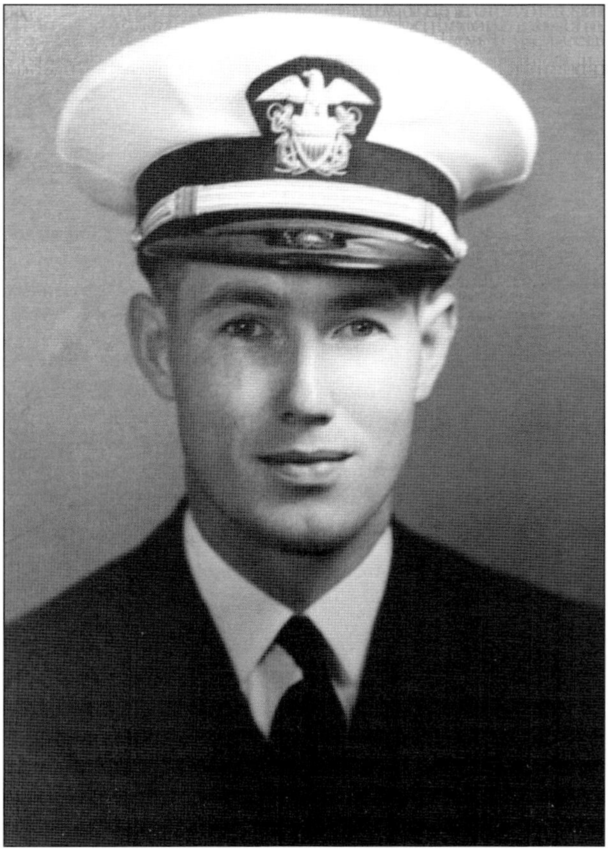

Ens. Mark C. Butler Jr. served as a midshipman on the USS *Silverbell* and participated in the liberation of the Philippines. Previously a social studies teacher at Trimble County High School, Butler completed his tour as commanding officer of a net-laying vessel. (Courtesy of the Trimble County Historical Society.)

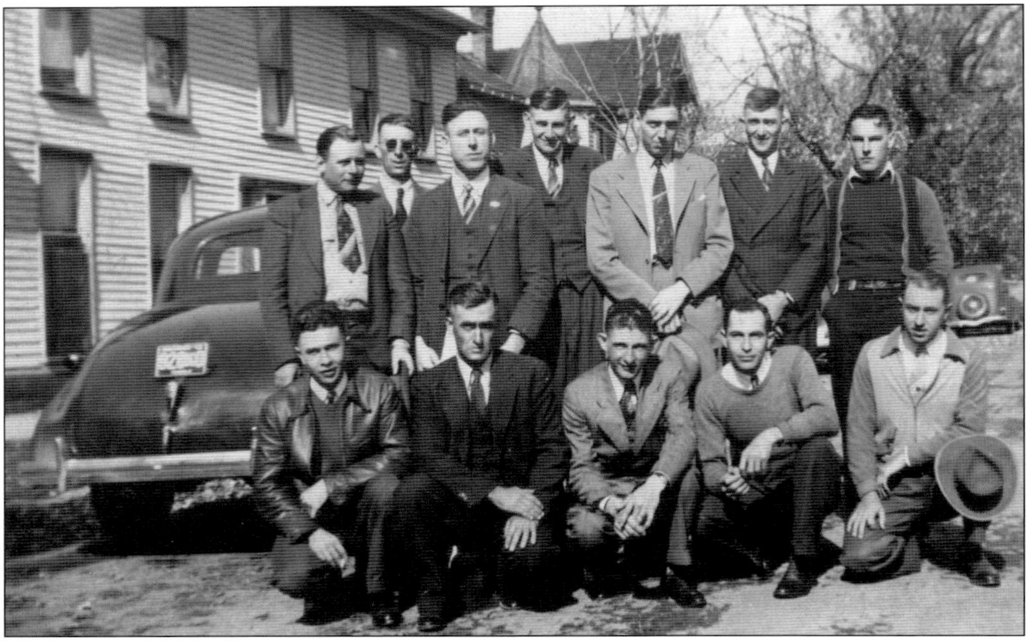

Gale Porter Young, kneeling at far left, poses with others called to duty by the Trimble County office of the Selective Service during World War II. Young served as a supply technician with the 1503rd Army Air Force based at Hamilton Air Force Base in California. (Courtesy of the Trimble County Historical Society.)

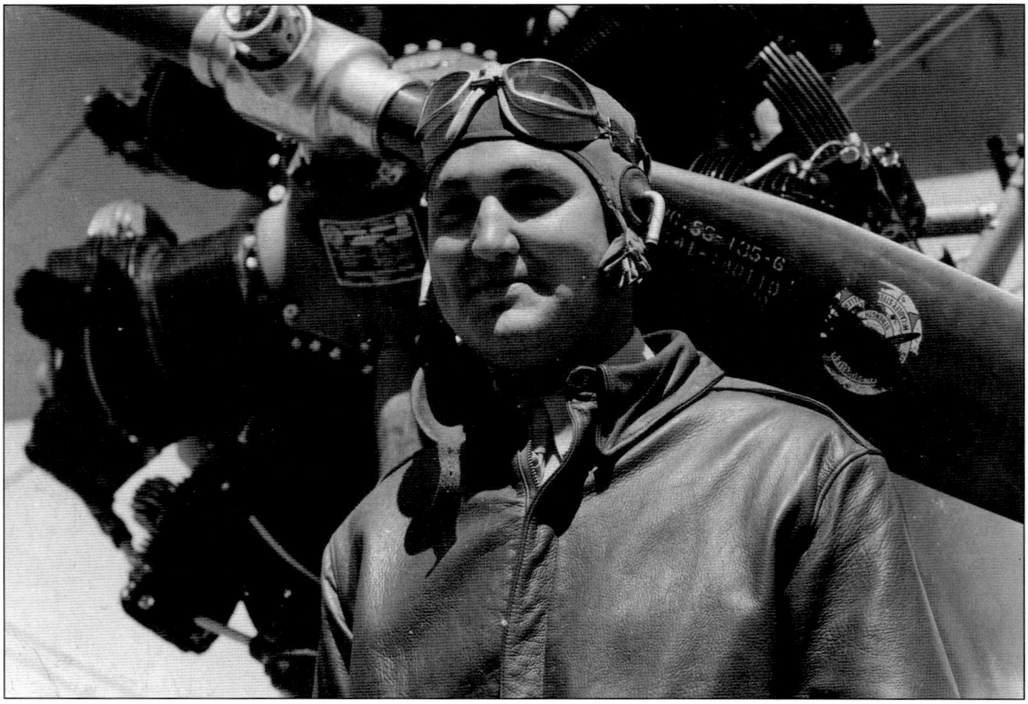

Robert A. Poland rose to the rank of major during his career in the military, which started in World War II. Here, he poses for the Tulane University yearbook. (Courtesy of the Trimble County Historical Society.)

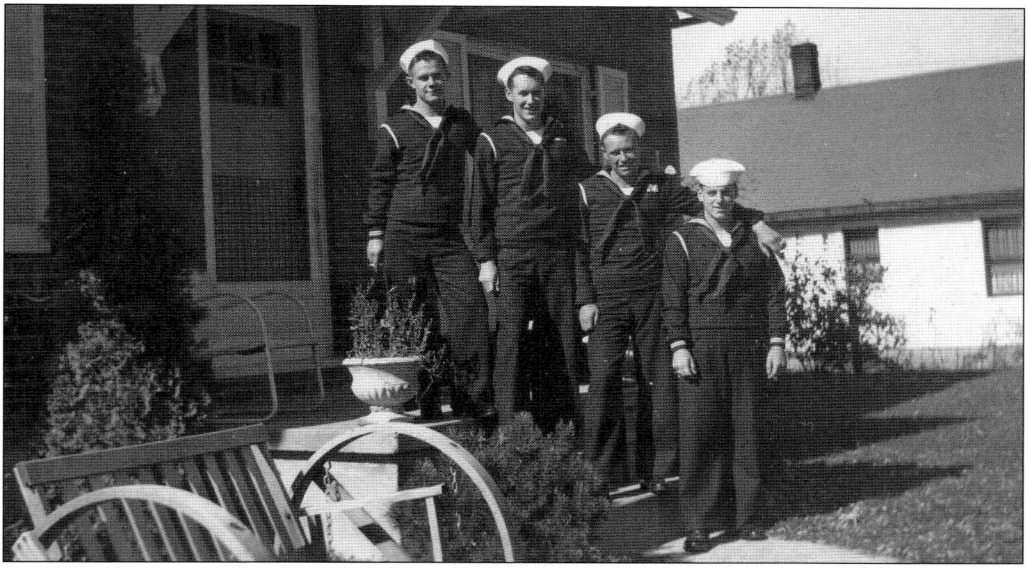

Buddies pose together before shipping off for the Navy. From left to right are Leonard Spillman, who served US Fleet Hospitals; John Bowman, who served on the USS *Gentry* in the North Atlantic and Pacific theaters; Kenneth Harmon, who served on the USS *Lough* in the Philippines; and Glenn Lee Hutcherson, who served on the USS *Willis* in the European and Pacific theaters. (Courtesy of the Trimble County Historical Society.)

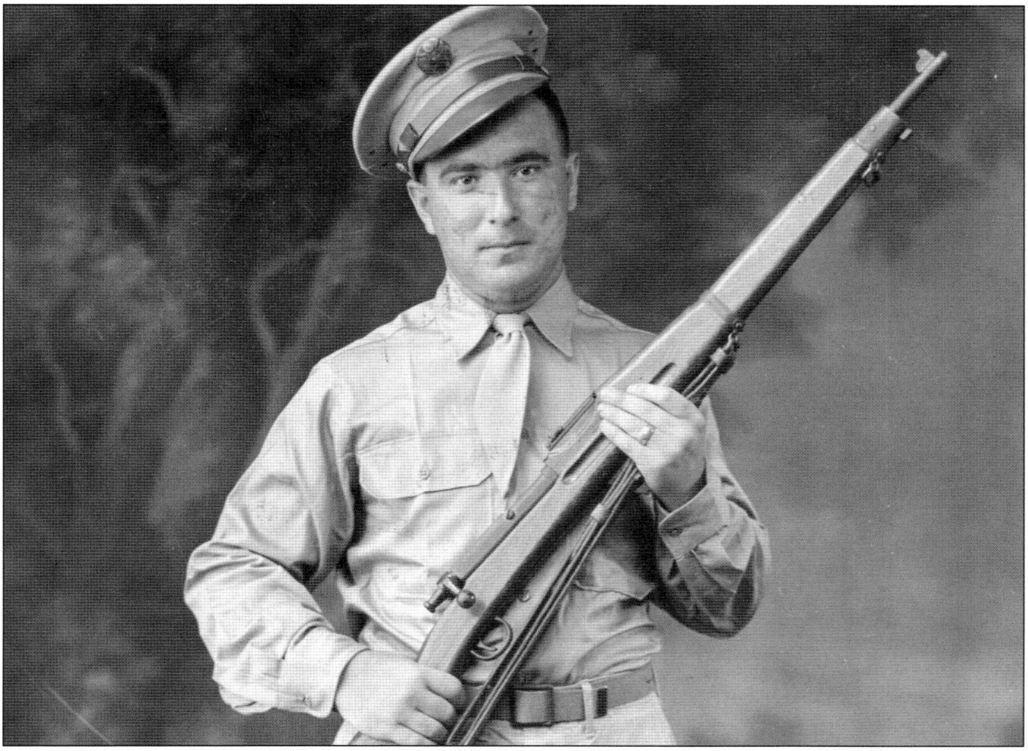

Private Arthur McDowell was inducted into Company L of the 310th Infantry in June 1944 and was wounded in combat fighting in Germany on April 7, 1945. Along with the Purple Heart, he earned a Bronze Battle Star. (Courtesy of the Trimble County Historical Society.)

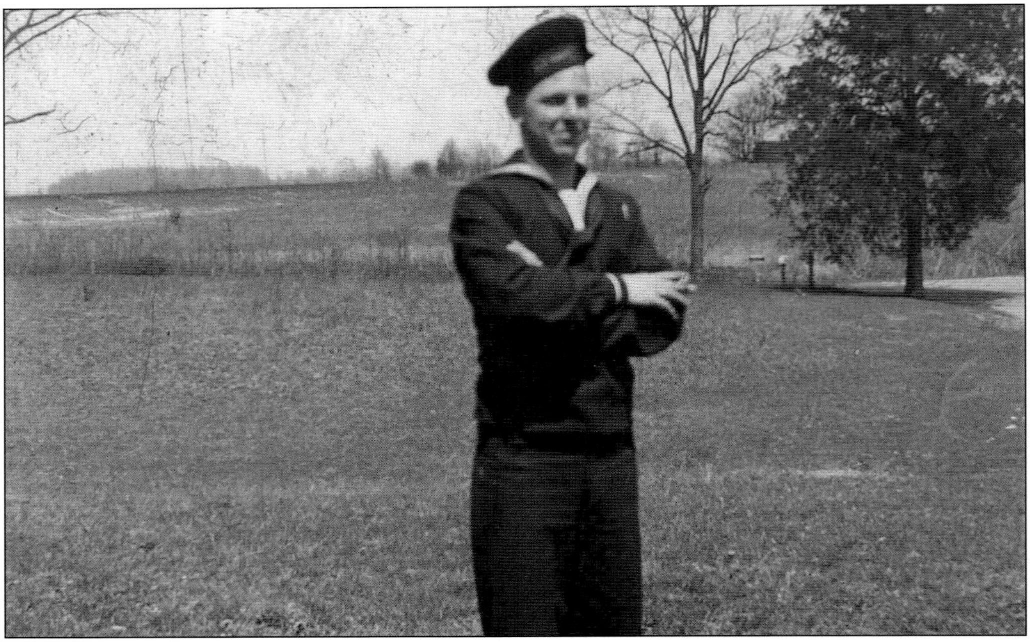

Robert Gausley Pendleton was reported missing in action on January 9, 1943, and was later listed as killed in action. The son of Ren Hurley and Susie Pendleton, he worked on his parents' Cooper's Bottom farm near Milton prior to his induction into the Navy. (Courtesy of the Trimble County Historical Society.)

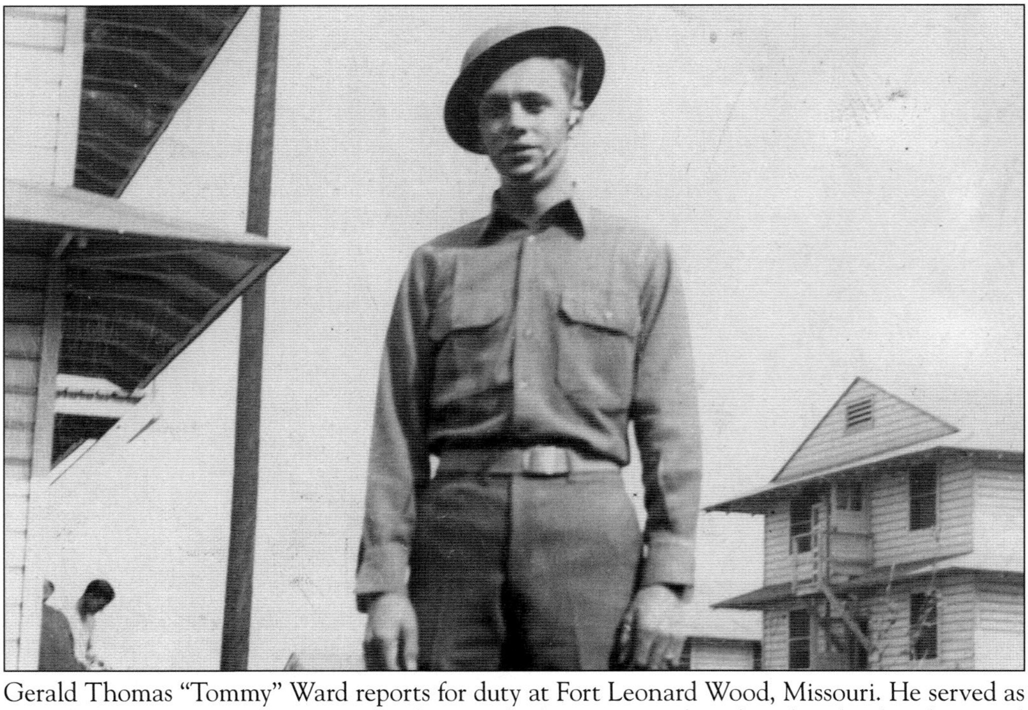

Gerald Thomas "Tommy" Ward reports for duty at Fort Leonard Wood, Missouri. He served as a truck driver in Company E, 63rd Infantry, which participated in the Rhineland and Central Europe campaigns in 1944. (Courtesy of the Trimble County Historical Society.)

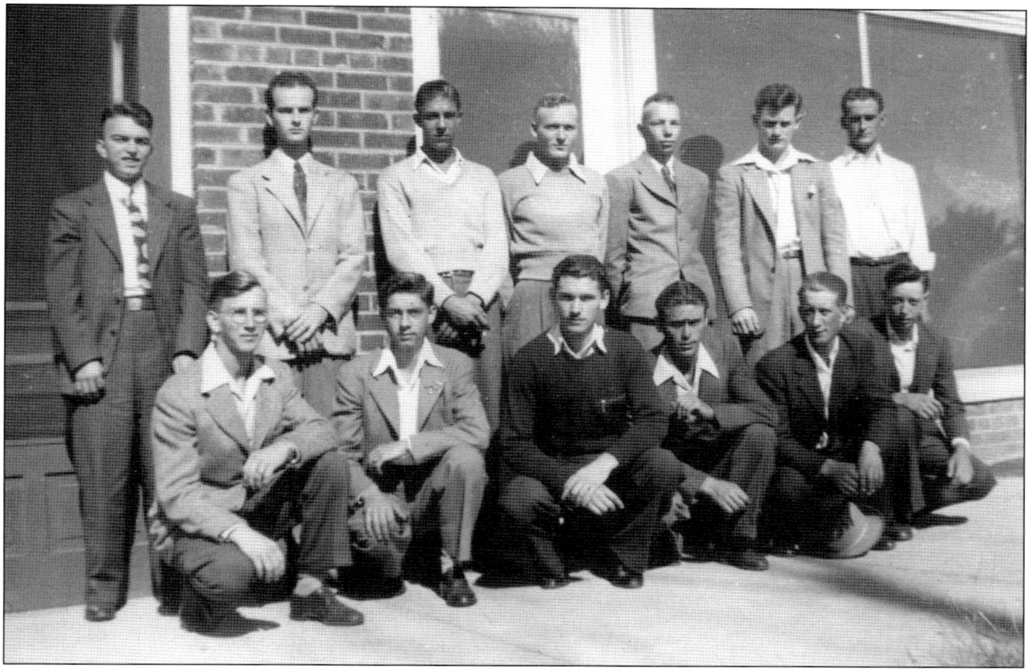

More inductees are, from left to right, (kneeling) Chris Sachleben, Leroy Barringer, Jack S. Payton, Albert Dalton, and two unidentified, including a Chadwell; (standing) Junior Powell, William Parson, Charles Percell, Kenneth Melvin, Bobby Joyce, Jimmy Black, and Oldham Peyton. (Courtesy of the Trimble County Historical Society.)

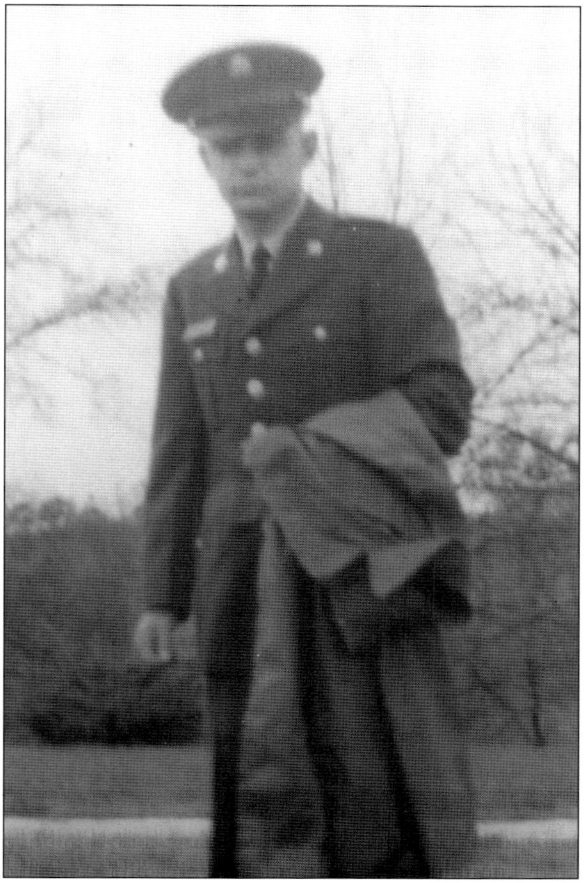

Mark Dwight Banta of Bedford served in the Army during the Vietnam War. (Courtesy of the Trimble County Historical Society.)

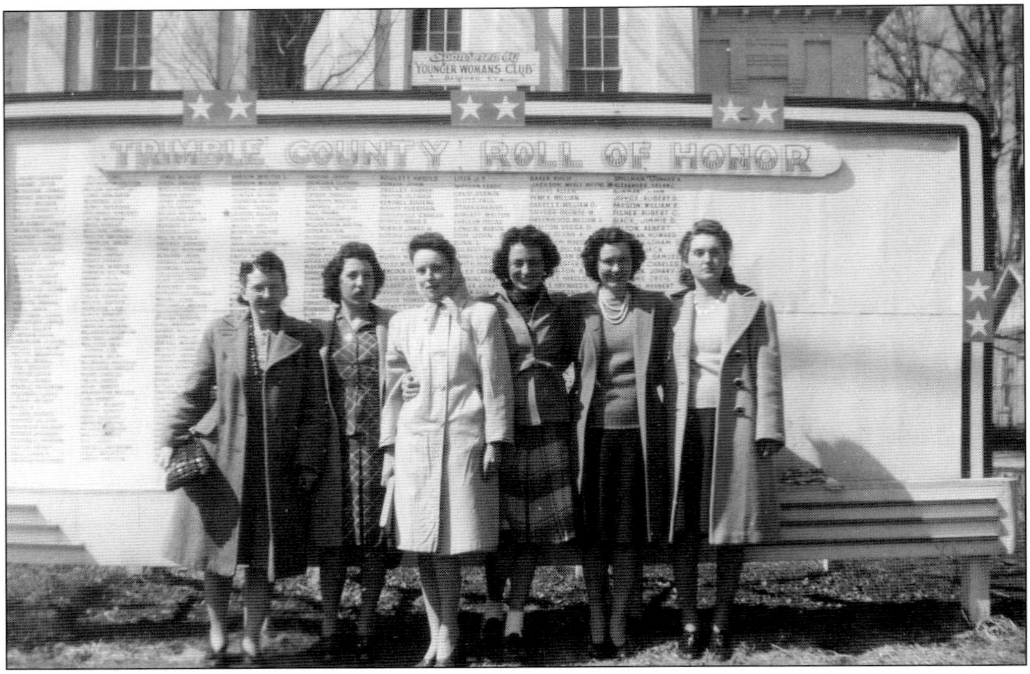

The Bedford Younger Women's Club sponsored Trimble County's Roll of Honor, a wall with the names of all local men who were called into service during World War II. Standing in front of the wall, erected on the front lawn of the Trimble County courthouse, are, from left to right, Mary White, Willanna Martinie Moore, Alean Pierce Gentry, Katherine Welch Callis, Lorene Powell Blakemore, and Evelyn Doyle. (Courtesy of Mildred Pardo Pruitt.)

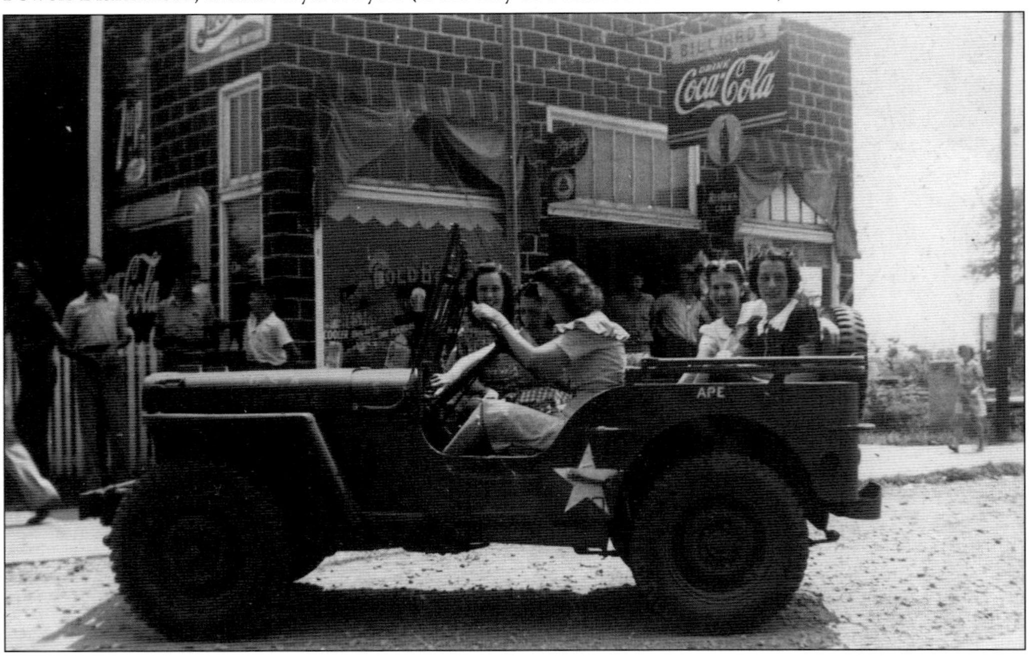

Lorene Powell borrows an Army Jeep from soldiers who made a stop at Bedford. She took several girlfriends for a quick ride, including Elizabeth Stockdale and Catherine Welch, who are seated in the back. (Courtesy of Mildred Pardo Pruitt.)

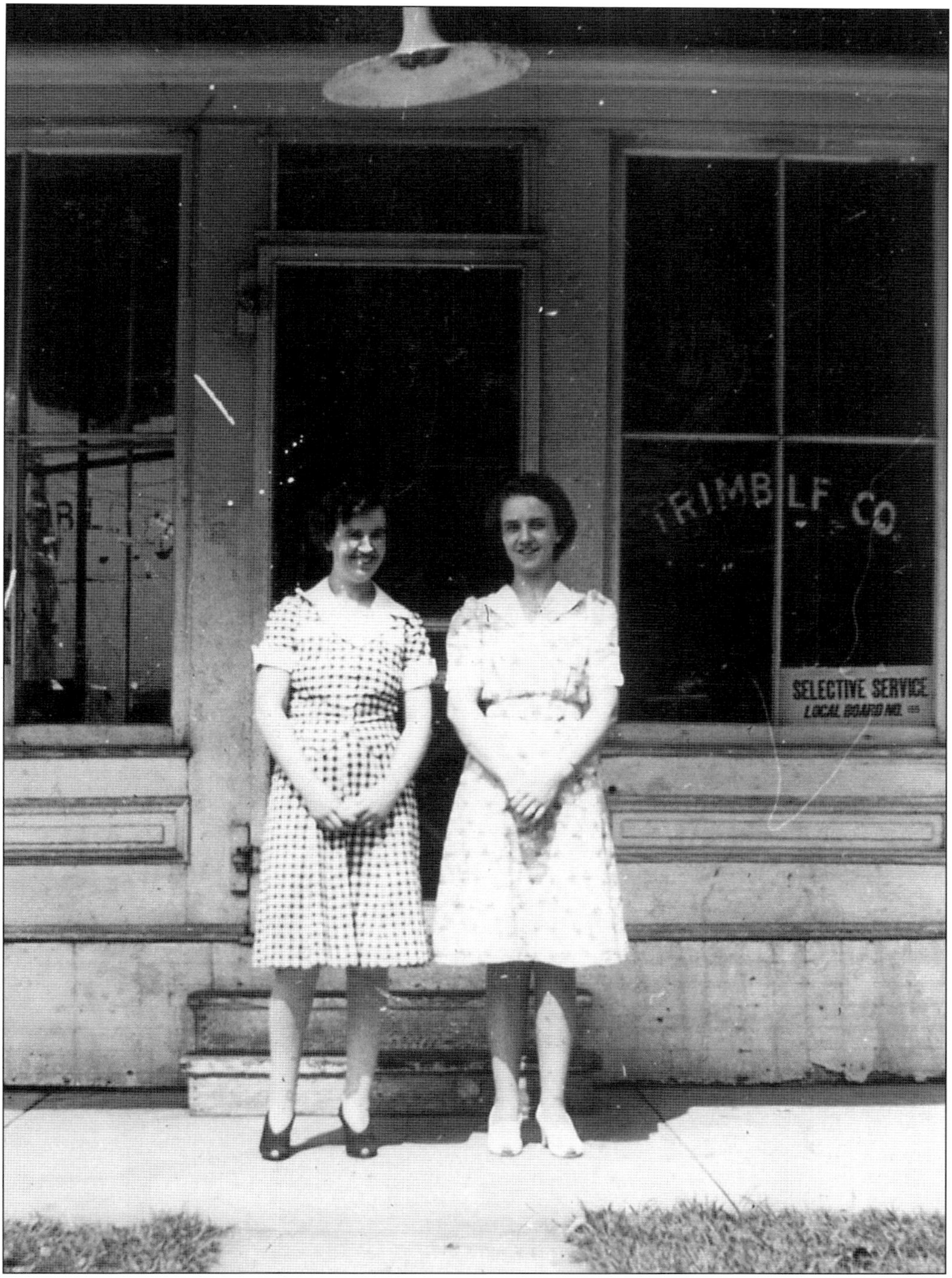

Gail Mosley and Catherine Nowlin stand in front of Trimble County's Selective Service office, Local Board No. 155, where local men and women signed up to join American fighting forces during World War II. All except three returned from the war. Seaman First Class George Stanley Abbot of Bedford, Fireman Third Class Willard Irvin Lawson of Milton, and Seaman First Class Robert Gausley Pendleton, also of Milton, were killed or died of wounds received in battle. (Courtesy of Mildred Pardo Pruitt.)

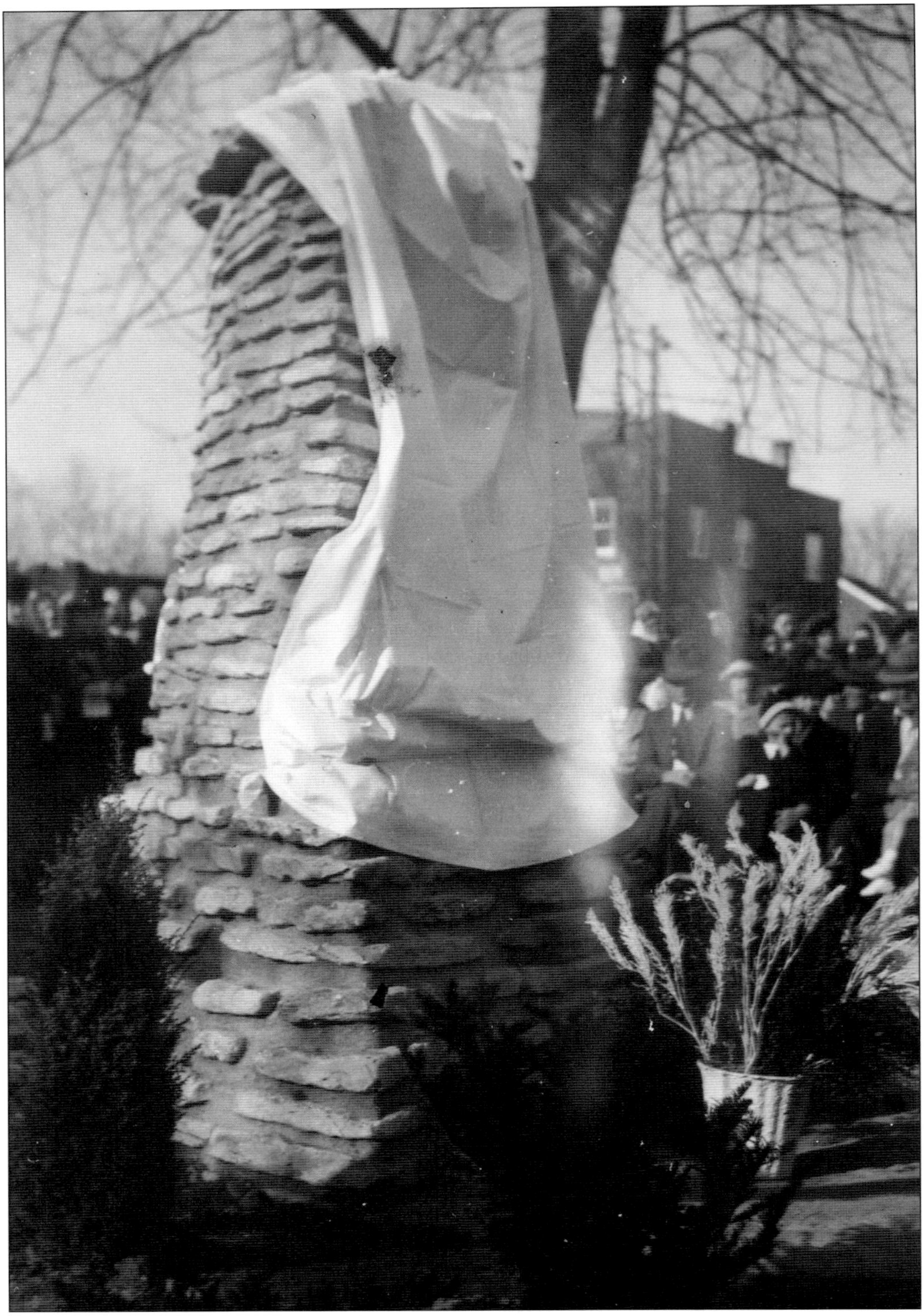

The Trimble County War Memorial remains shrouded prior to its dedication ceremony. The memorial includes the names of men killed in World Wars I and II, and other conflicts. (Courtesy of Reggie Rand.)

Four

Out on the Farm

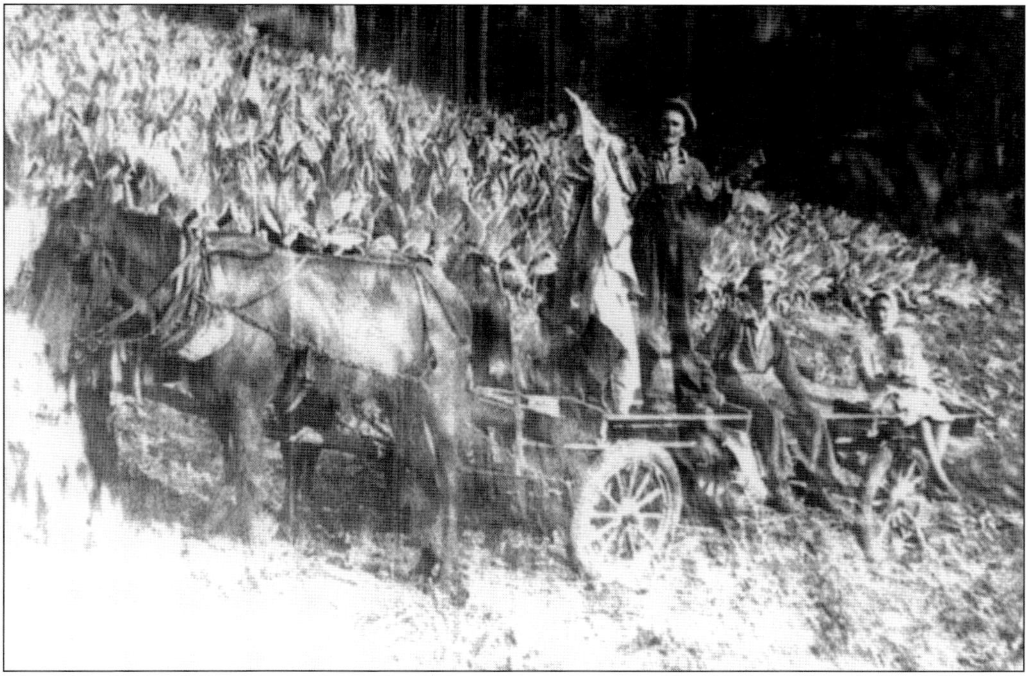

Bob Carter cuts tobacco while family members pose on the back of the wagon. Tobacco has been one of the top cash crops in Trimble County for generations and is still grown, though not in the quantities of the past. Tobacco remains one of the few crops that is planted, topped, and harvested by hand. (Courtesy of Lucy Webster Smith.).

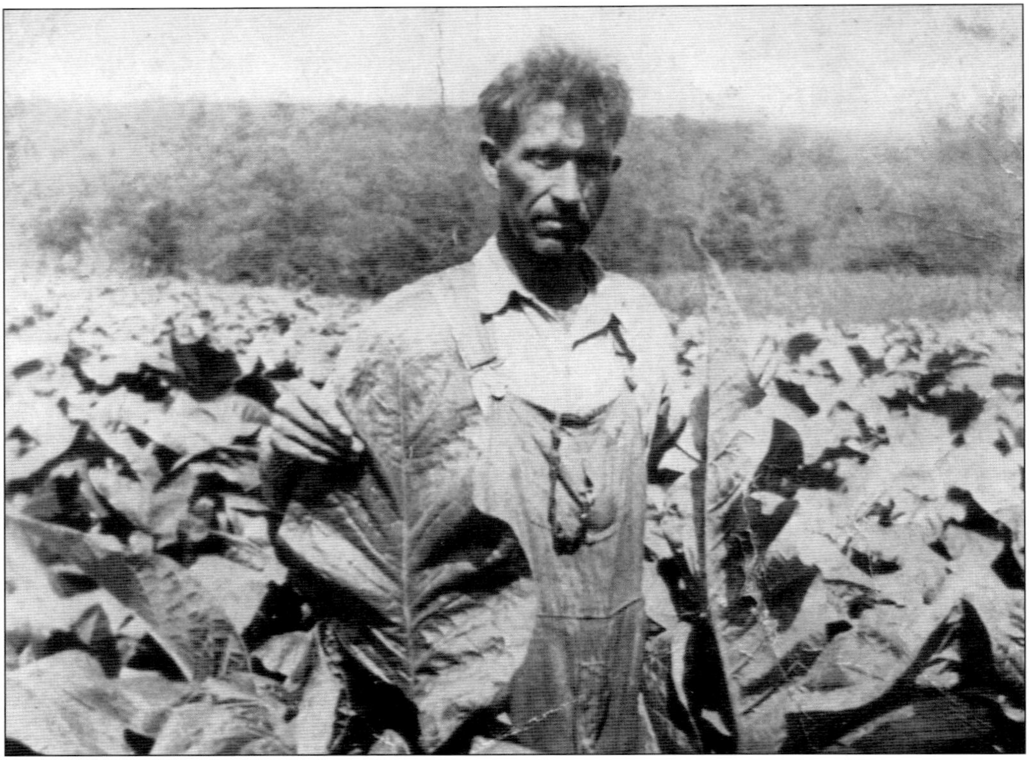

Burley tobacco is most common in Kentucky, particularly in Trimble County. Here, Henry Wingham displays a leaf from a maturing plant. Toward the end of summer, flowers develop, and these are topped. Harvest is usually in late August or early September. (Courtesy of Ted Taylor.)

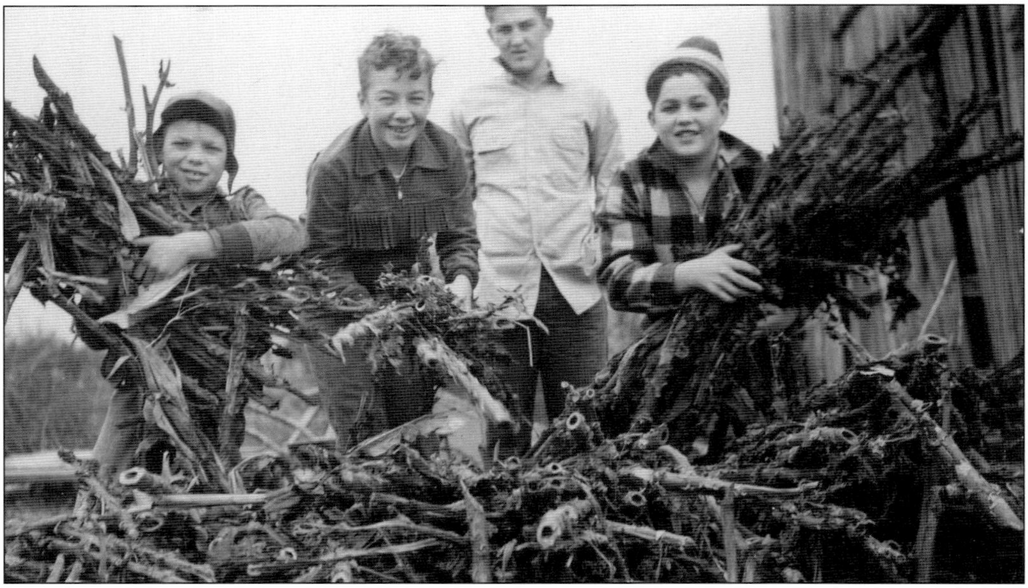

After a hard day stripping tobacco on the Rand farm in the fall of 1949, from left to right, Donald "Duck" Ward, Oscar "Spookum" Ward, Buddy Rand, and Reggie Rand pose for this photograph. The farm, near Bedford, raised seven acres of the crop at that time. (Courtesy of Reggie Rand.)

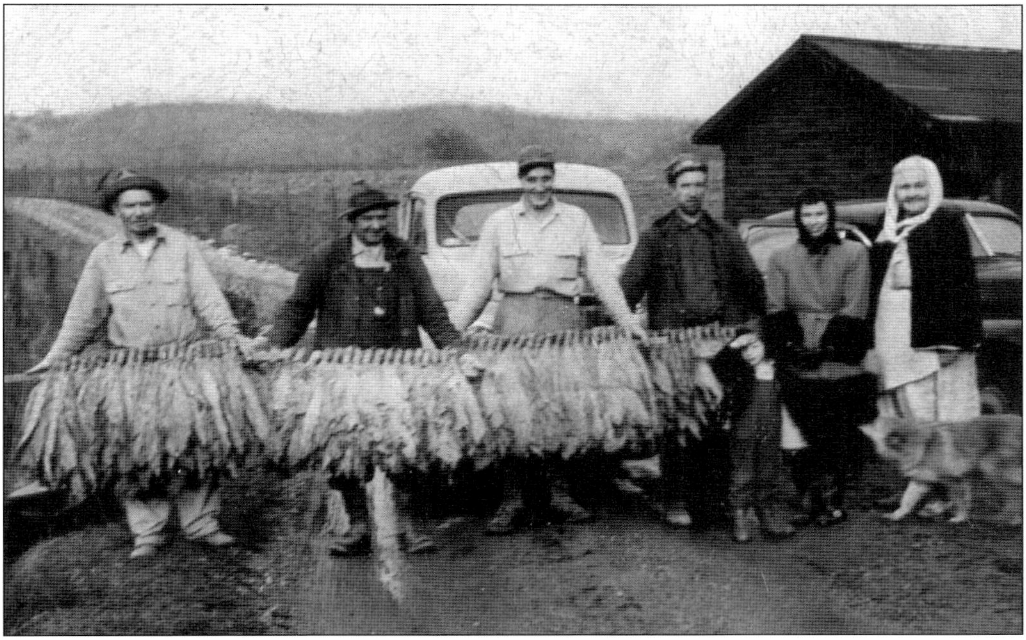

Tobacco leaves are tied together and placed on sticks that will hang in a tobacco barn for several weeks to cure. Showing off part of a harvest are (from left to right) Otis Brown, Herbert Hancock, John Hancock, Keith Taylor, Della Taylor, Anna Hancock, and young Ted Taylor (in front). (Courtesy of Ted Taylor.)

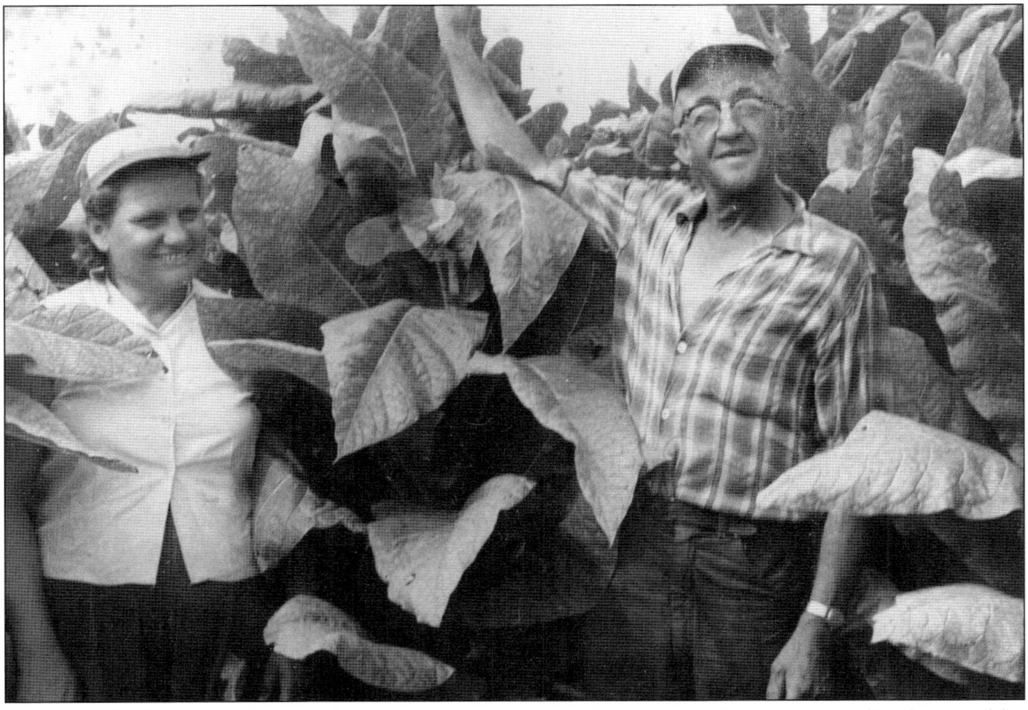

Luther and Elizabeth Fitzgerald were tenants raising tobacco on a farm near Bedford owned by James and Lurlene Mosley and Joseph and Laura Ogden, the Moselys' daughter and son-in-law. (Courtesy of JoDeva Ogden.)

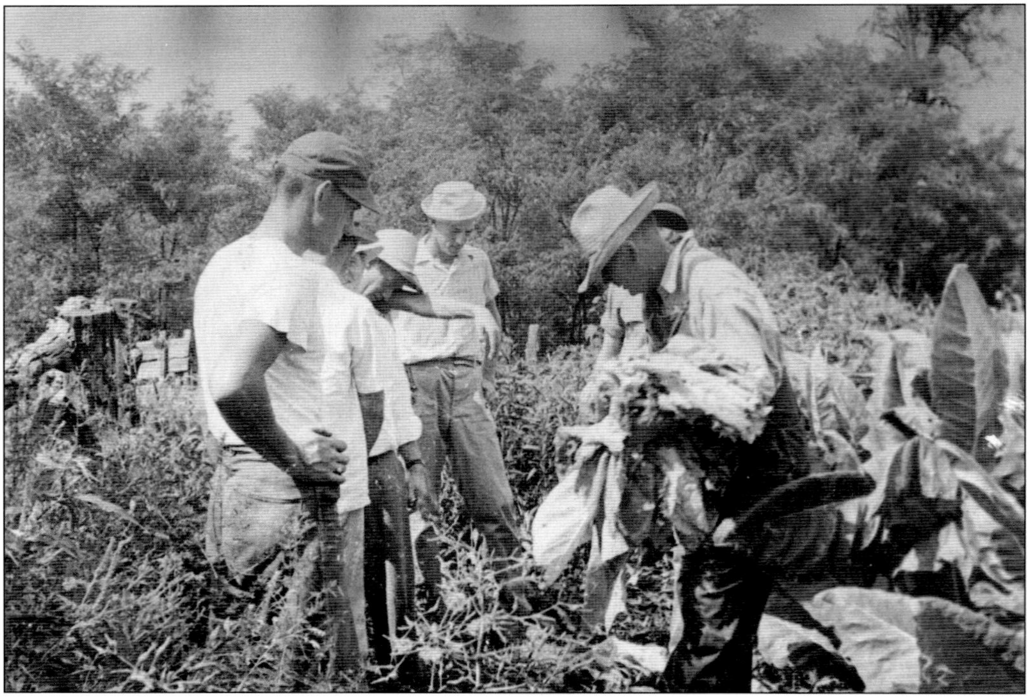

Harvey Paul Stewart (left) and neighbor Curt Dunaway (right) watch as the county agricultural extension agent demonstrates how to spear tobacco in the mid-1940s. This method replaced slicing the entire stalk before hanging it on sticks and hauling the crop to the barn for curing. (Courtesy of Robert Bruce "Bob" Stewart Jr.)

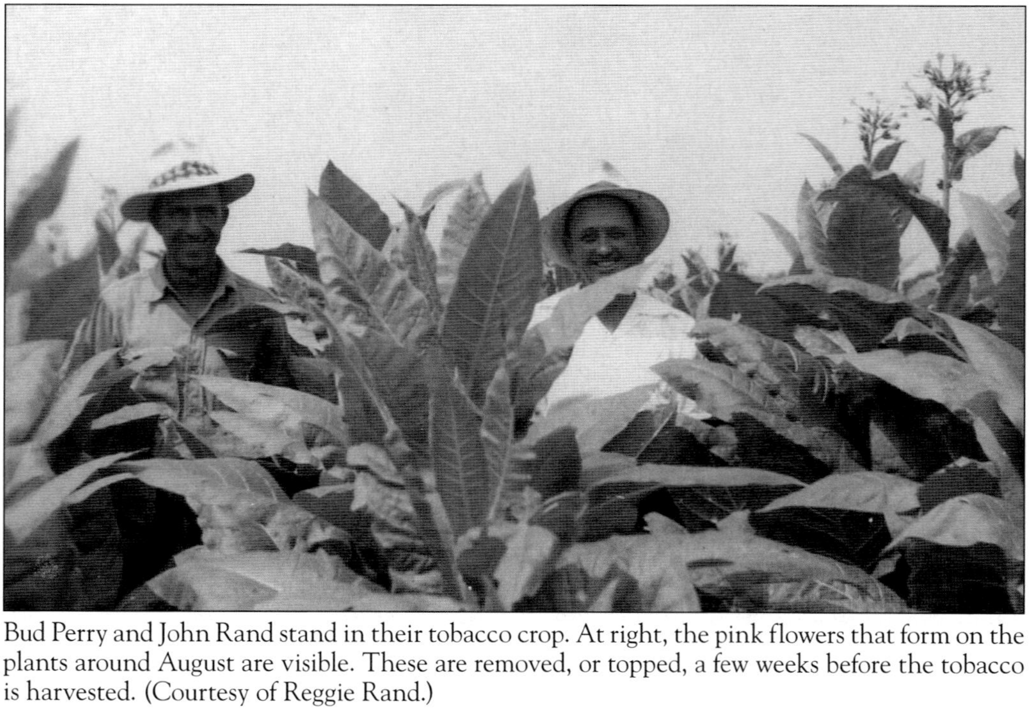

Bud Perry and John Rand stand in their tobacco crop. At right, the pink flowers that form on the plants around August are visible. These are removed, or topped, a few weeks before the tobacco is harvested. (Courtesy of Reggie Rand.)

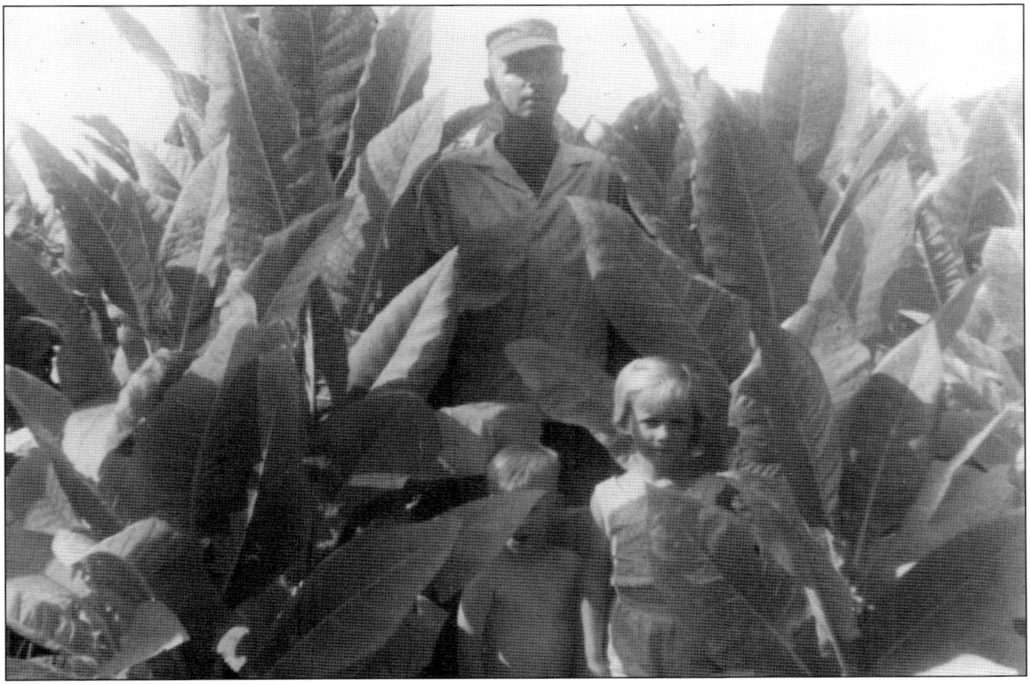

Forrest Burkhardt stands with his children, Cathie and Keith, in their tobacco field in Burkhardt's Bottom west of Milton along the Ohio River. The family has been farming the same land for several generations. (Courtesy of Betty Burkhardt.)

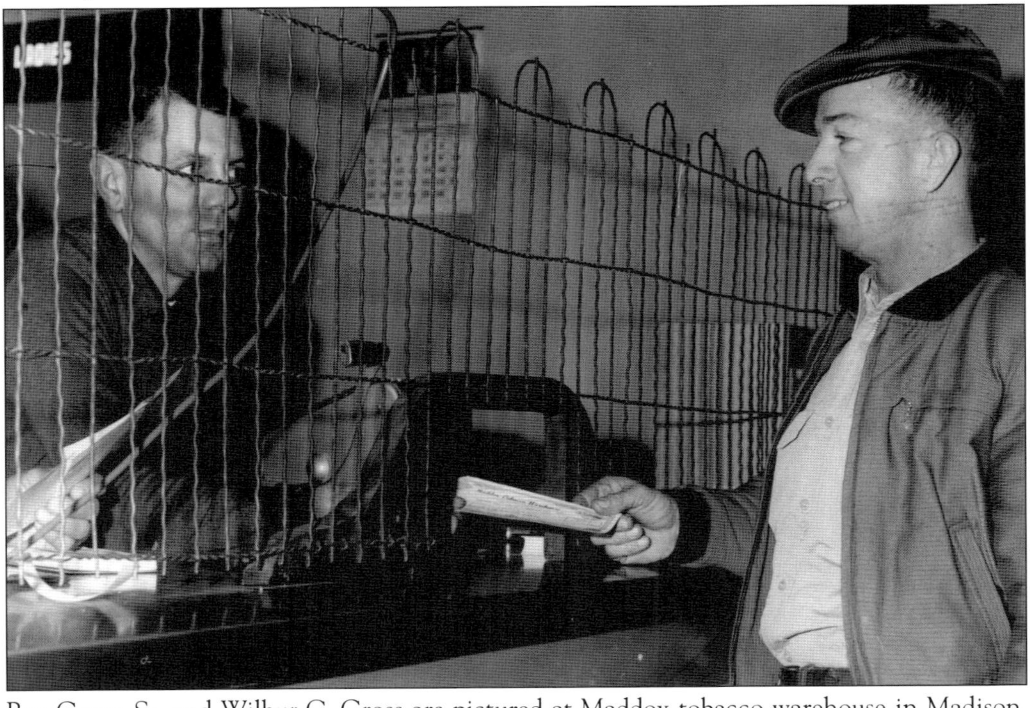

Ray Green Sr. and Wilbur C. Gross are pictured at Maddox tobacco warehouse in Madison, Indiana, one of dozens in the area where Trimble County farmers would sell their crops of burley tobacco. (Courtesy of Mike Gross.)

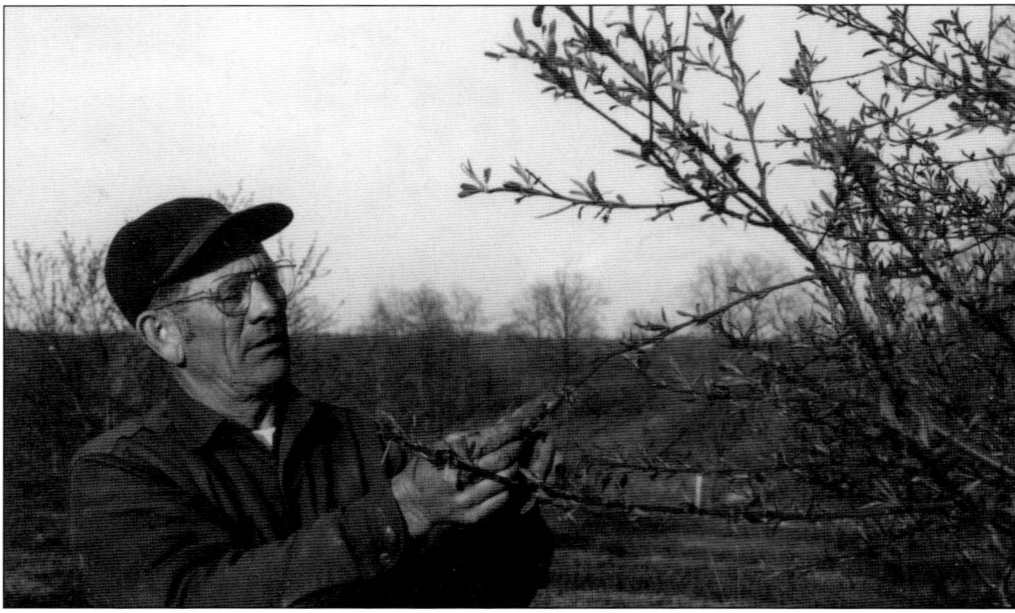

Above, Cecil Staples checks the buds of peach trees in his orchard in early spring. Staples operated a roadside fruit market, shown below. At one time, there were as many as 16 roadside stands selling locally grown produce throughout Trimble County. Though the Staples' stand is no longer being used, the building still stands on property next to Trimble County Park. (Both, courtesy of Gary Greenwood.)

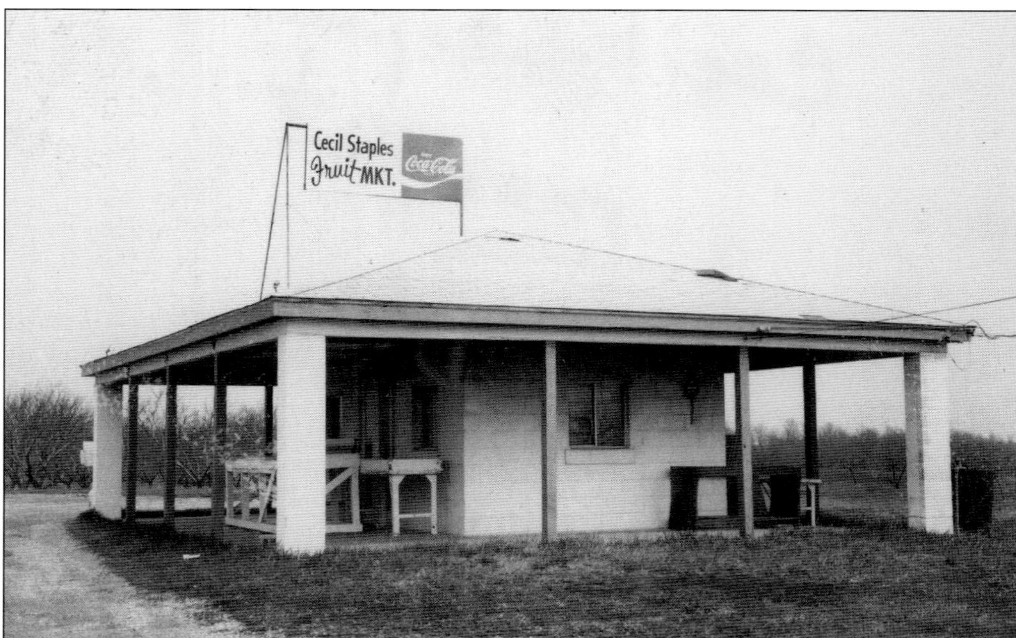

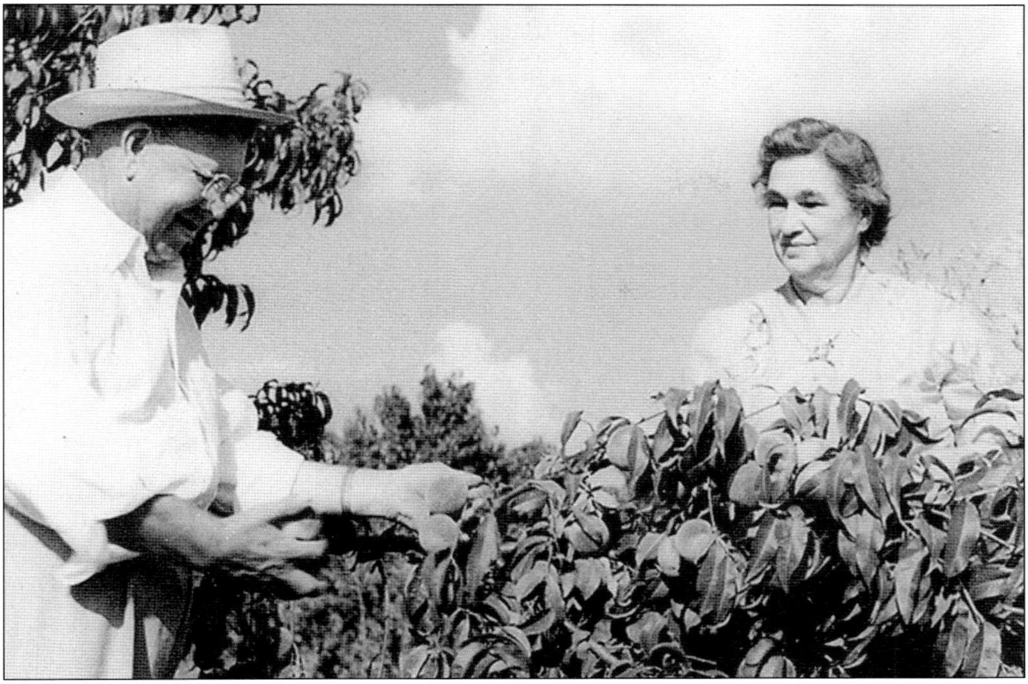

Joseph and Carrie Bray check the ripening fruit in their peach orchard in the early 1950s. In the 1930s, the Brays opened a roadside market (below) selling peaches and other produce on US 42 near Bedford. Bray's Roadside Market, built in the 1930s, is still in operation today, though there have been additions to the store to make room for an ice cream parlor and a market for fresh vegetables. The market also sells locally made honey and other local products. (Both, courtesy of Jamey Bray.)

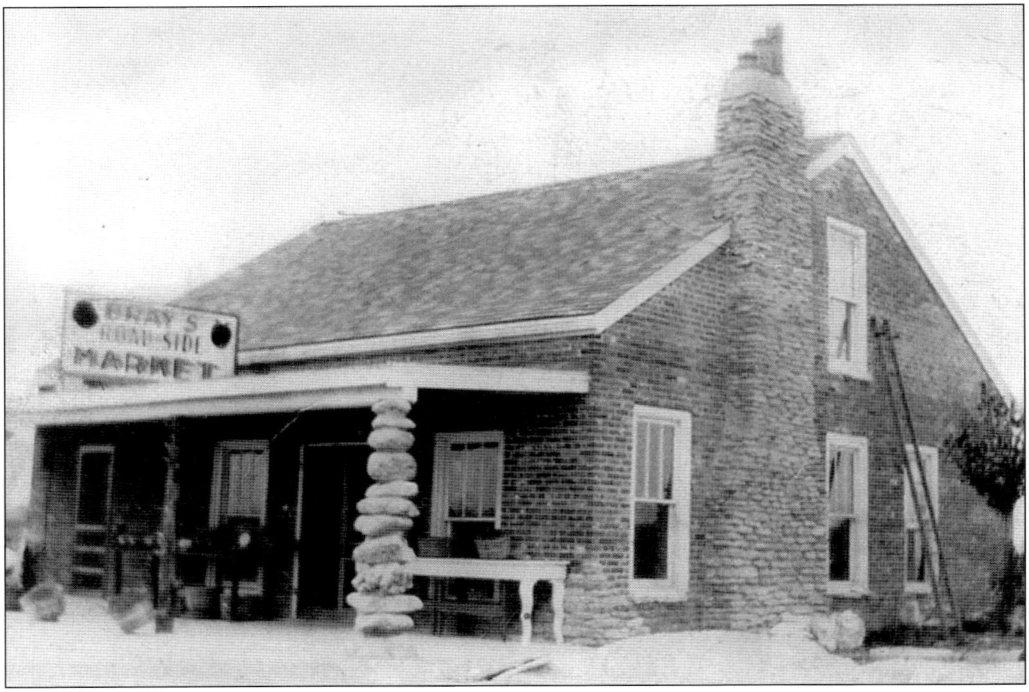

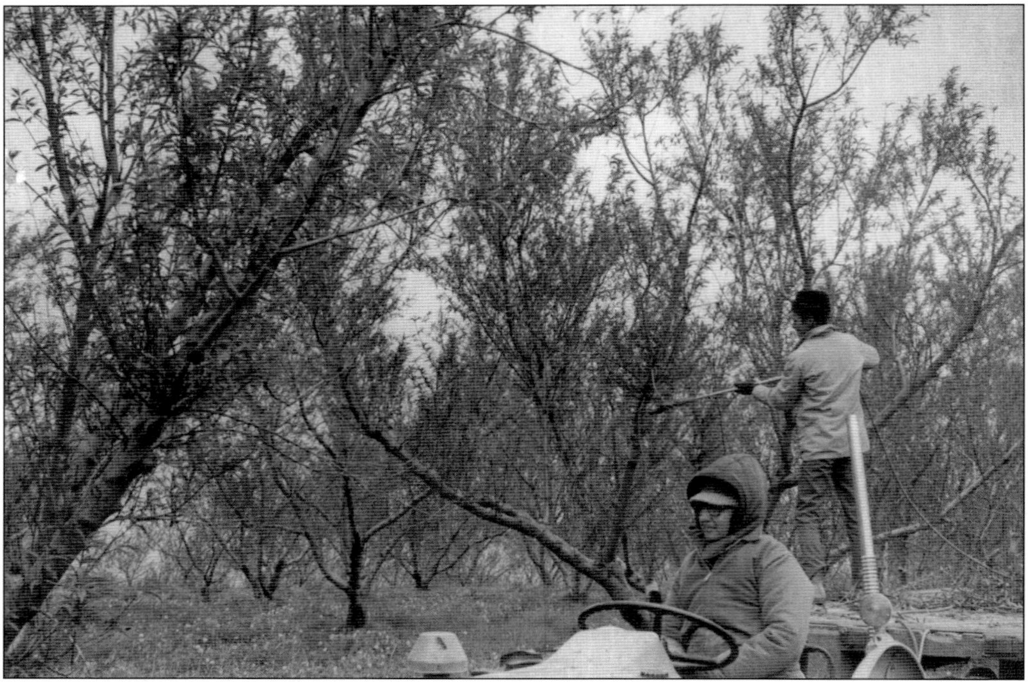

A crew of workmen brave the cold weather to prune peach trees in a local orchard. While tobacco has declined as a cash crop, peach and apple orchards still dot the Trimble County countryside. (Courtesy of Hilda Parrish.)

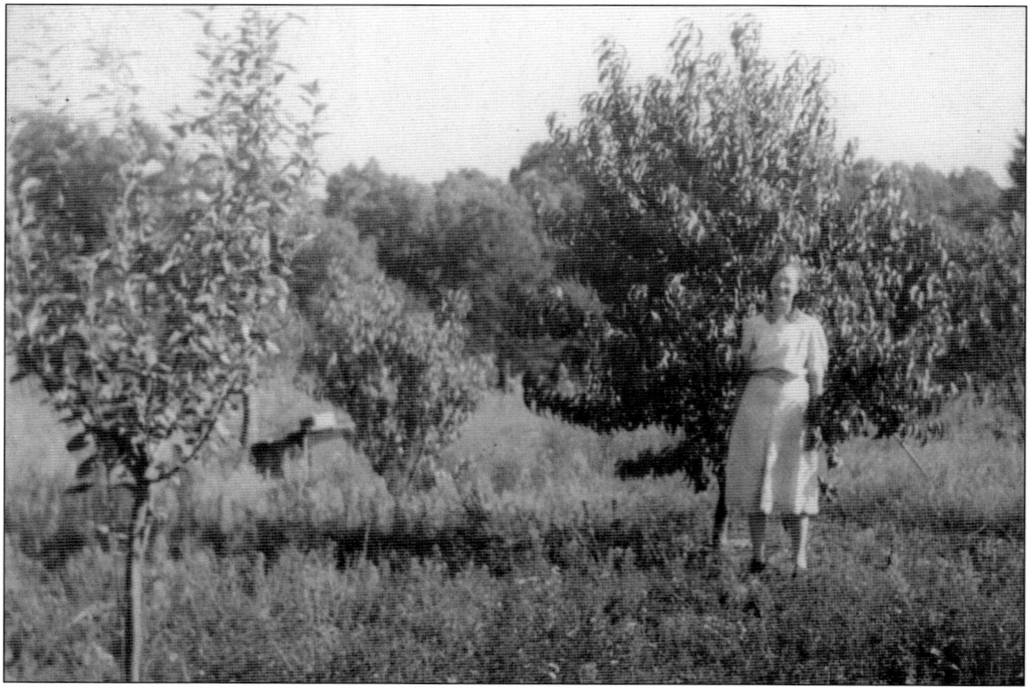

Ethel Greenwood stands among the trees in the peach orchard. Trimble County is known regionally for producing some of the juiciest cling and freestone peaches, most of which are sold at several roadside stands in the county. (Courtesy of Gary Greenwood.)

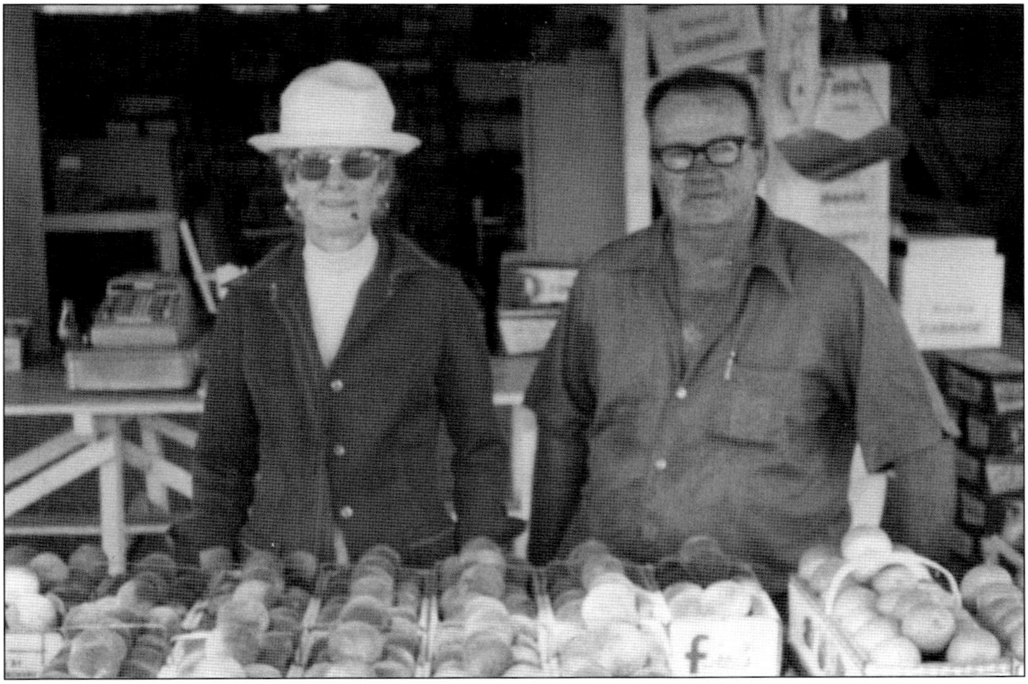

Bessie and Clarence Callis pose in front of their stand, located near the intersection of US 421 and New Hope Road. Callis was known for flying his single-engine plane, taking off and landing on an airstrip across the road from the orchard and roadside stand. (Courtesy of Gary Greenwood.)

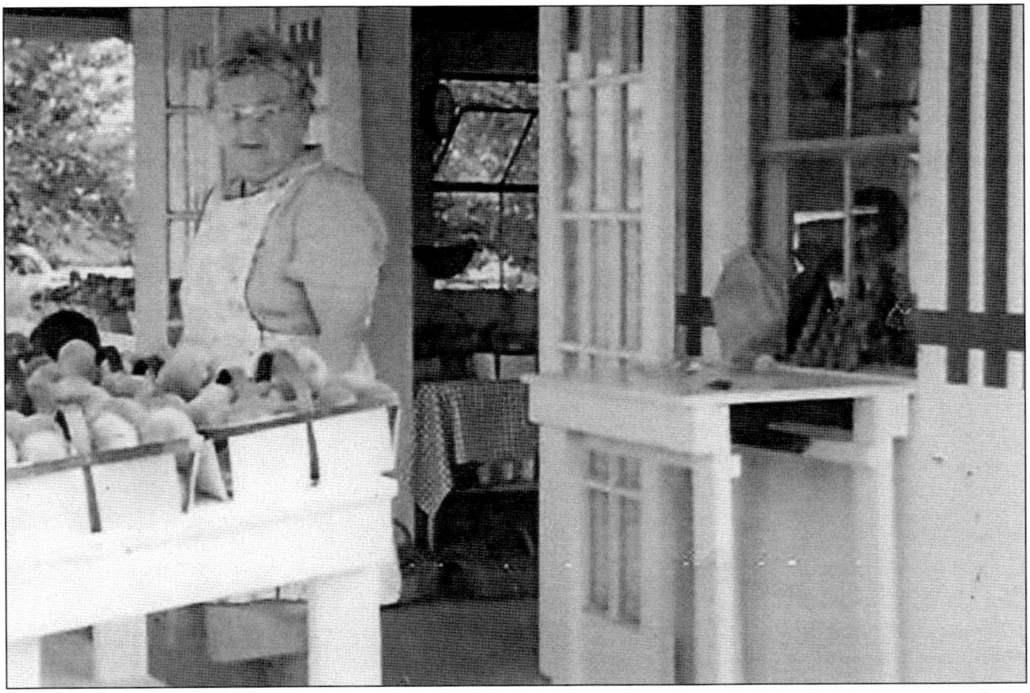

Mabel Wise Craig minds the store at Craig's Market on US 42, west of Bedford. At one time, there were as many as 16 local fruit-and-vegetable stands operating on US 42 and US 421 in Trimble County. (Courtesy of Jamey Bray.)

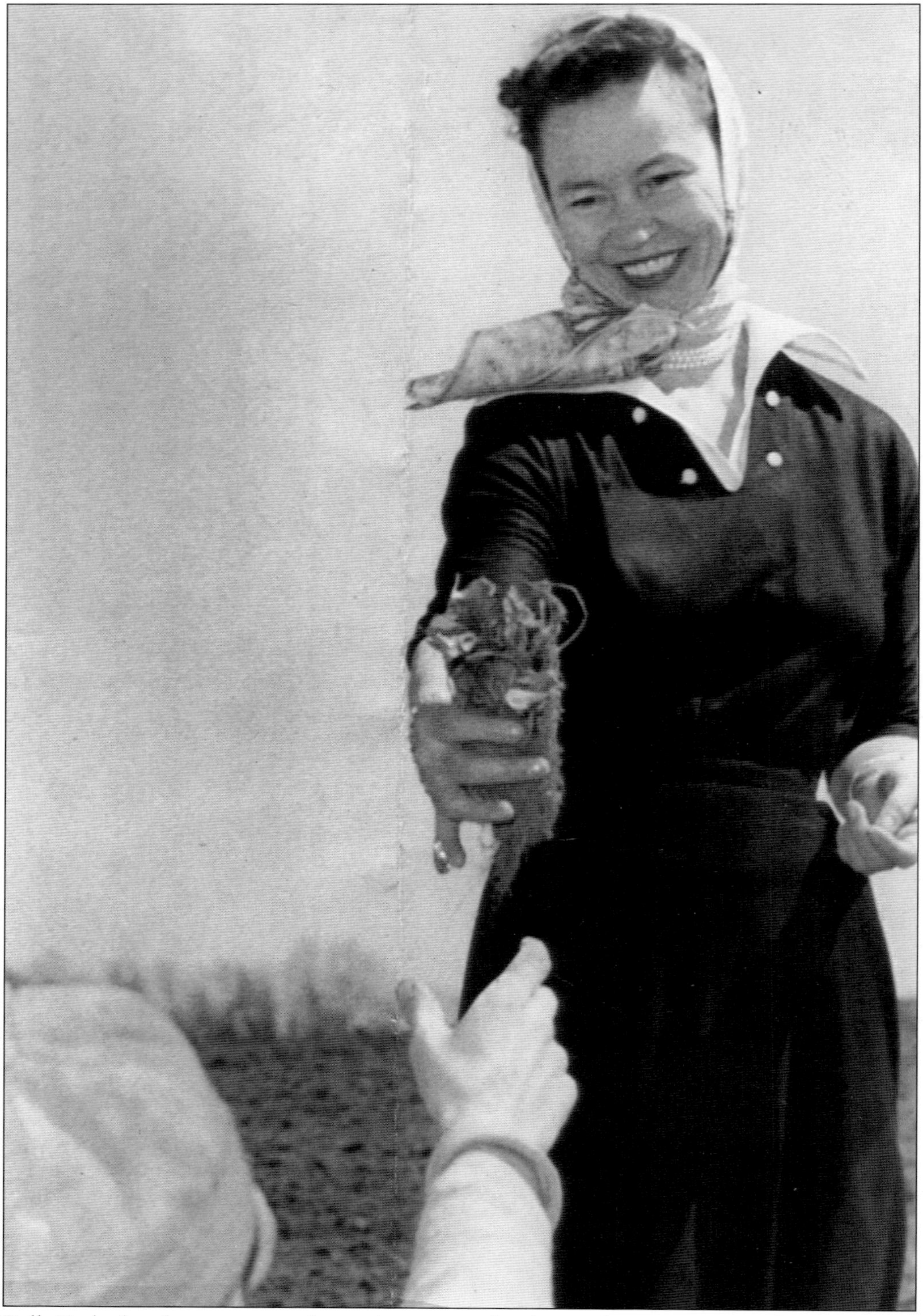

Della Taylor hands a young strawberry plant to a worker during planting season in the early spring. Like tobacco, strawberries were planted and harvested by hand. (Courtesy of Ted Taylor.)

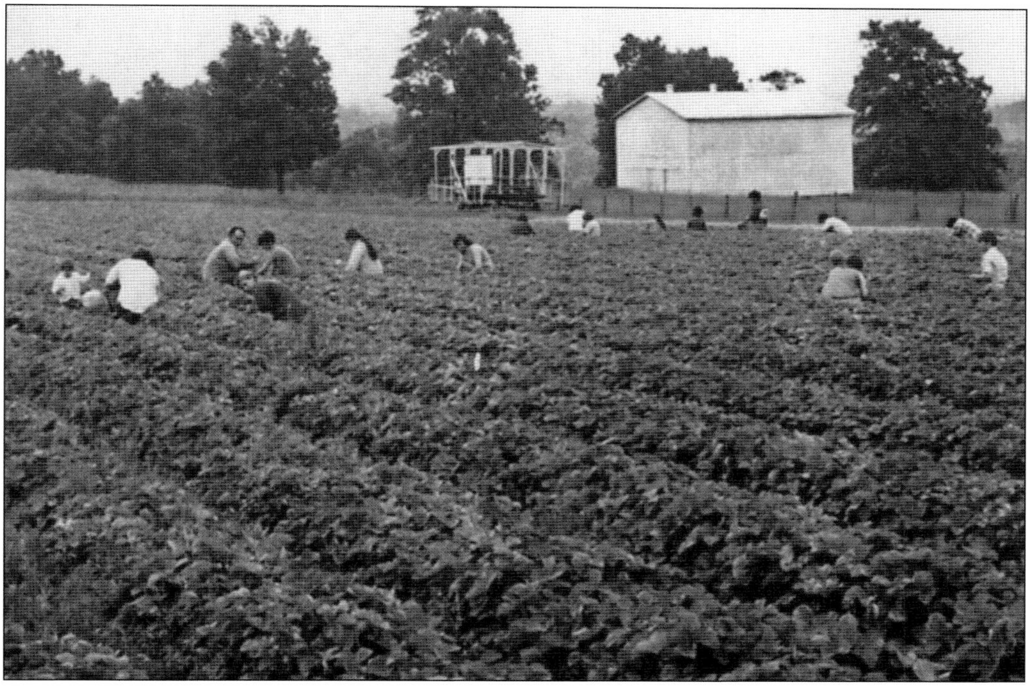

Above, hired hands go row by row picking strawberries at the Taylor farm outside Milton in the northern part of Trimble County. Below, Della Taylor poses with ribbons she won at the Kentucky State Fair for that year's crop of strawberries. She sold the harvest each year at a roadside stand that still can be seen on US 421 across from the new Milton Elementary School. (Both, courtesy of Ted Taylor.)

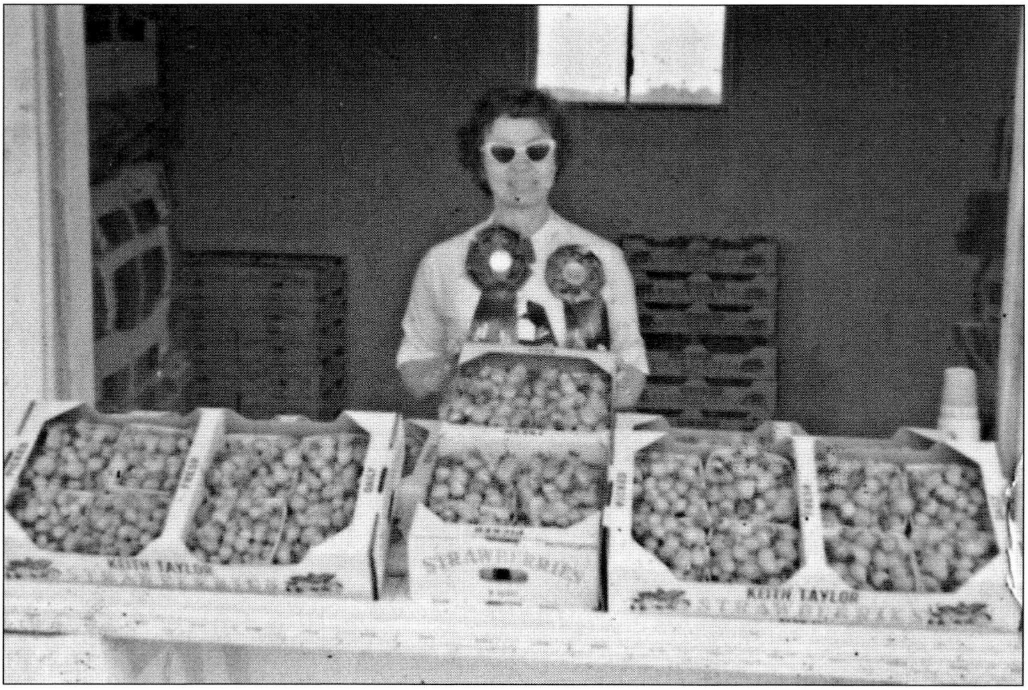

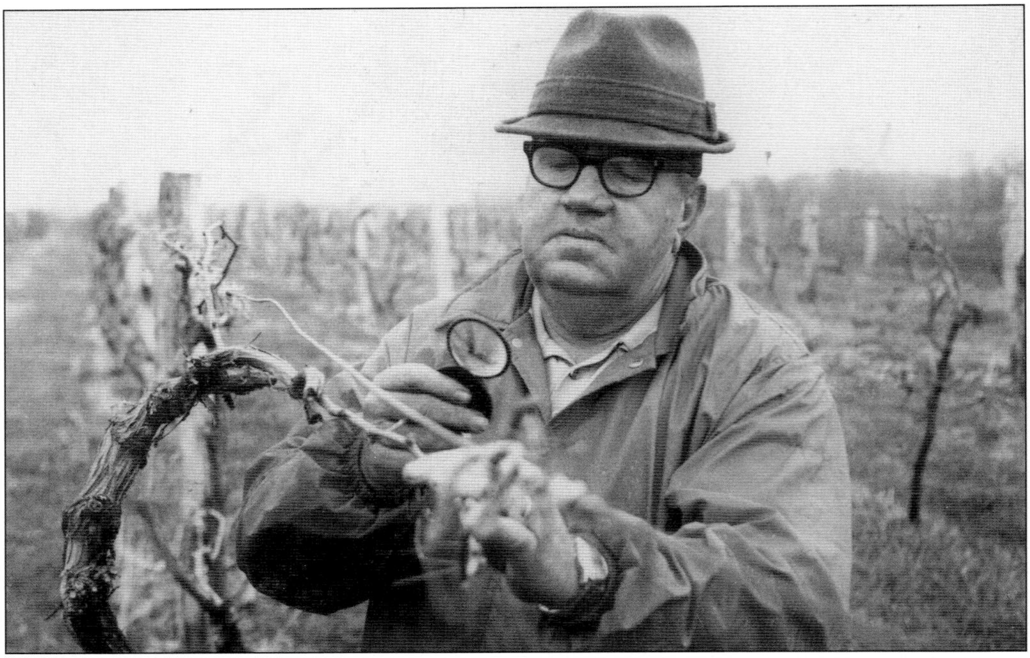

Clarence Callis checks grapevines in the 1970s. The Callis family still sells peaches and fresh vegetables, such as sweet corn, tomatoes, and zucchini, at a roadside stand next to the peach orchards. Grapes were at one time a top crop in Kentucky, but very few commercial vineyards exist in Trimble County today. (Courtesy of Gary Greenwood.)

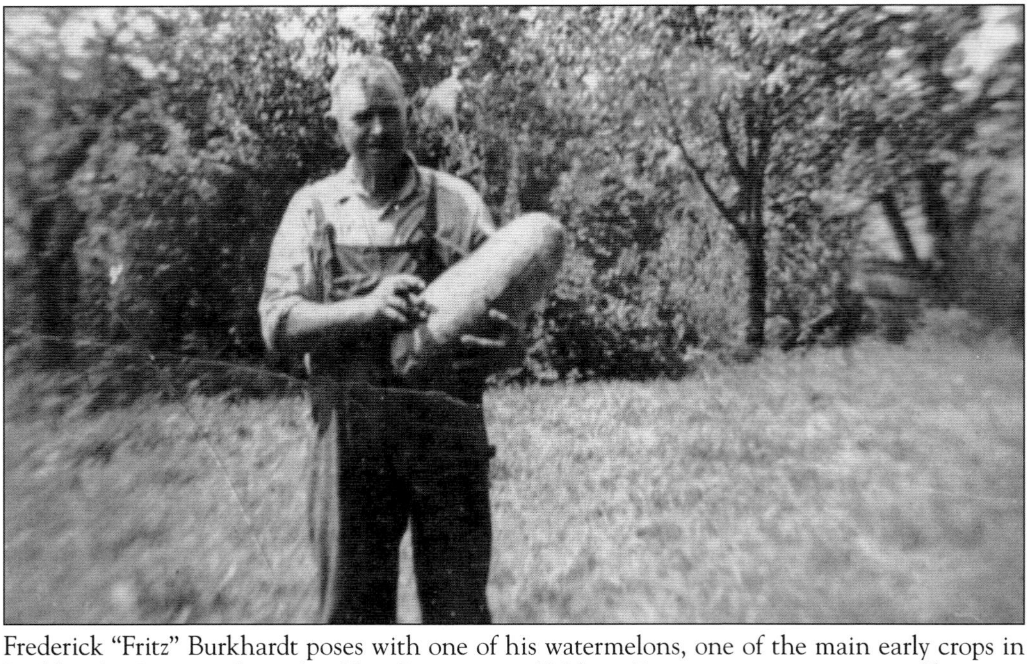

Frederick "Fritz" Burkhardt poses with one of his watermelons, one of the main early crops in Burkhardt's Bottom along the Ohio River west of Milton. Fritz was very protective of his crop, always on the lookout for poachers who accessed the patches by boat. Burkhardt supplied fruit sellers in Madison, Indiana, and would go to town and exchange them for groceries and other supplies. (Courtesy of Betty Burkhardt.)

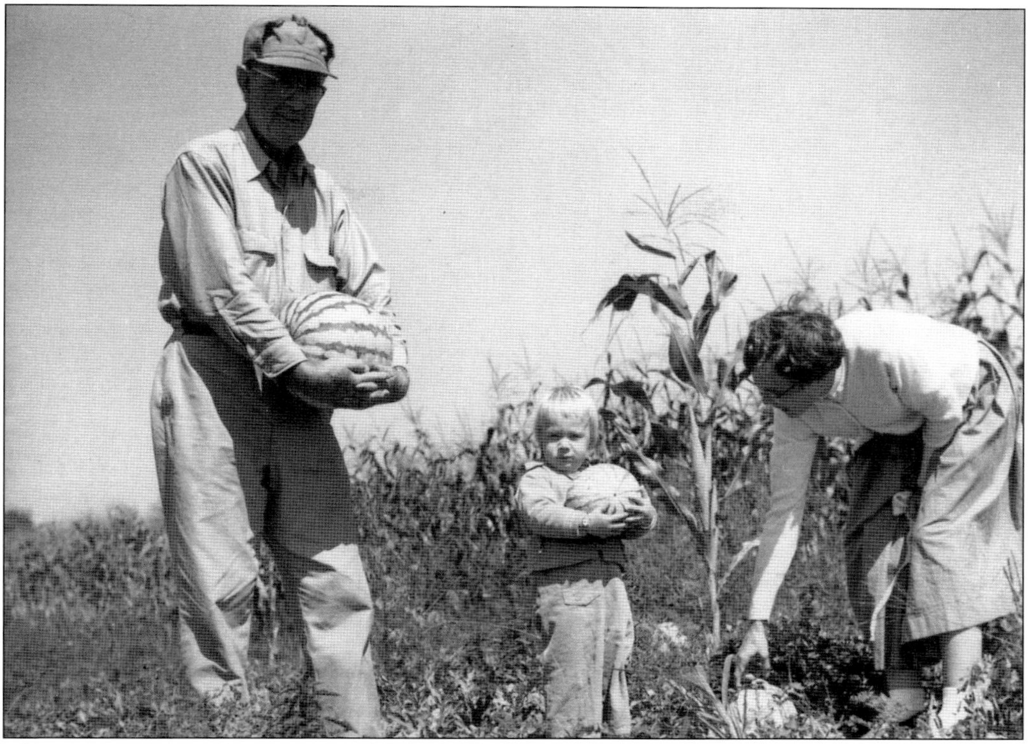

Three generations of Stewart family watermelon pickers are shown here from left to right: Robert Bruce Stewart Sr.; his granddaughter, Susan; and his daughter-in-law Jean Crutcher Stewart. Watermelon and pumpkins are late summer and early fall crops planted in many parts of Trimble County. (Courtesy of Robert Bruce "Bob" Stewart Jr.)

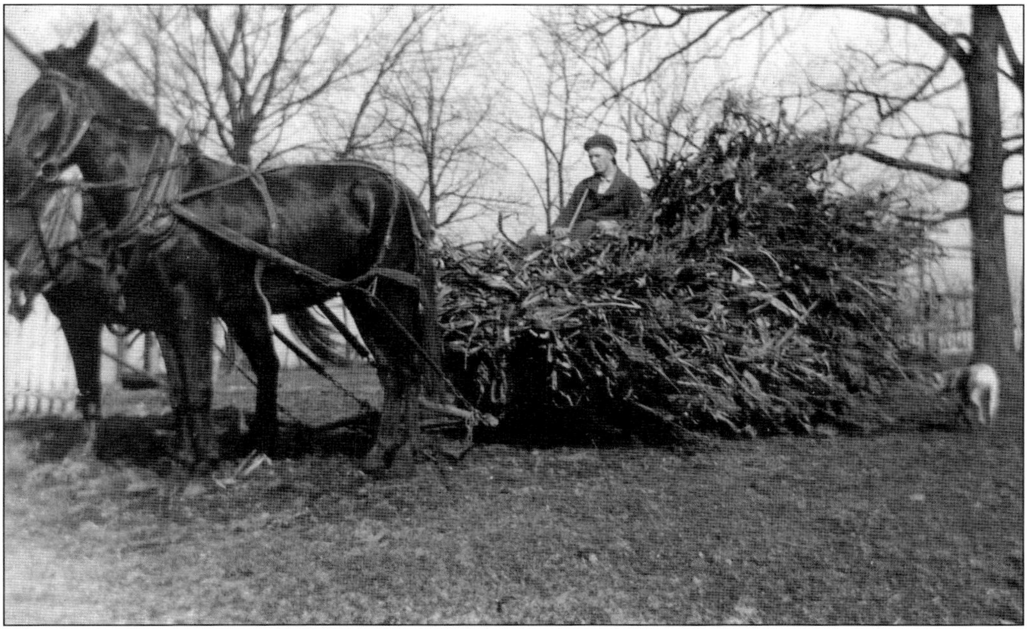

Lyle Pardo hauls a wagonload of harvested sorghum from the field around 1920. Sorghum was cooked over an open fire to make a kind of molasses. (Courtesy of Mildred Pardo Pruitt.)

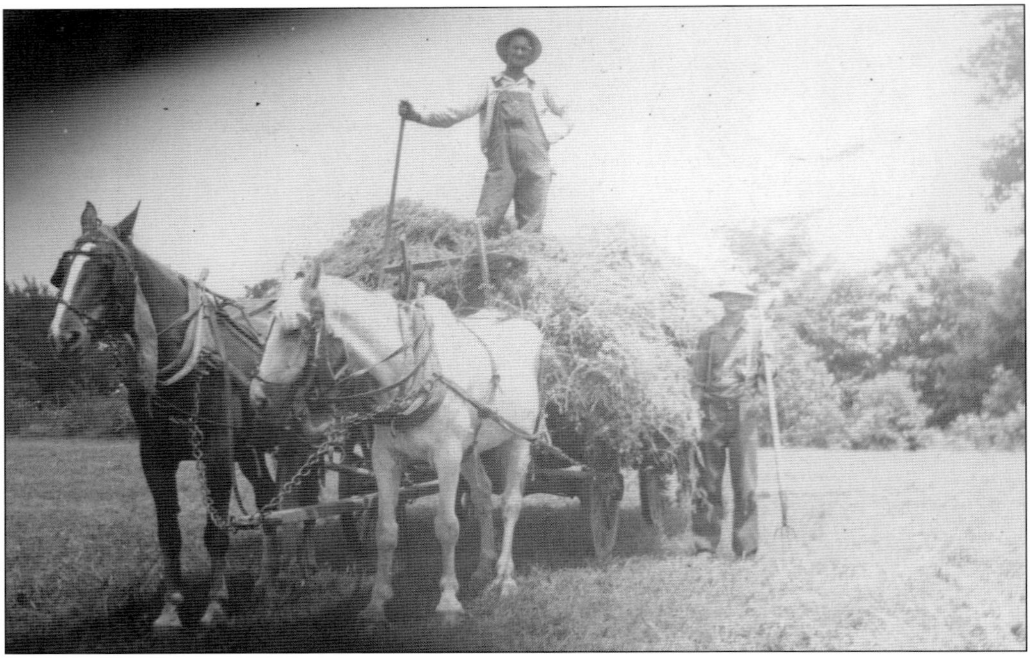

Brothers Leroy Thomas "Tom" and Jennings Bryan Greenwood pose with a recent harvest on their father's farm near Milton. Jennings served in the Navy during World War I, and Tom was a veteran of World War II. (Courtesy of Gary Greenwood.)

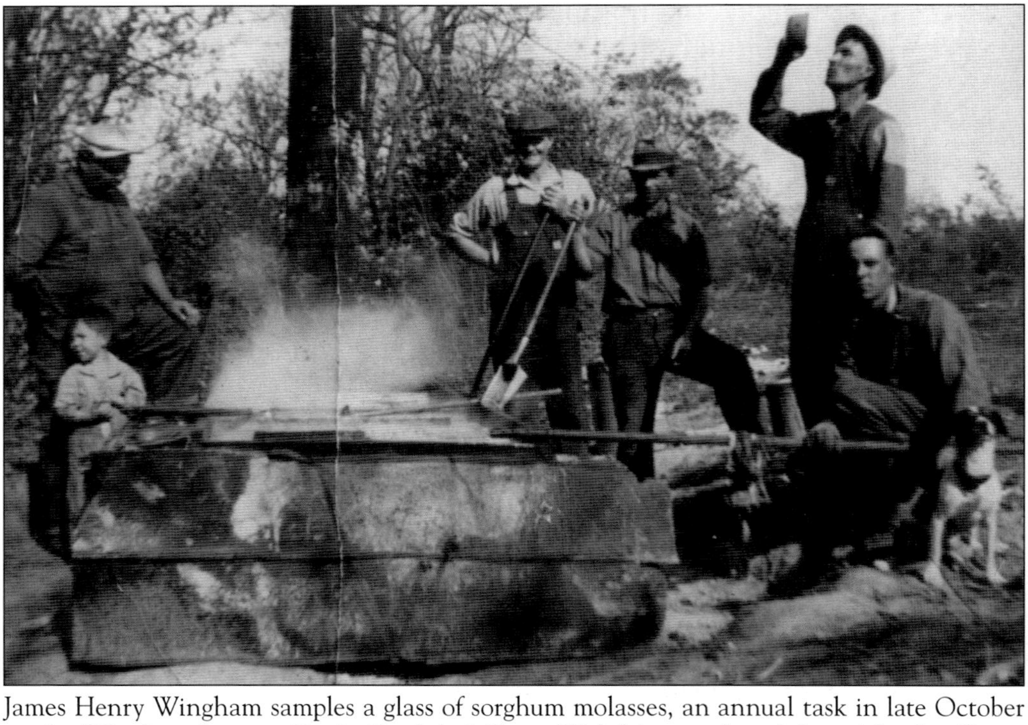

James Henry Wingham samples a glass of sorghum molasses, an annual task in late October on the Wingham farm on Canip Creek in Milton. With him are, from left to right, Joe Gross, Clifford Wingham, Bill Raker, Ted Wingham, and Bill Wingham. This photograph was taken on the farm around 1938. (Courtesy of Ted Taylor.)

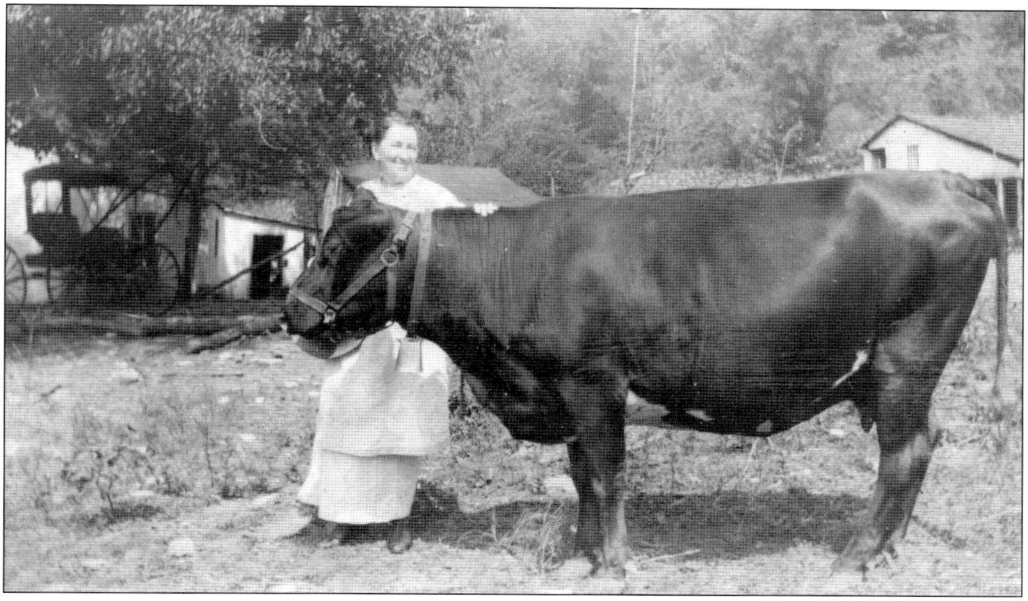

A member of the Gross family stands in the barnyard with a prized bull on a Trimble County farm near Milton. (Courtesy of Mike Gross.)

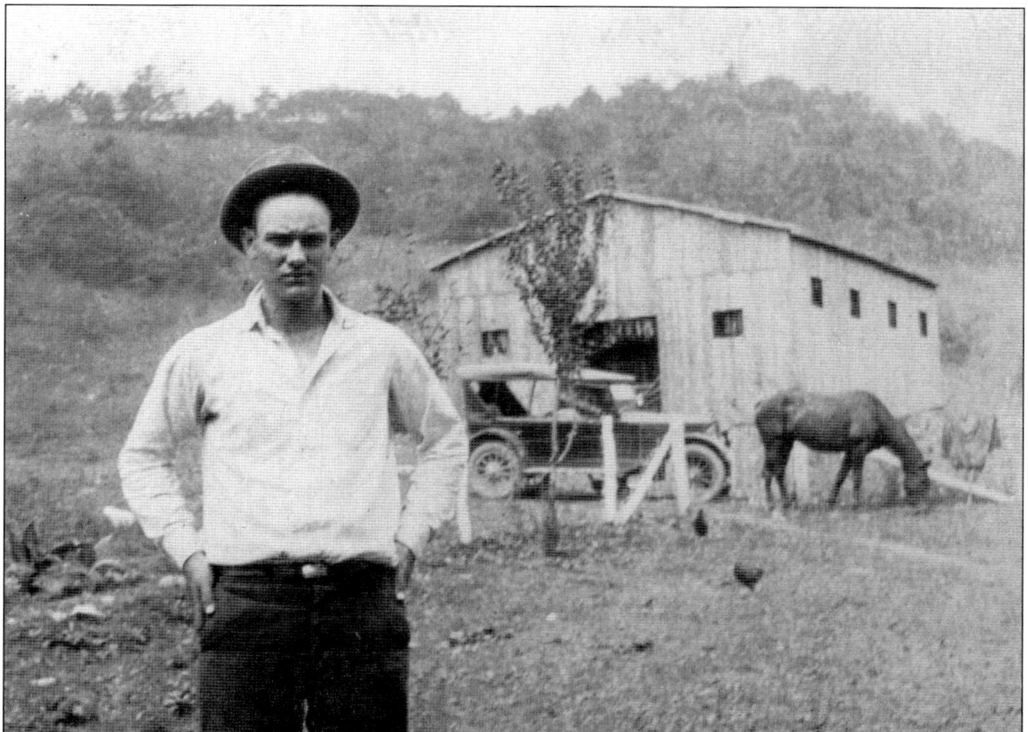

James William "Billy" Egerton Sr. poses on his farm near Bedford. Born in Carroll County, he lived most of his life in Trimble County, serving as a deputy sheriff when his brother, Clarence Egerton, was the county sheriff. (Courtesy of Frederica Congleton.)

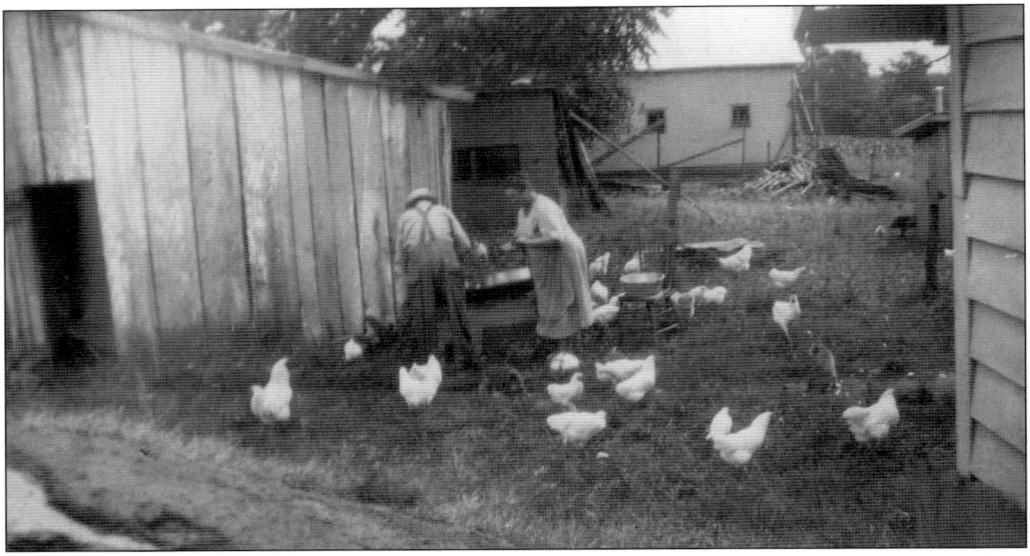

John and Mary Pardo tend to the chickens and do other chores on the family farm on Mount Pleasant Road east of Bedford. Their daughter, Mildred Pardo Pruitt, sold a portion of the family farm on Mount Pleasant Road to the Trimble County School District, where the new Bedford Elementary School was built in 2002. (Courtesy of Mildred Pardo Pruitt.)

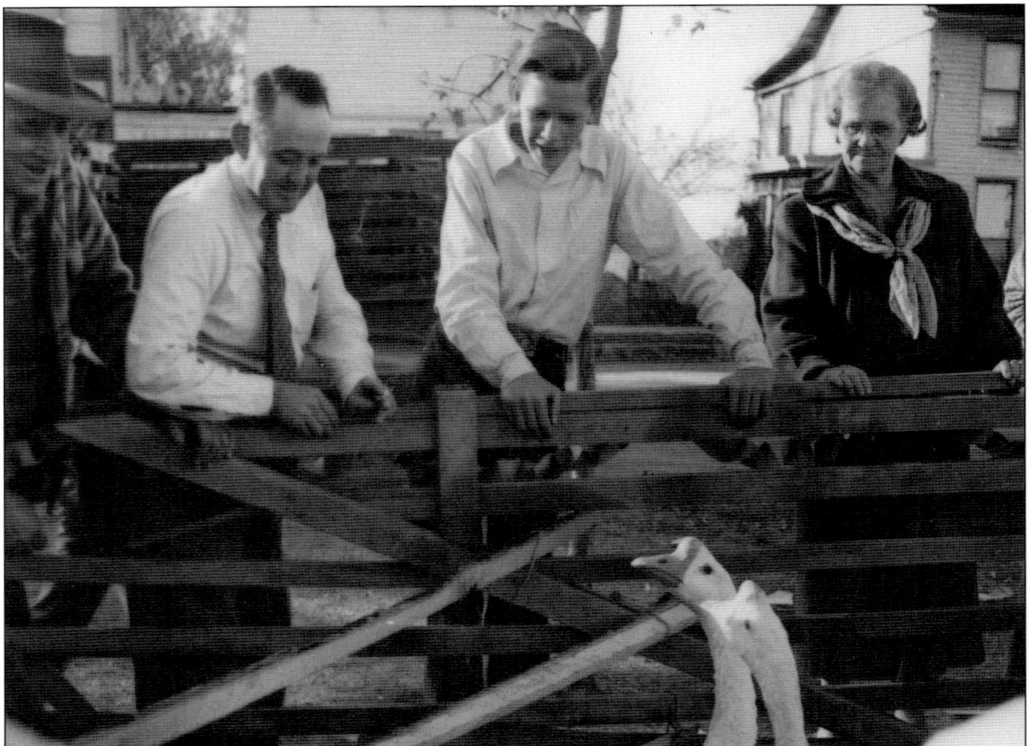

John Rand, in tie, helps feeds the geese and talks with Charlie Smith (center) and his family at their Trimble County farm. Rand's son Reggie says his father, a leader in the county Democratic Party, was either on the campaign trail or trying to sell the family insurance, which was his day job. (Courtesy of Reggie Rand.)

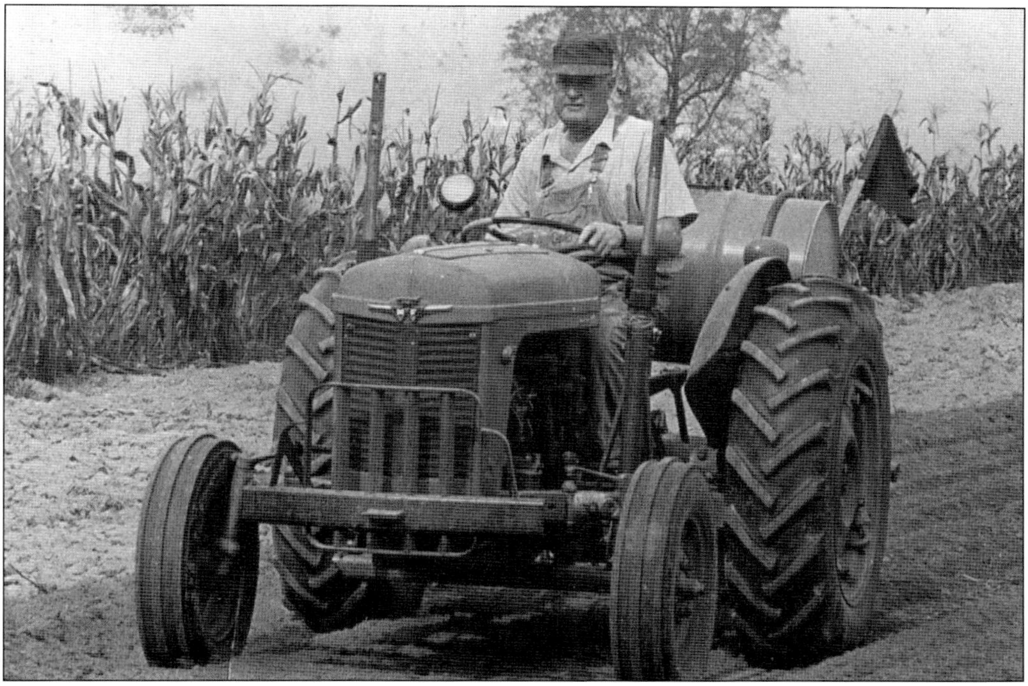

Bill Raker plows a field near an unharvested crop of corn. He is riding a Massey-Ferguson tractor. (Courtesy of Ted Taylor.)

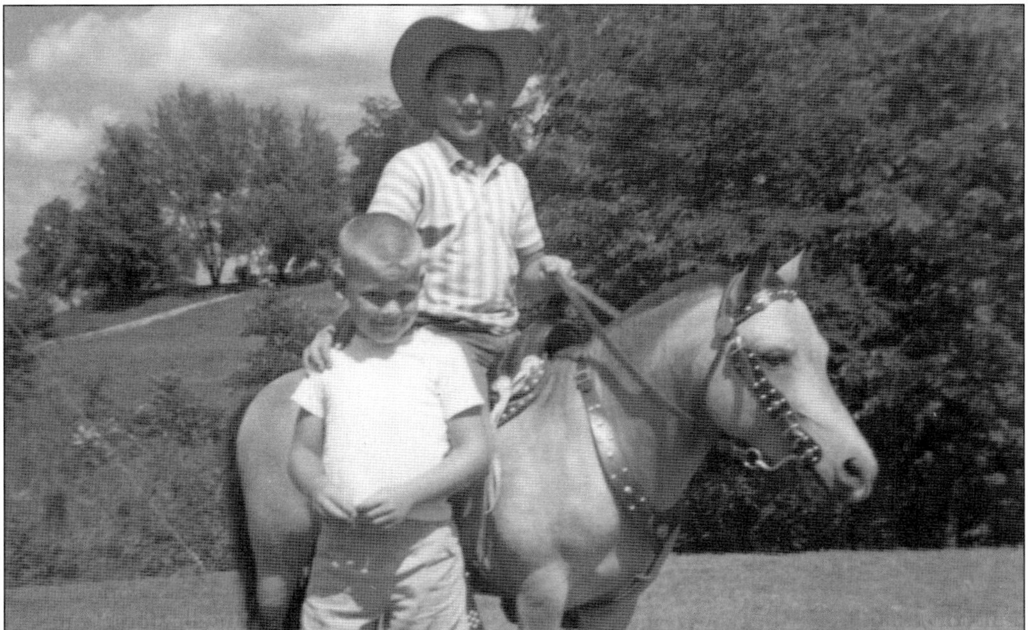

Joe Tingle poses with his brother Jeff while riding a miniature pony on Charlie Ransdell's farm near Bedford. Ransdell started raising miniature horses in Trimble County in the 1950s. (Courtesy of Frederica Congleton.)

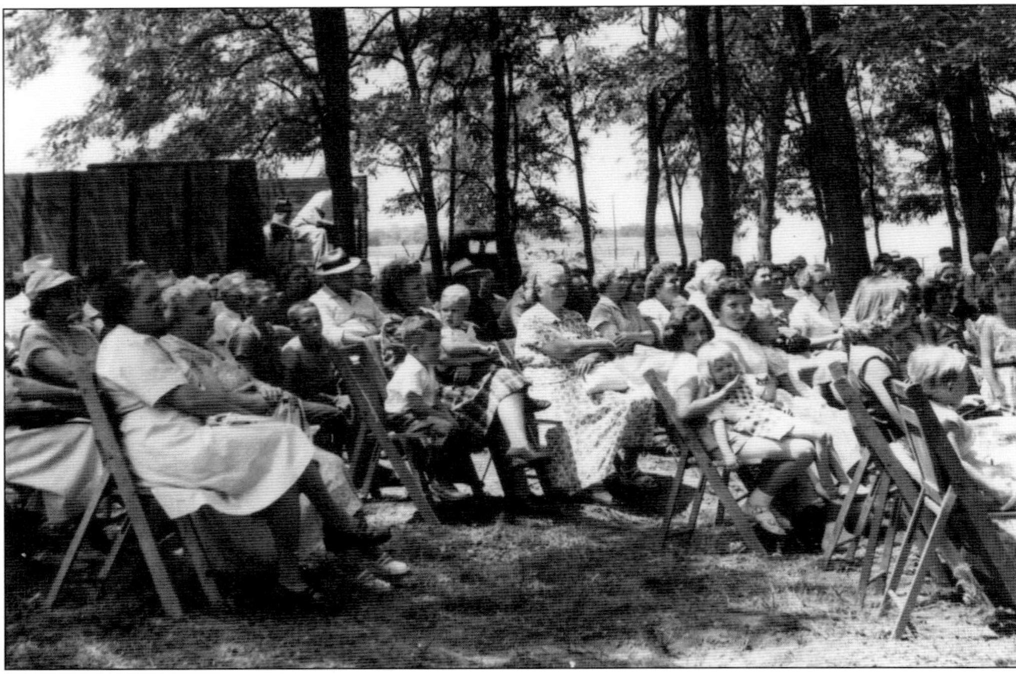

The John Rand farm was one of many that hosted Trimble County Field Day for the Trimble County Extension Service. Field Days traditionally feature agricultural experts who speak on a variety of farming-related topics. Here, men, women, and children listen to a speaker in a shady grove on the farm near Bedford. (Courtesy of Reggie Rand.)

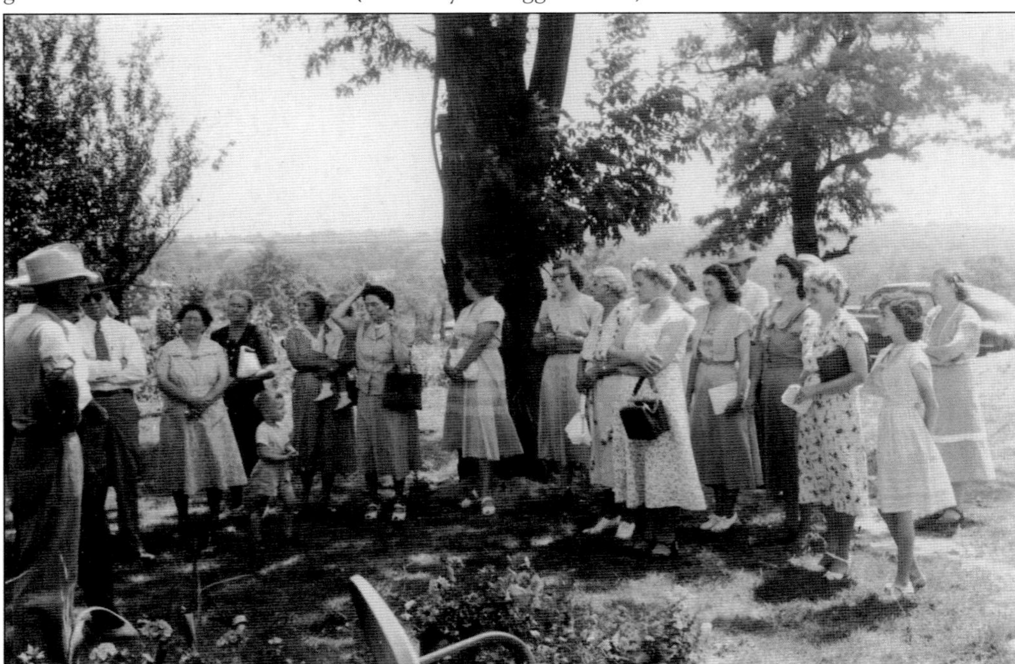

Another year, the Extension Service hosted its Field Day on the Stewart farm, located in the southern portion of Trimble County near the Henry County line. (Courtesy of Robert Bruce "Bob" Stewart Jr.)

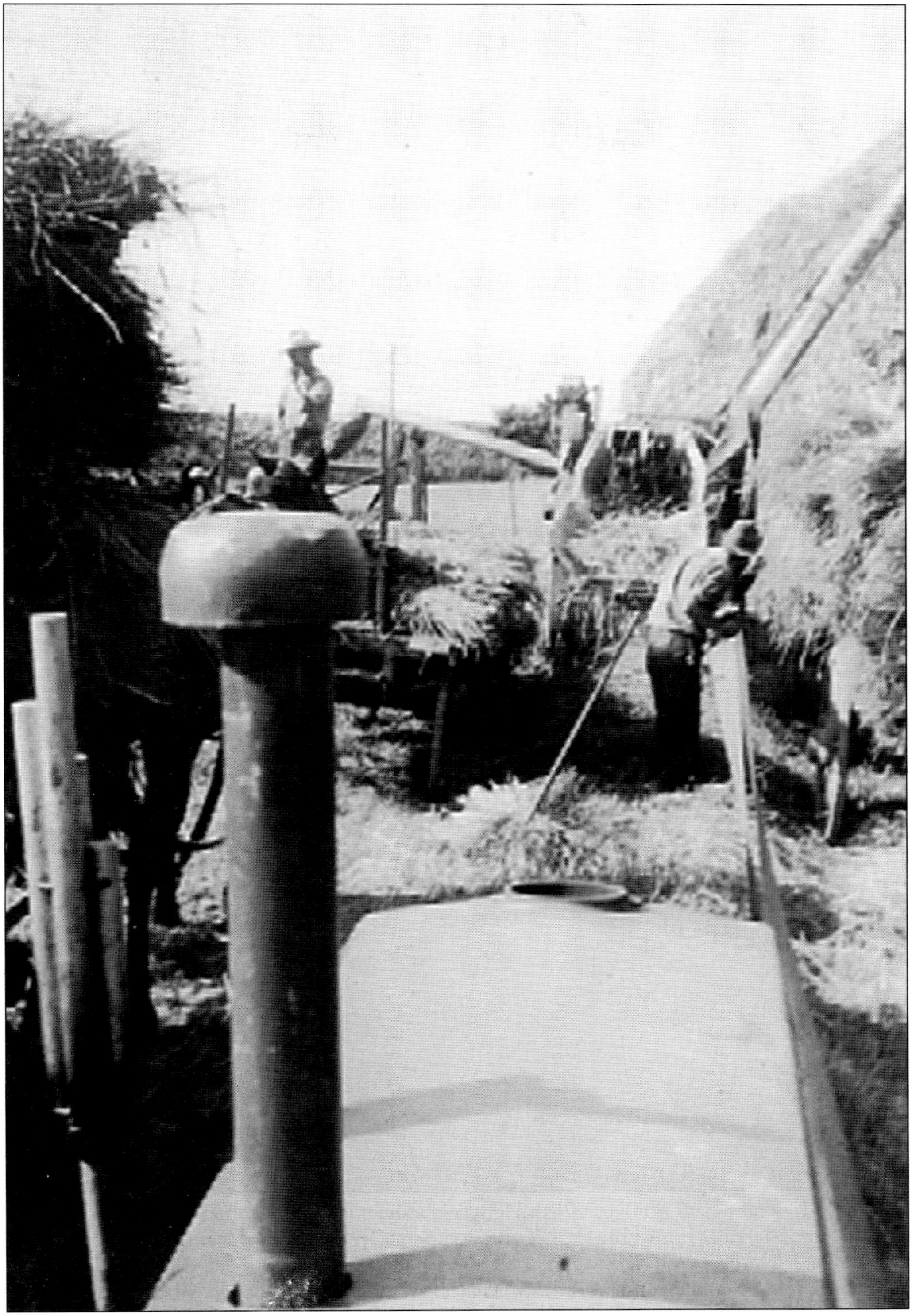

An ancient Case threshing machine was put to good use on a sunny fall day during the local wheat harvest. (Courtesy of Kay Sachleben Barnes.)

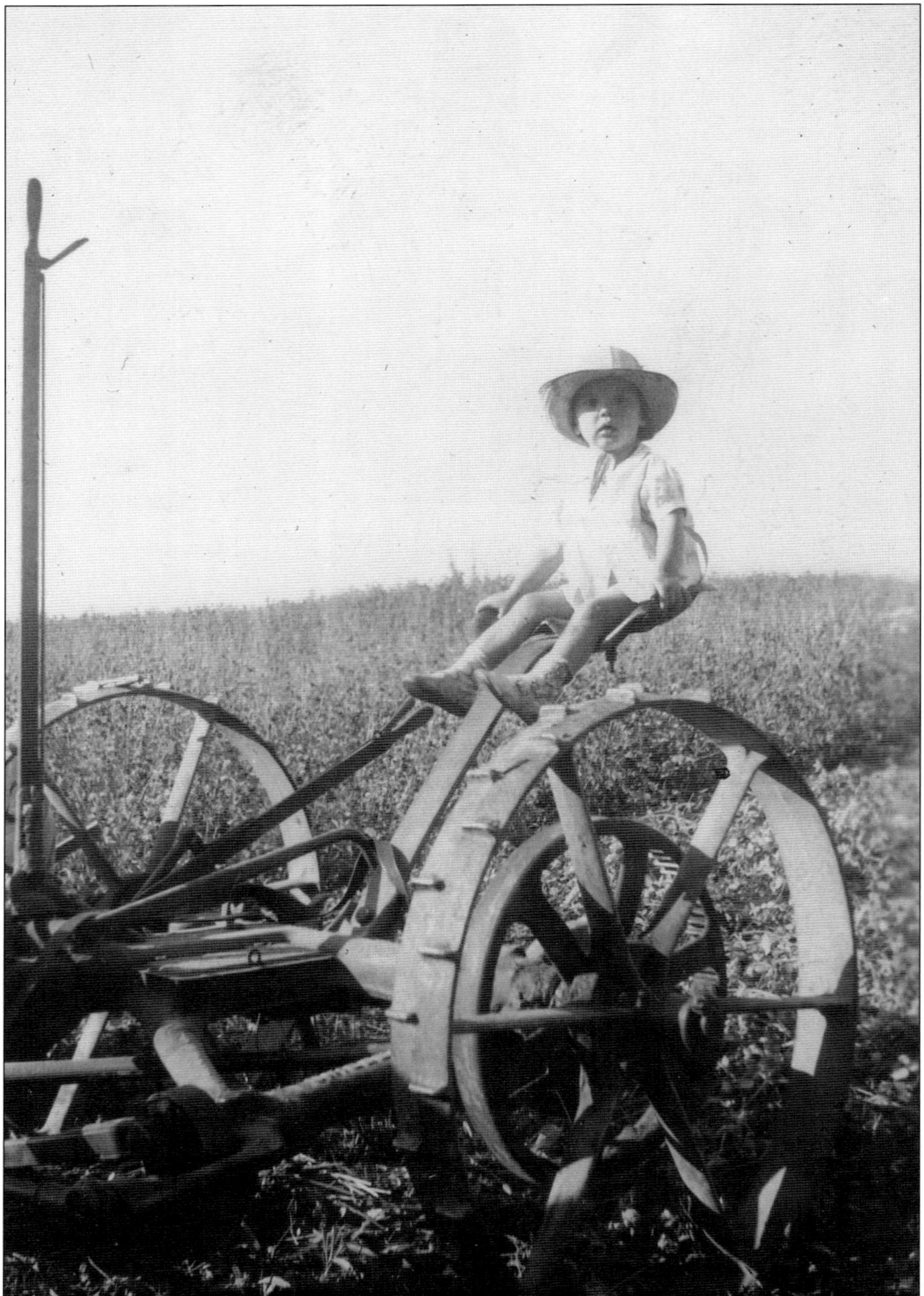

Alma Doris Ogden is perched on the seat of this ancient piece of farm equipment on the Mosley-Ogden farm near Bedford. The farm was owned by her grandparents James and Lurlene Mosley and her parents, Joseph and Laura Ogden. (Courtesy of JoDeva Ogden.)

Five

Readin', 'Ritin', and 'Rithmetic

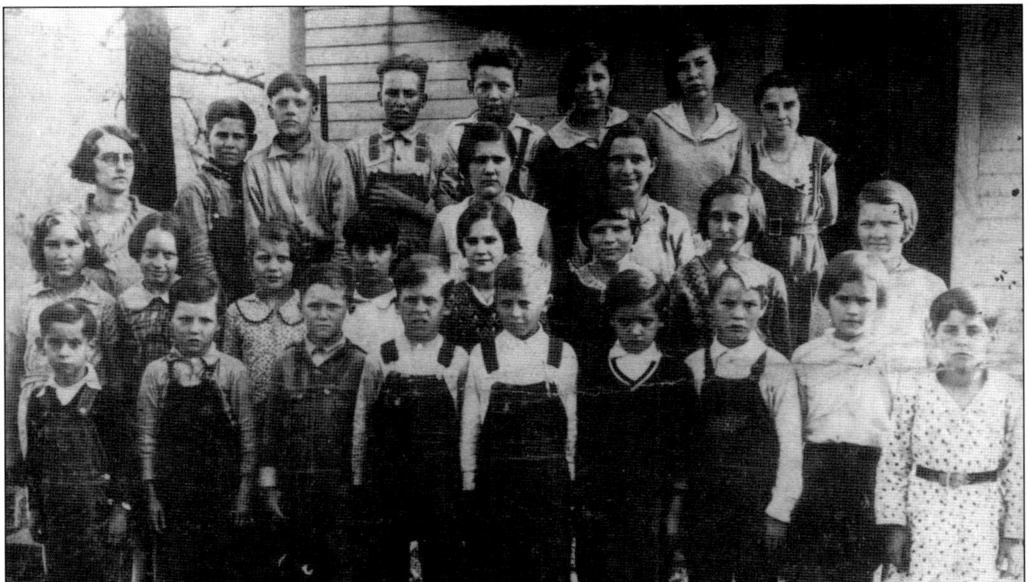

Before consolidation in the early 20th century, there were 33 one-room schoolhouses dotting the landscape of Trimble County. Pictured here are students in the 1930 class at the Norfolk School, located just south of the Preston Plantation. From left to right are (first row) Clifford Williams, Roy Boldery, Verda Crafton, Rudy Barnes, Claudie Jones, Clifford Rowlett, Raymond O. Williams, Francis Horner, and Evelyn Williams; (second row) Doris Crafton, Johnny Conard, Lois Rowlett (Liter), Hazel Williams, ? Purvis, Viola Perry, Goldine Boldery, and Doca Horner; (third row) teacher Miss Elizabeth Ball and two unidentified; (fourth row) Obbie Barnes, Andy Horner, Dick Law, Raymond Rowlett, Mary Conard, Roberta Crafton, and Ruby Mae Willis. (Courtesy of Carolyn Crafton Adams.)

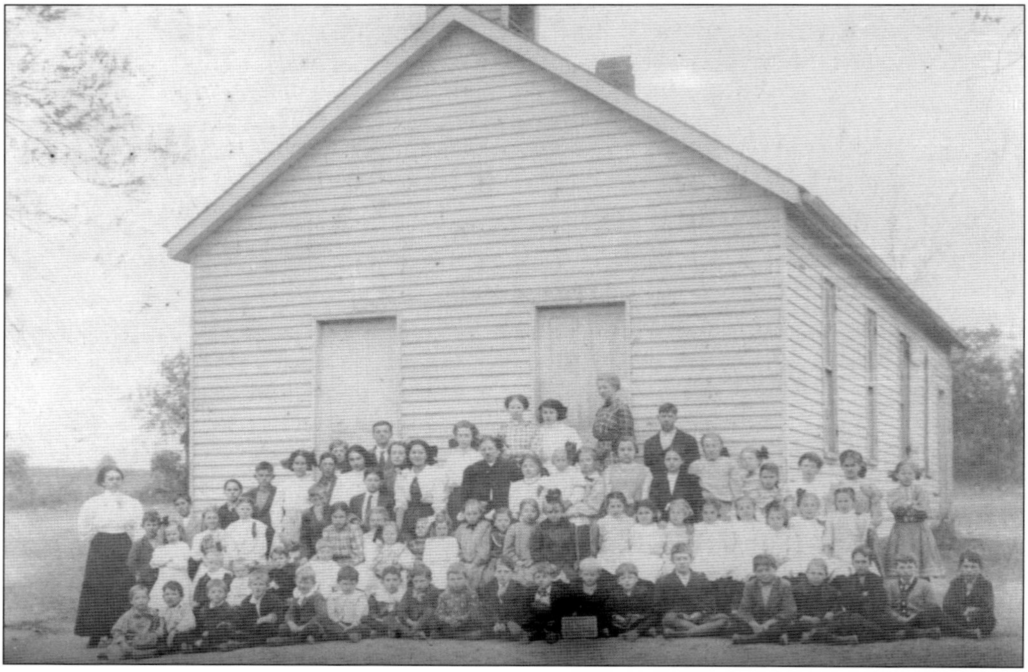

The Pryor Hill School in 1913 provided education to families in the Carmel district of northeast Trimble County. It was built in the 1860s on land donated by Jonathan Markely. The original building burned in 1927 and was replaced in 1928. Those attending included the family names of Abbott, Stewart, Woods, Holsclaw, Richmond, Bird, Buchanan, Mosser, Perkinson, Wright, Mikesell, and Welsh. (Courtesy of Gary Greenwood.)

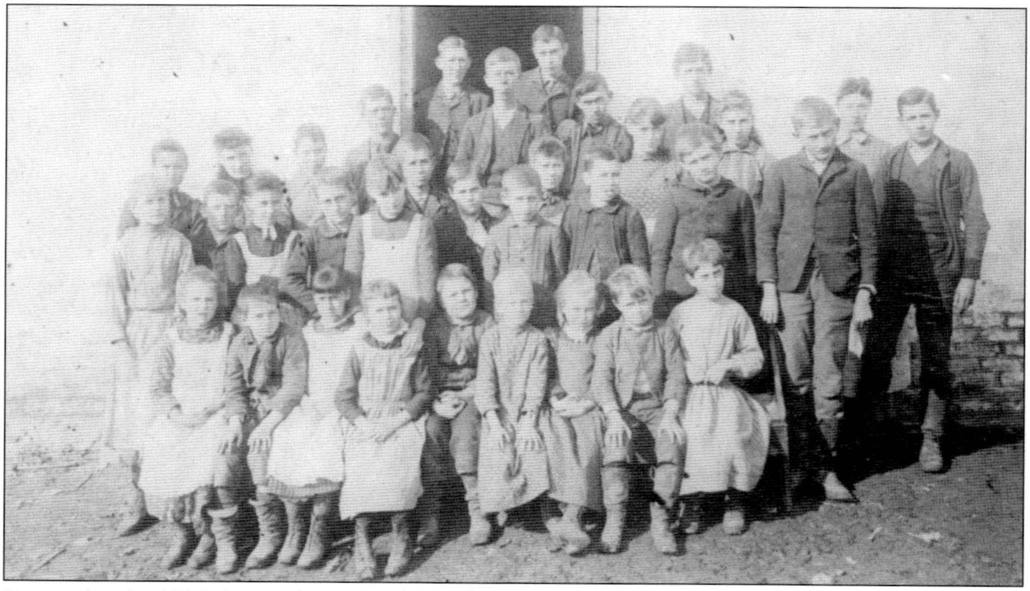

Pictured is the 1890 class at Corn Creek Academy. This school was built on the old Milton-Bedford Pike on land donated by Drakeford Gray in the early 1800s. The original school was built of bricks made on the William Powell farm. A new building was completed in 1911 and was used until 1935. The oldest in Trimble County, the Corn Creek School operated continuously for 126 years. (Courtesy of Gary Greenwood.)

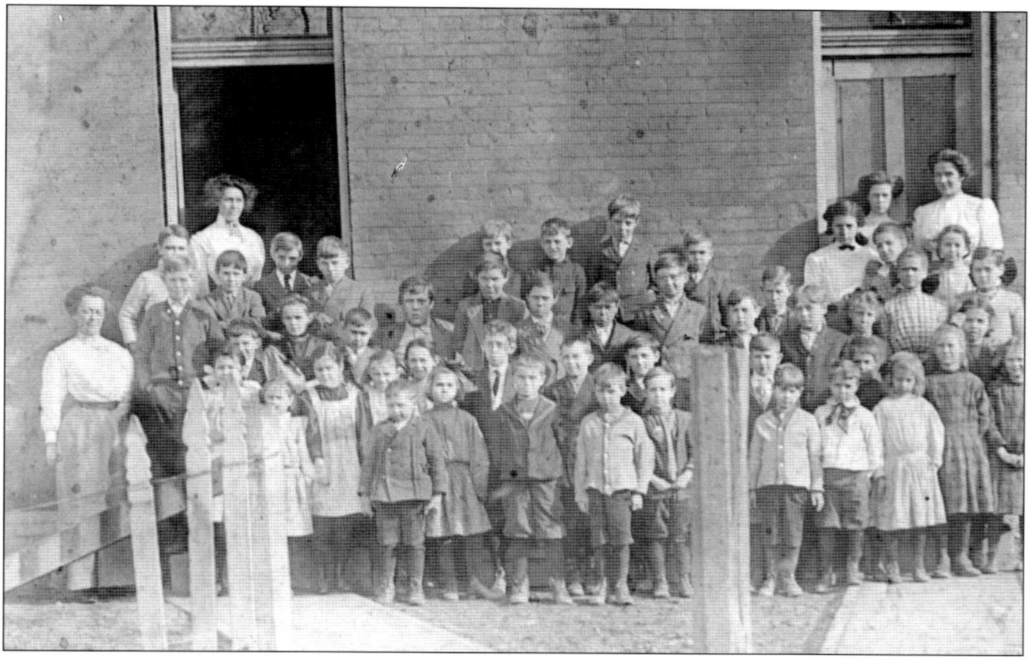

The first public school in Milton was located in the village of Kingston, on the south side of Tiber Creek. Above is Milton's second schoolhouse, built in 1877 next to Tiber Creek at the corner of what is now Highway 36 and School Hollow Road. Recurring flooding caused the school to be replaced by one about a half mile south in the hollow. (Courtesy of Gary Rowlett.)

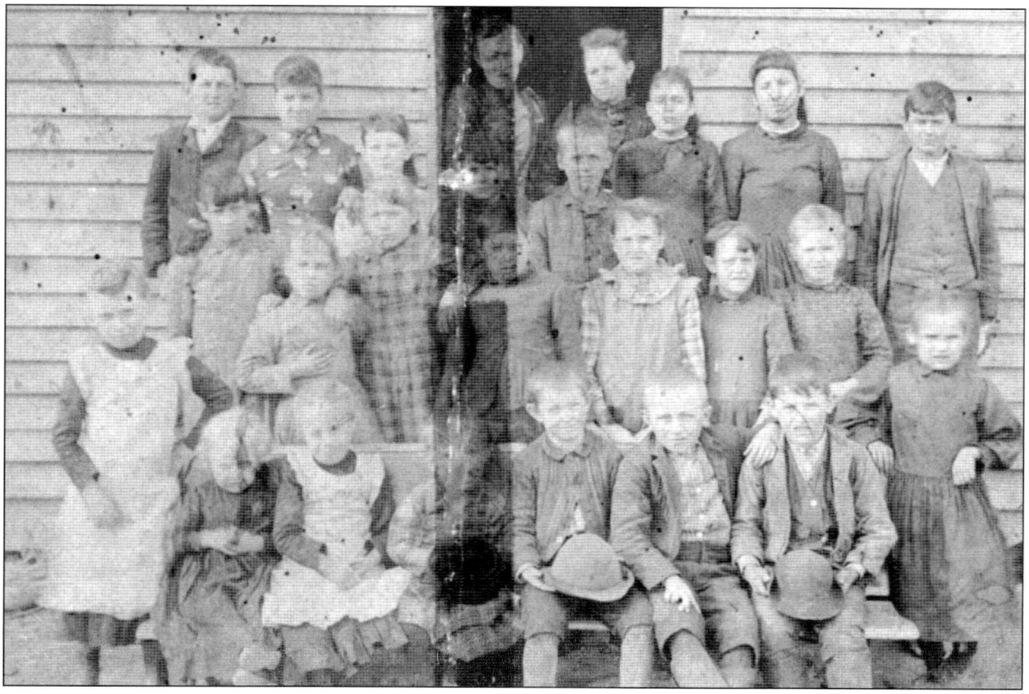

By 1908, there were 32 one-room schools serving children in Trimble County, three of which were for African American children. This school was located in the northern part of the county. (Courtesy of Charlene Boatwright Ellis.)

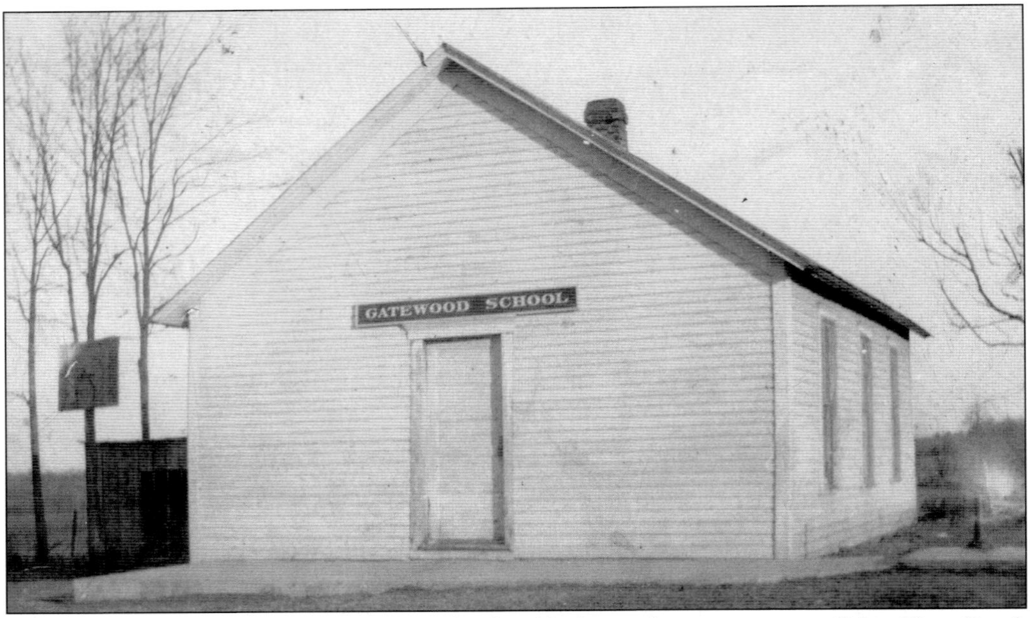

The Gatewood School was two miles north of Bedford near the intersection of New Hope Road. Gail Mosley Ransdell started her teaching career there. In addition to being a noted local educator, Randsell also wrote for newspapers and magazines. (Courtesy of Gary Greenwood.)

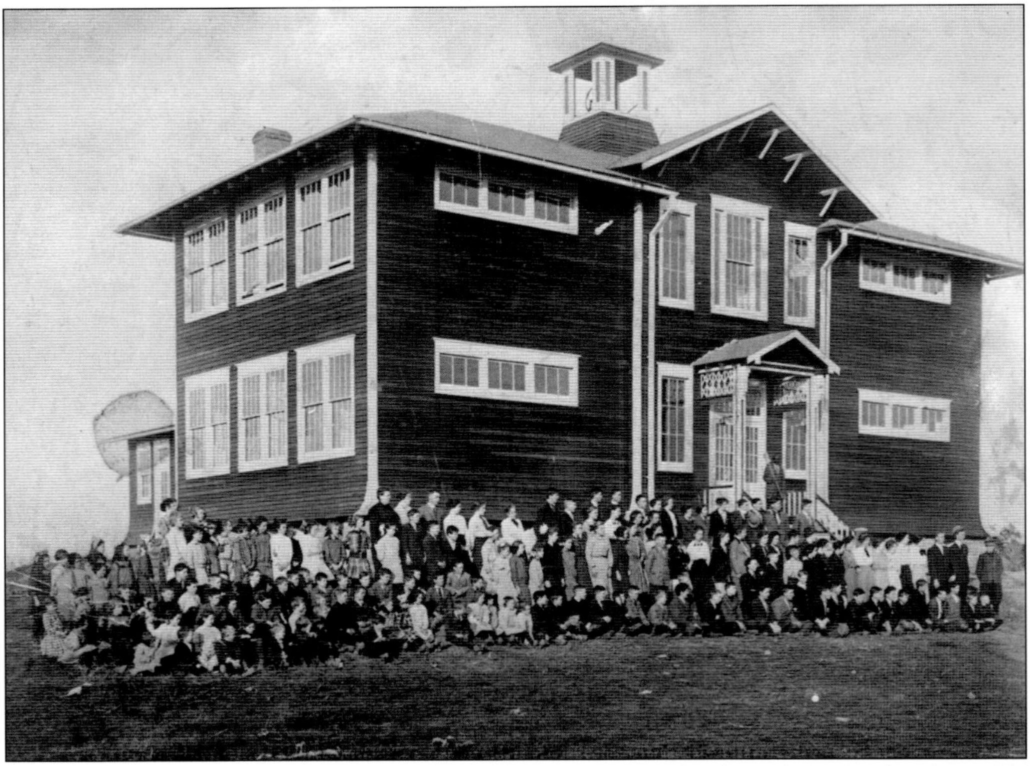

The eight-room school built in 1912 accommodated both the Bedford Graded School and Trimble County High School. It was built by H.G. Mitchell on the James Wentworth farm. Here, students pose for a group photograph in 1913. (Courtesy of Gary Greenwood.)

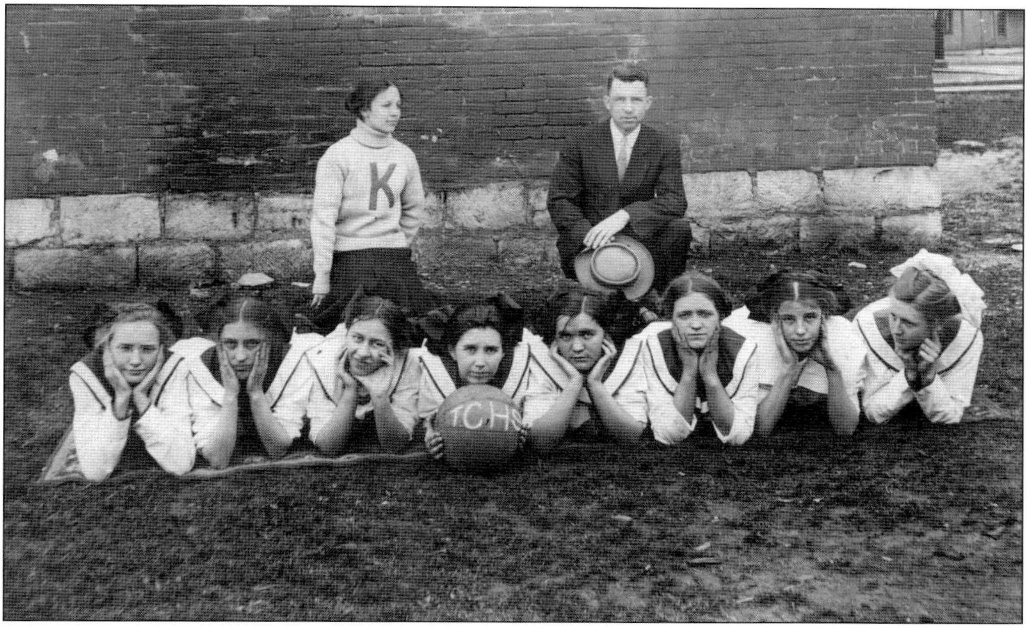

These Trimble County High School girls basketball team members are, from left to right, Mamie Stanley, Mary Peak, Lena Clem, Pauline Cook, Ola Edwards, Muriel McMahan, May Hancock, and Sadie Colbert. Miss Vaughn and Mr. Edwards are the adults in back. (Courtesy of Trimble County Public Library.)

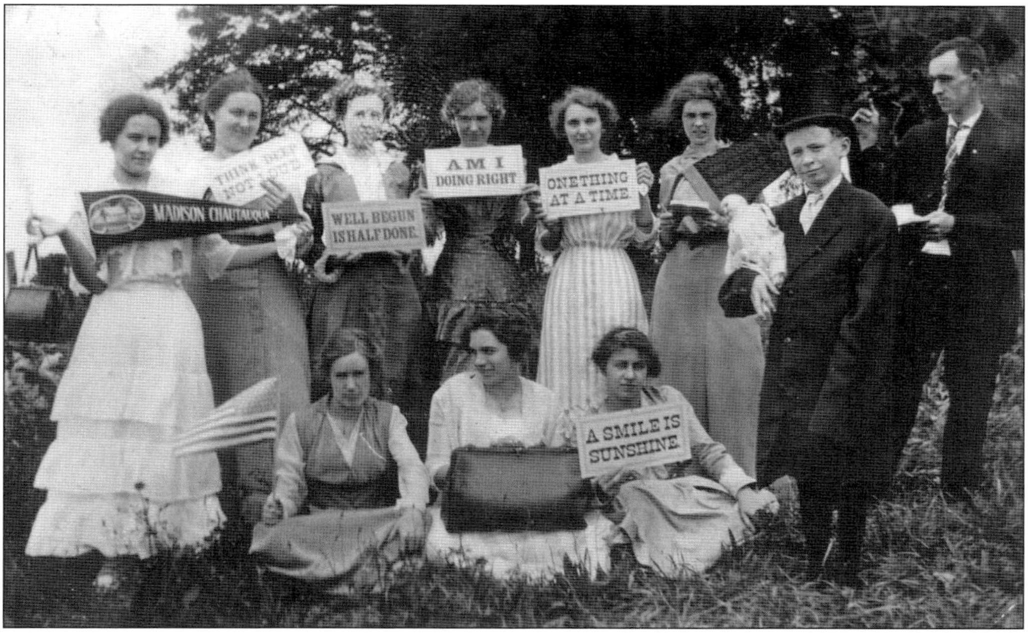

Bedford High School members of the class of 1909 pose with affirmations: from left to right are (seated) Olive Suddith, Vera Cutshaw, and Lena Clem; (standing) Allie Clem, Mattie Morgan, Alice Baker, Lottie Logan, Rose Morgan, unidentified, I.T. Stanley, and R.E. Clem (son of A.B. Clem, who owned one of the grocery stores). (Courtesy of Mildred Pardo Pruitt.)

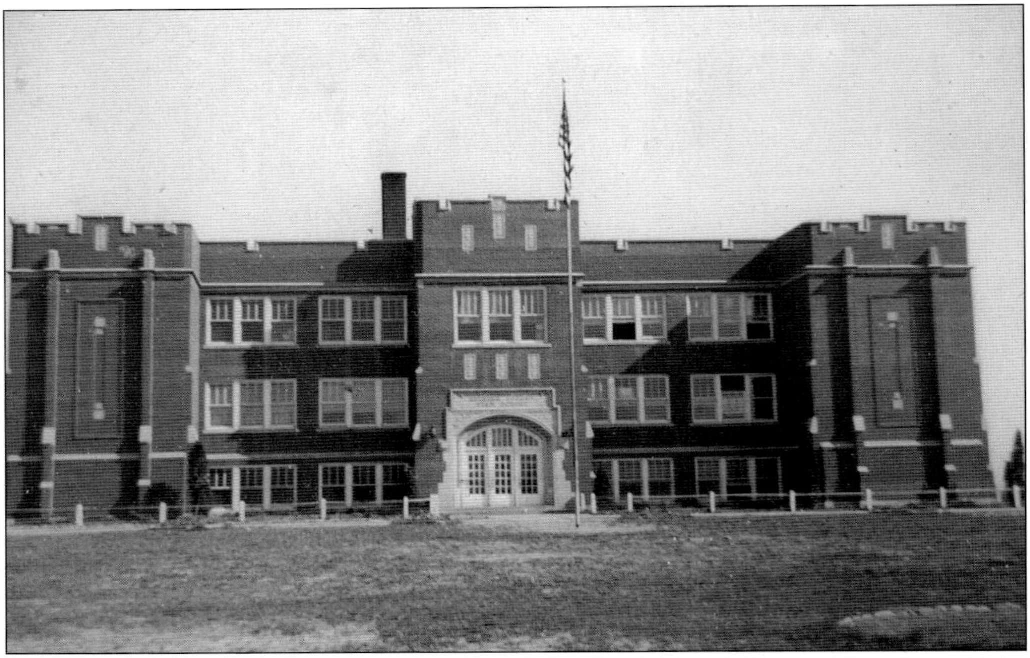

In 1930, the Bedford Grade School District consolidated with Trimble County High School. The Trimble school board built this traditional three-story brick building that included 14 classrooms and a gymnasium, the first for Bedford's schools. It was replaced in 1969 by the existing Trimble County High School just north of Bedford city limits. A portion of the old high school exists as part of the Trimble County Middle School. (Courtesy of Lucy Webster Smith.)

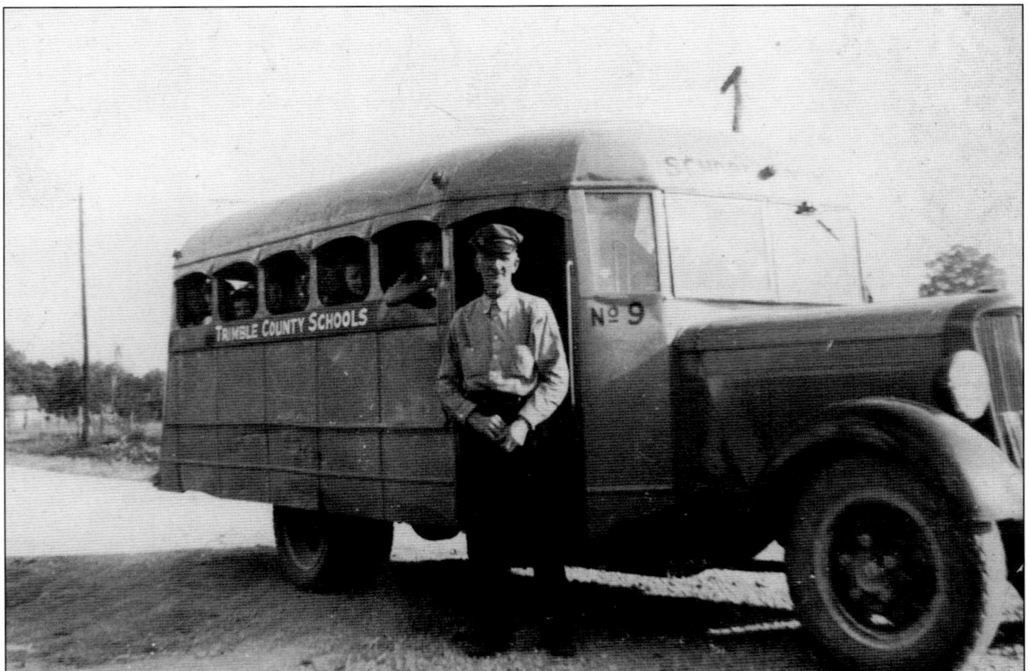

Edward Sachleben was a bus driver for Trimble County High School. Here, he poses in front of a busload of his charges. (Courtesy of Kay Sachleben Barnes.)

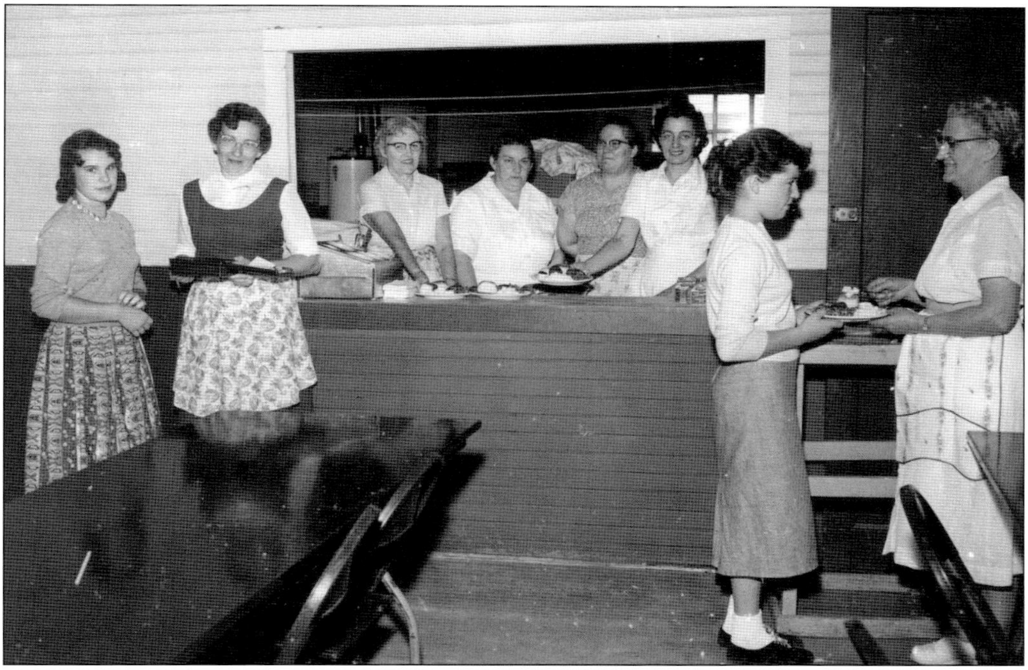

Hard at work in the Trimble County High School cafeteria, lunchroom ladies pose with students. From left to right are Mary Bailey, Louise Pierce, Ruth Leach, Marian Newman, Amy Burrows, Kathryn Callis, and two unidentified. (Courtesy of the Trimble County Public Library.)

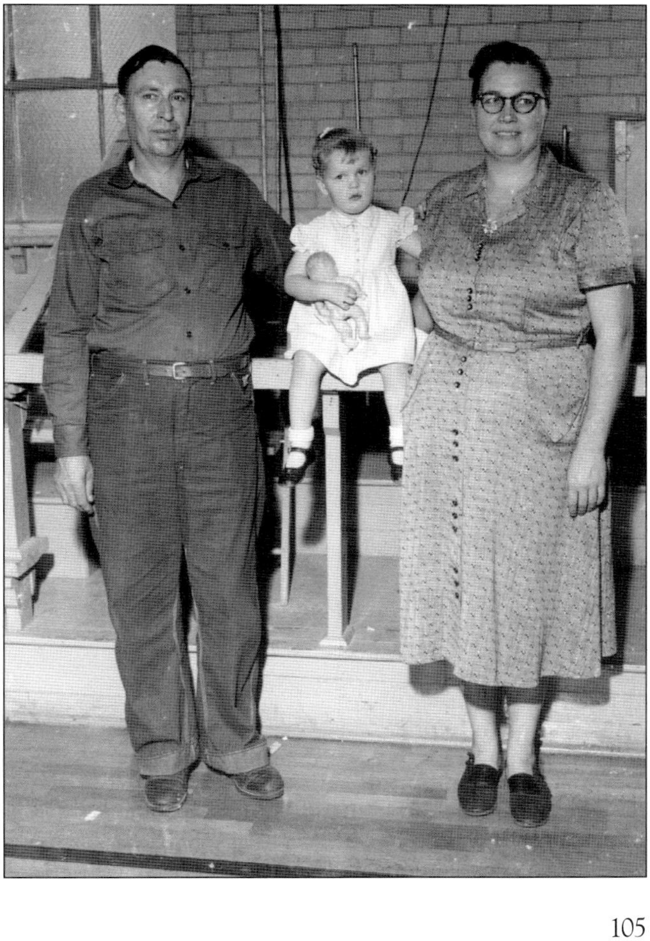

Robert and Gladys Penick worked as janitors at Trimble County High School. Here, they pose for a yearbook photograph with their daughter, Dorothy. (Courtesy of the Trimble County Public Library.)

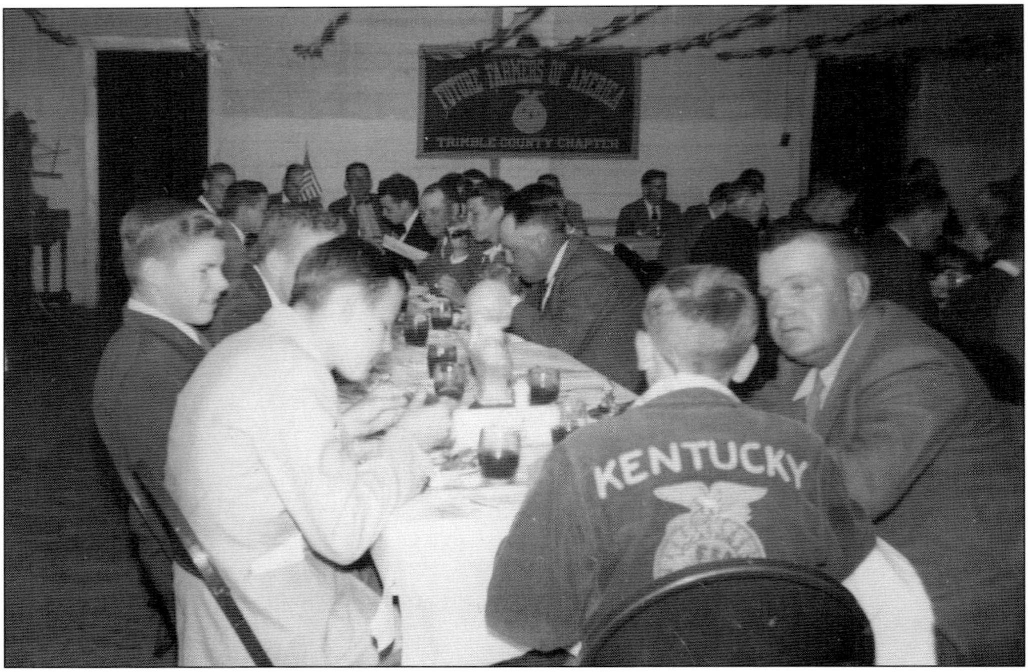

Members of the Trimble County High School Future Farmers of America enjoy their annual banquet in 1952, long before girls were allowed to join. In the foreground, from left to right, are Hubert Stark, Clarence Callis, and Bobby True. (Courtesy of Reggie Rand.)

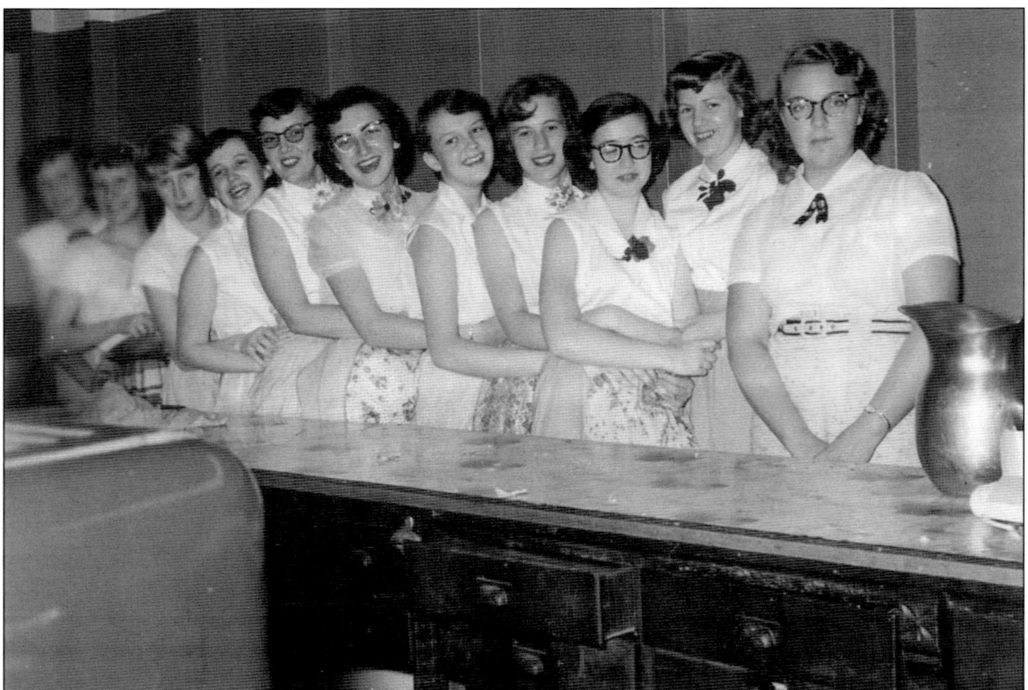

Most likely members of the Future Homemakers of America, these Trimble High School girls were on hand to cook the meal served at the FFA dinner in 1952. (Courtesy of Reggie Rand.)

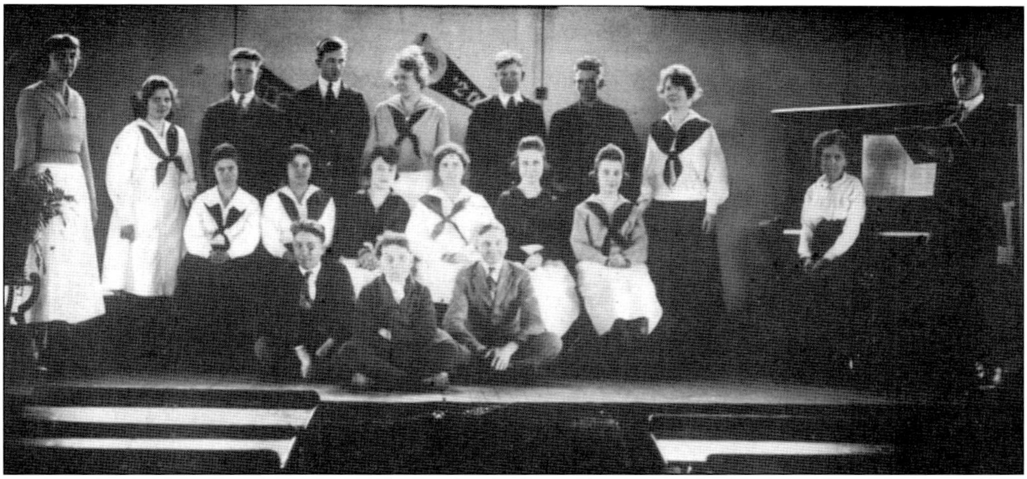

Robert B. Clem was director of the Trimble County High School Glee Club, which featured members (in unknown order) Helen Lee, Vera Brown, Ethel King, Claudys Carson, Dorris Spillman, Erby Spillman, Jessie Peak, Kathleen Harmon, Daisy Garriott, Keith Hood, Guy McClure, David H. Beetem, Charles Lee, Wilbur Coghill, Glen Hancock, and Fred Hosley. Miss Lottie Logan served as manager, while Mrs. Florence Anderson was pianist. (Courtesy of Mildred Pardo Pruitt.)

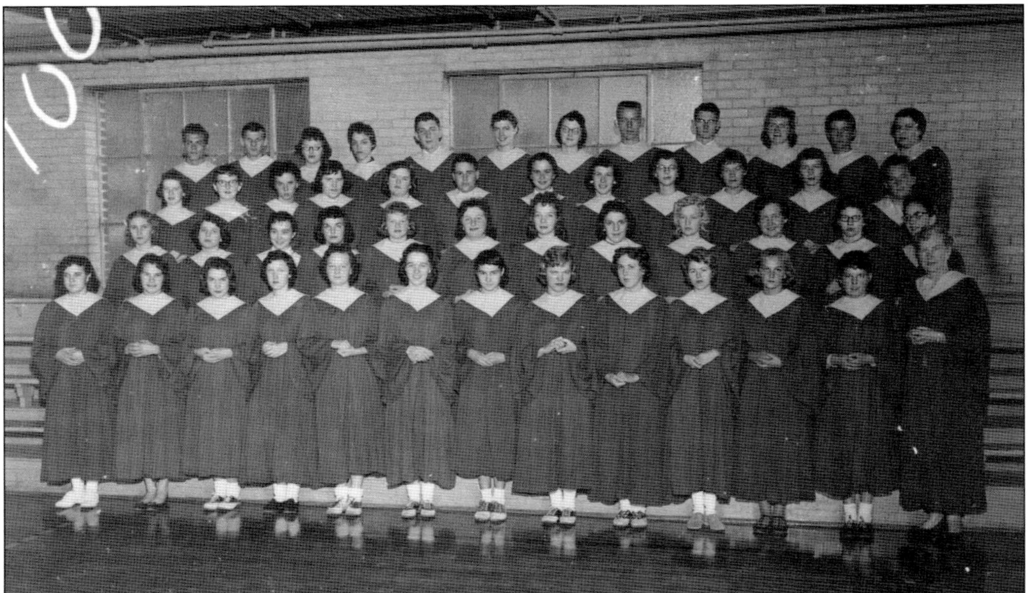

Standing on risers in the gymnasium for a yearbook photograph are members of Mrs. Neal's Glee Club at Trimble County High School. (Courtesy of the Trimble County Public Library.)

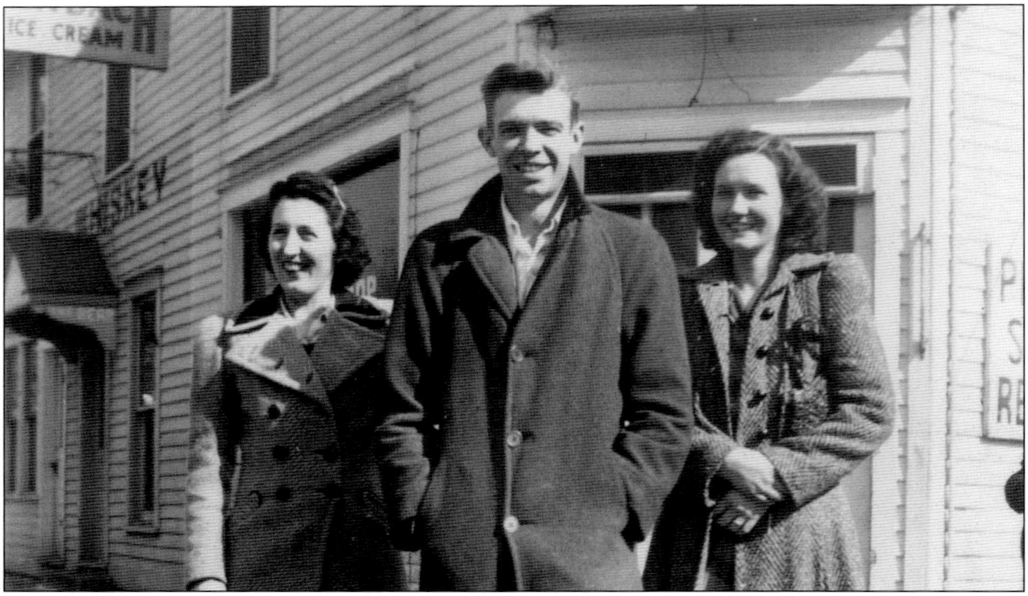

From left to right, Willana Martinie, Robert Jackson "Jack" Tingle, and Lorene Powell stand in front of Bedford Sweet Shop, which also was the location of a sandwich shop and the Community Store, a grocery store established by Mr. and Mrs. Watts. Tingle was a legendary basketball player. He played for the University of Kentucky on a scholarship and played professionally for the Washington Capitals, the Minneapolis Lakers, and the New York Nationals. (Courtesy of Mildred Pardo Pruitt.)

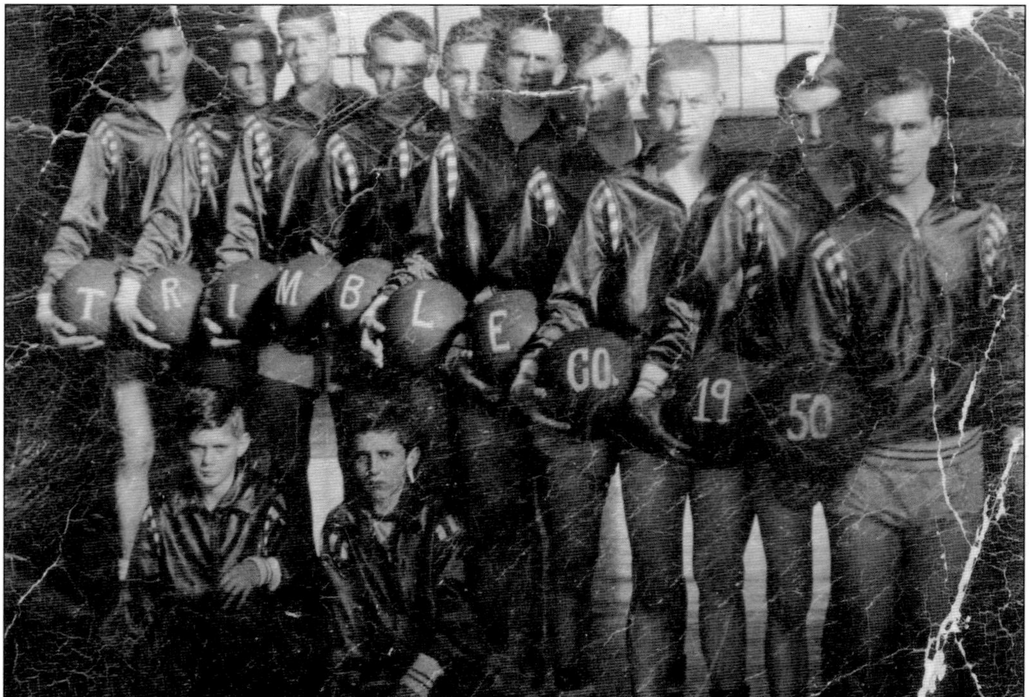

Members of the 1950 Trimble County High School basketball team pose for their yearbook picture. (Courtesy of Frederica Congleton.)

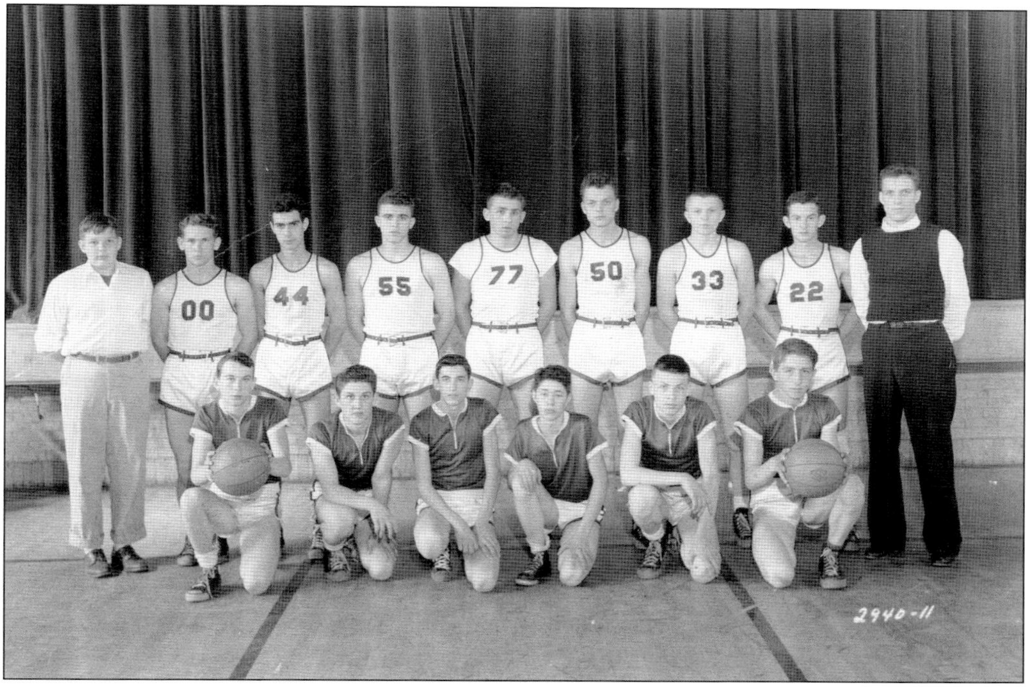

Another Trimble County High School basketball team from the early 1950s poses with its manager, Reggie Rand (far left). Basketball has always been one of the major high school sports in the region. (Courtesy of Reggie Rand.)

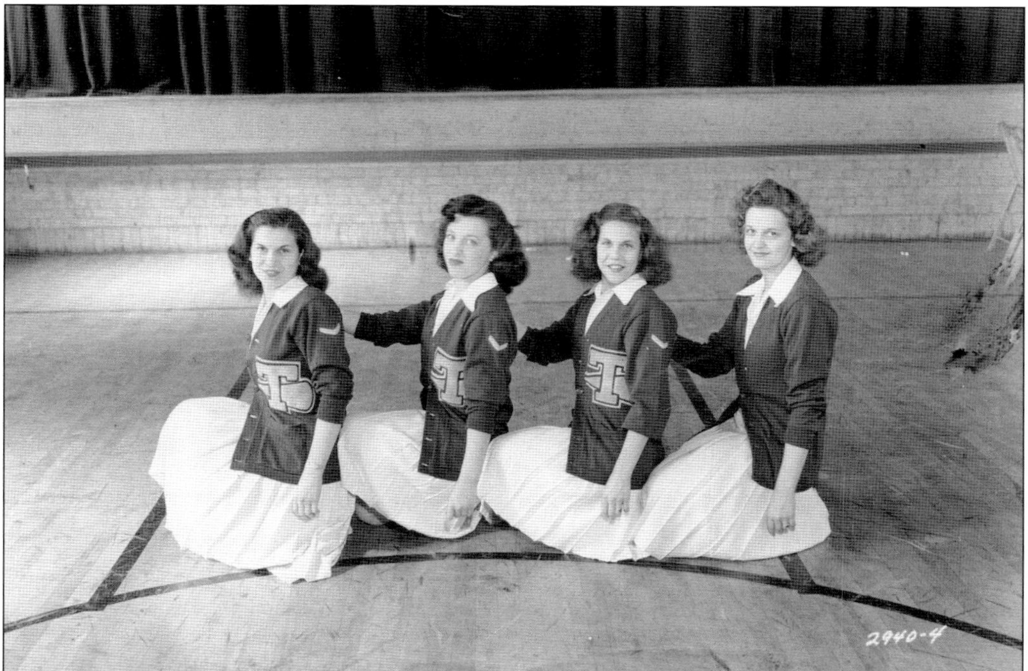

These Trimble County High School basketball cheerleaders from the early 1950s pose for the *Elbmirt*, the high school's yearbook. "Elbmirt" is "Trimble" spelled backward. (Courtesy of Reggie Rand.)

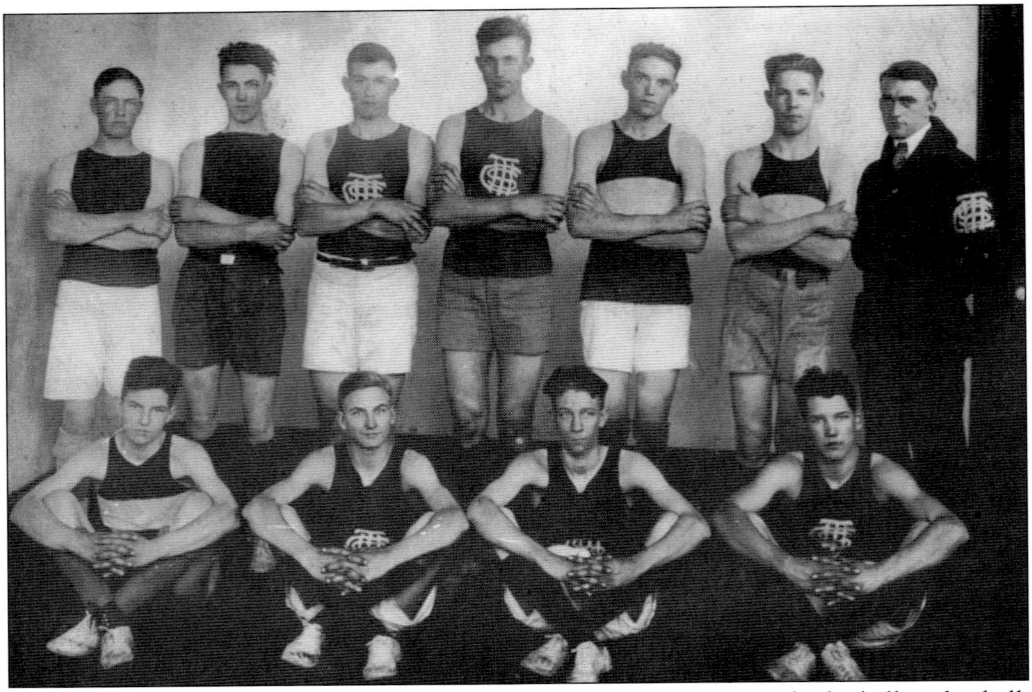

Trimble County High School has always offered more sports than just basketball or football. This photograph of the track team was included in the 1920 edition of the *Elbmirt*. (Courtesy of Mildred Pardo Pruitt.)

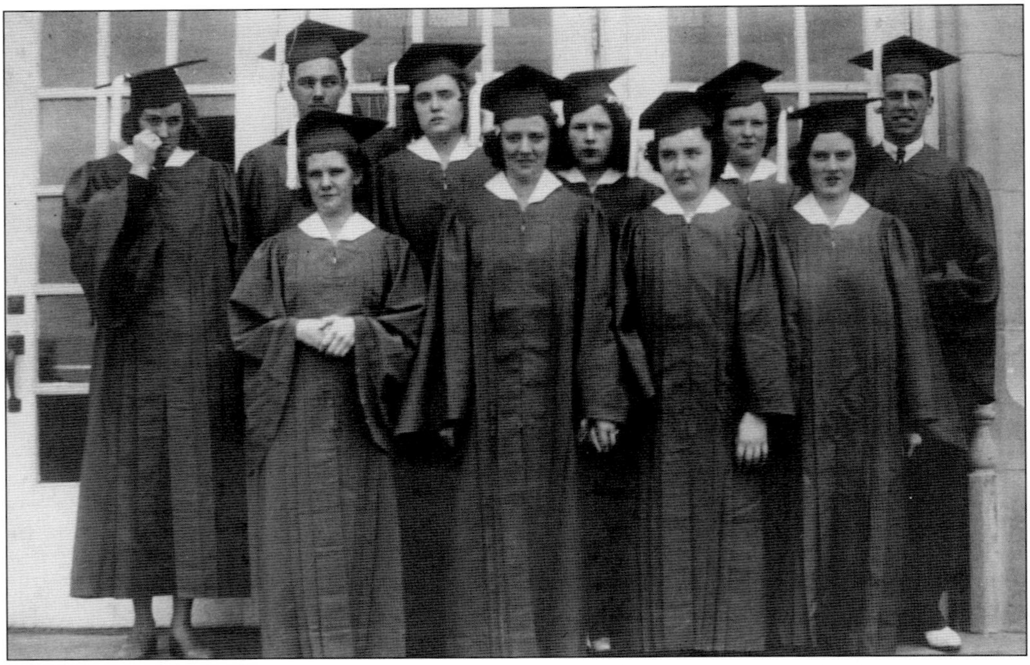

The 1941 Trimble High School graduating class included, from left to right, (first row) Lois Pryor, Lucille Sherrill, Mildred Pardo, and Mary Fisher; (second row) Martha Raisor, John Earl Jones, Naomi Miller, Mary Spillman, Alice Ginn, and Rudolph Barnes. Of the 10 classmates shown, five are still living. (Courtesy of Mildred Pardo Pruitt.)

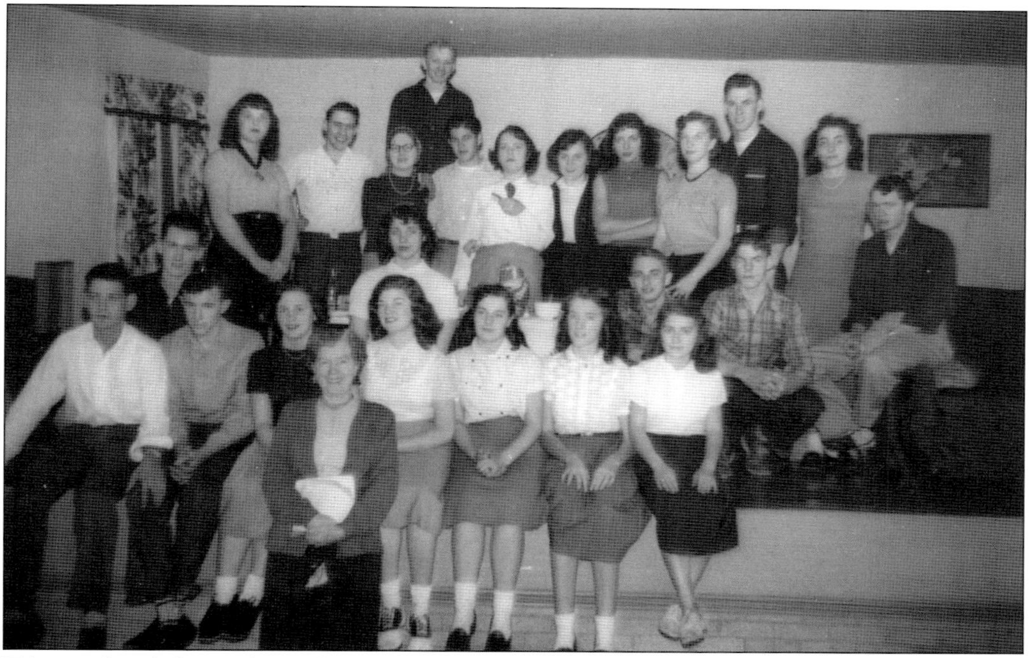

Taking a break from rehearsal, Trimble County High School seniors in the 1953 class play *Sing for Your Supper* pose for the yearbook photographer. (Courtesy of Reggie Rand.)

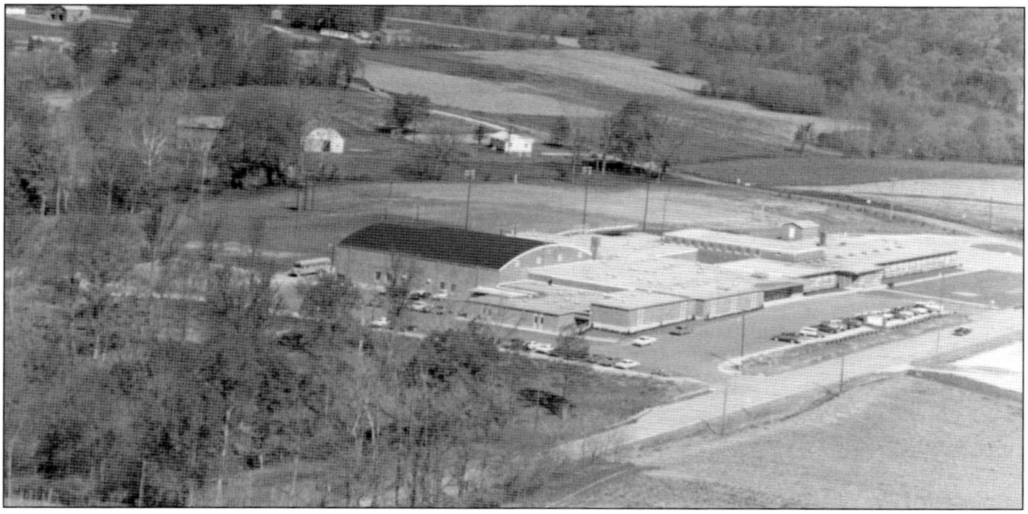

This is an aerial view of the current Trimble County High School, shortly after it was built in 1969. The new Bedford Elementary School was built in 2002 just across Mount Pleasant Road. The field on the right is where the future school would be constructed. New baseball, softball, and tennis facilities were built there, too, in 2012. In 2014, a new football field and track were built. (Courtesy of Gary Greenwood.)

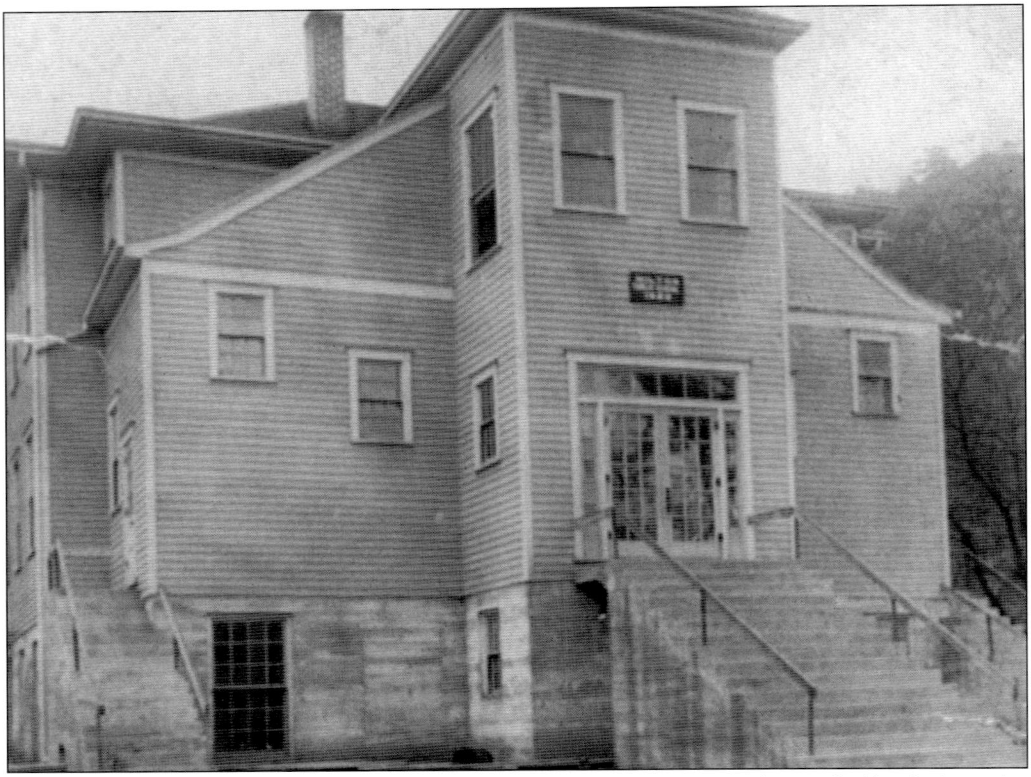

The third Milton School, above, was built in School Hollow in 1920, about a half mile from the Ohio River. The original structure had 10 classrooms. The gymnasium, shown below, was added in 1928. A separate lunchroom was added later. The Milton Graded School District dissolved in 1933 and merged with the Trimble County School System. This school was replaced by Milton Elementary School in 1953. (Both, courtesy of Gary Rowlett.)

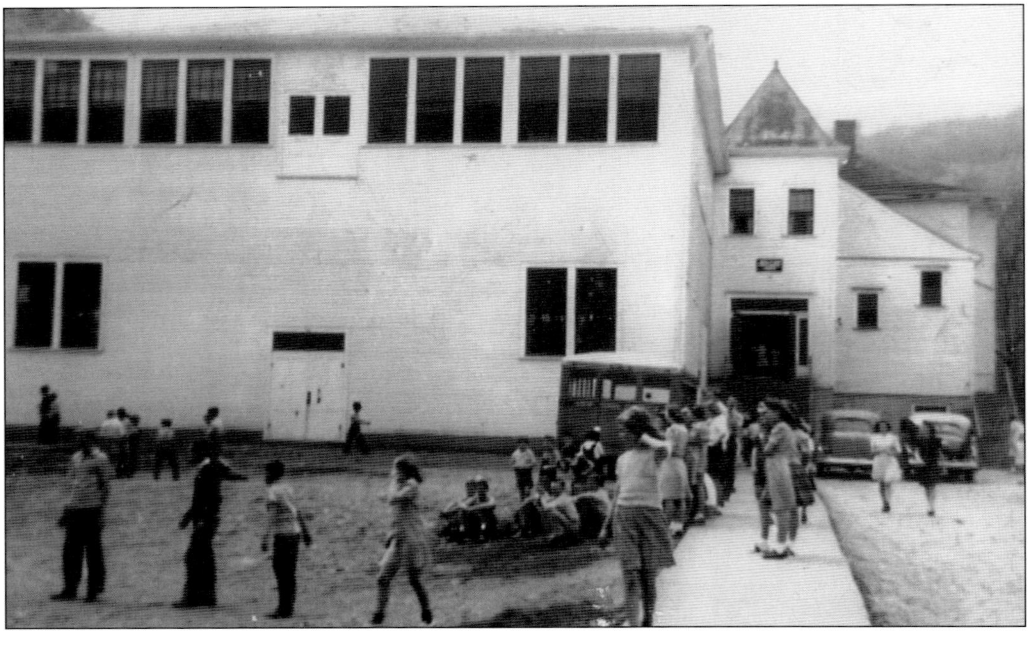

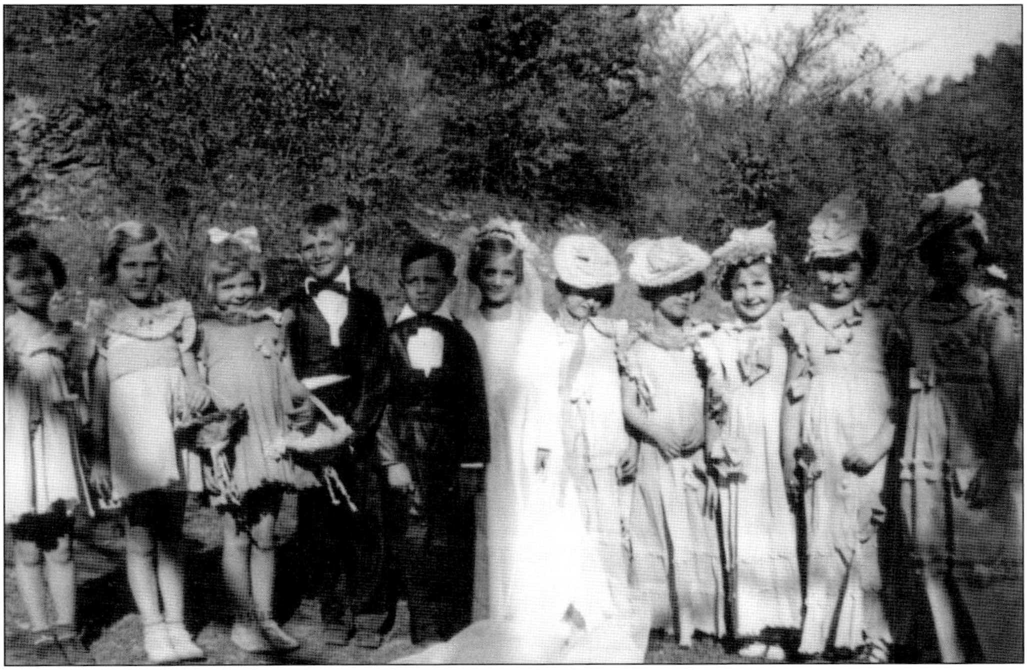

Younger Milton school students pose in costume before the annual performance of *Tom Thumb's Wedding*. The play was a tradition at the school and was based on the script published in 1898 by Walter H. Baker & Co. of Boston. It portrayed the actual 1863 wedding of Charles Stratton and Lavinia Warren. Stratton was known as Gen. Tom Thumb at P.T. Barnum's American Museum in New York City. (Courtesy of Bill Henderson.)

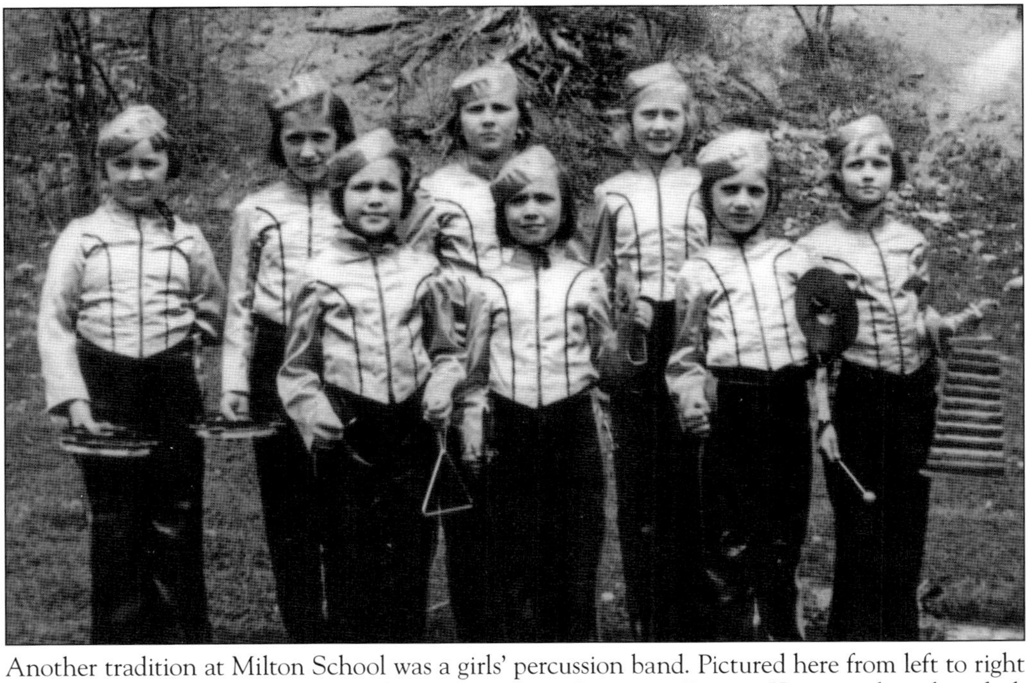

Another tradition at Milton School was a girls' percussion band. Pictured here from left to right are (first row) Clara Mae Kruse, Evelyn Bayne, Maria Strasmeir, Bonnie Kruse, and unidentified; (second row) Thelma Chandler, Patty Gossom, and Jo Bayne. (Courtesy of Bill Henderson.)

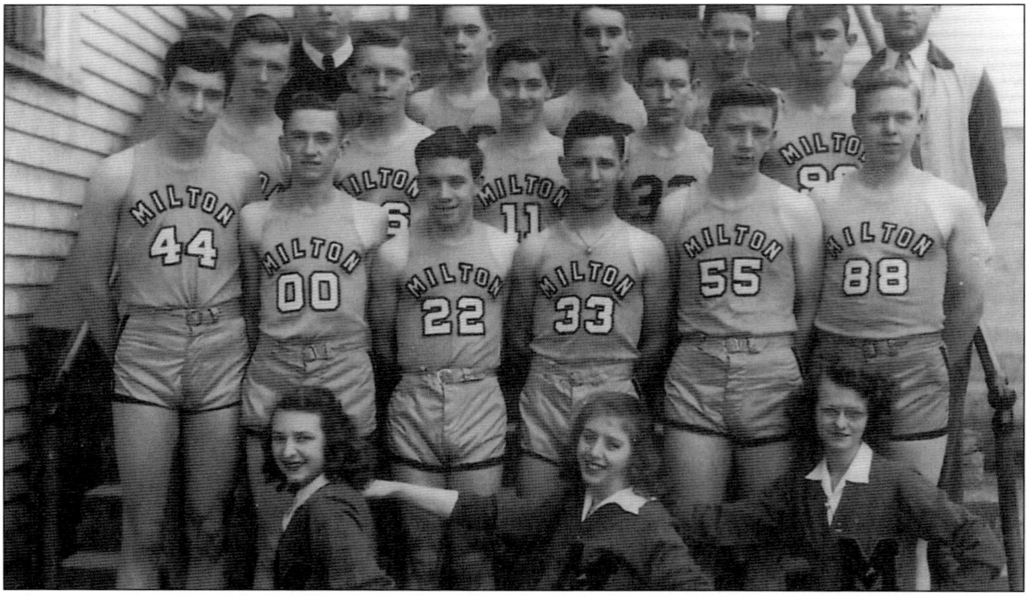

Milton High School also had its own sports teams. Members of this basketball team from around 1946–1948, include, from left to right, (first row) cheerleaders Jeanie Spillman, June Hereford, and Evelyn Thieman; (second row) Junior Shelley, Richard Bradley, Gene Hereford, Norman Williams, Jesse Glenn Bell, and Dickey Tandy; (third row) Bobby Coghill, Carl Schafer, Randall Richmond, Bobby Duncan, and Sam Maddox; (fourth row) Klein Mahoney, Frank Green, Gayle Bird, Russell McConnell, and Coach Allen. (Courtesy of Ted Taylor.)

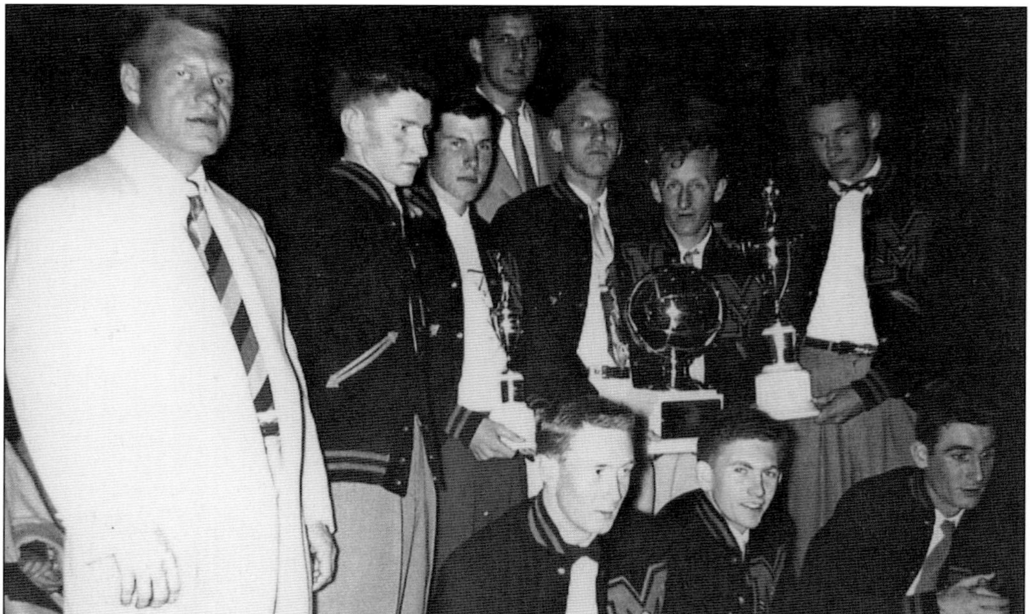

Milton High School's basketball team poses at the annual banquet. In the fall of 1953, the school consolidated with Trimble County High School. From left to right are (kneeling) Gary Rowlett, Bill Ward, and Pete Maddox; (standing) Coach "Skid" Johnson, Bill Richmond, Kenny Burkhardt, Phil Detmer, Jewell "Skeeter" Long, and Joe Brown. In the back is Bill Spivey, a University of Kentucky All-American player who spoke at the event. (Courtesy of Ted Taylor.)

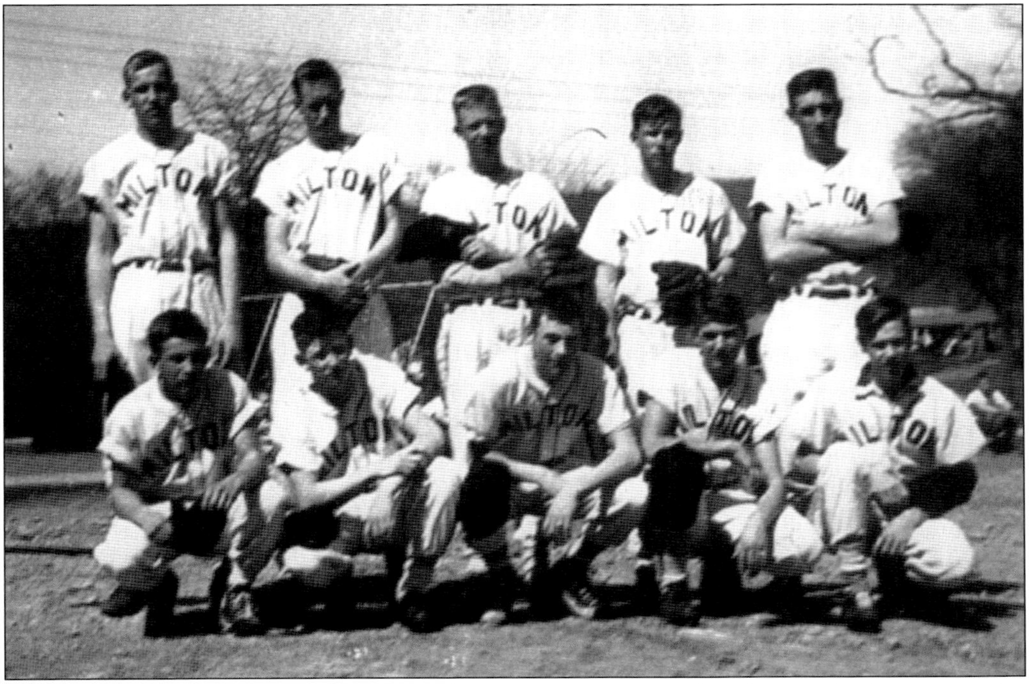

Milton High School's last baseball team played in the spring of 1953. In the fall of that year, the high school consolidated with Trimble County High School. From left to right are (kneeling) Billy Ward, Billy Richmond, Bobby Bebout, Ronnie Mahoney, and Larry Schwers; (standing) Phil Detmer, Gary Rowlett, Ted Taylor, Kenny Burkhardt, and Pete Maddox. (Courtesy of Ted Taylor.)

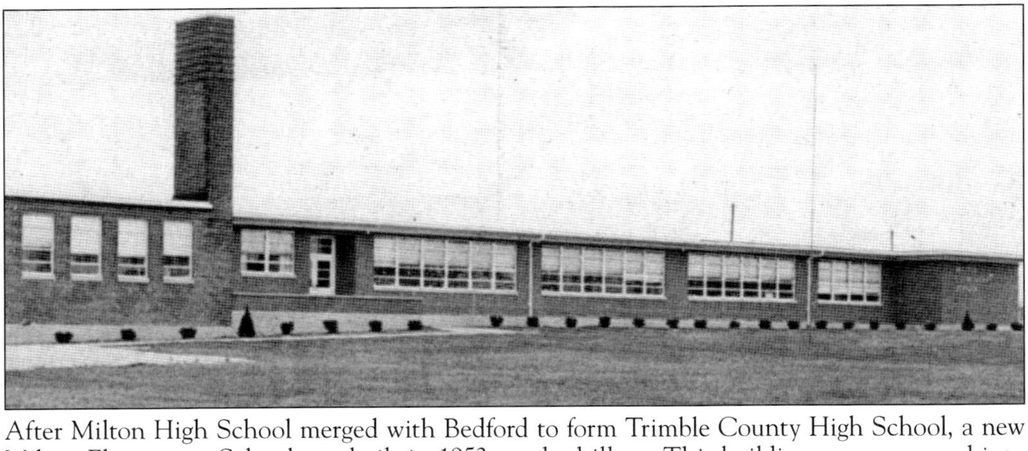

After Milton High School merged with Bedford to form Trimble County High School, a new Milton Elementary School was built in 1953 on the hilltop. This building was renovated into apartments in 2012. A new Milton Elementary was built south of the city limits. (Courtesy of the *Trimble Banner*.)

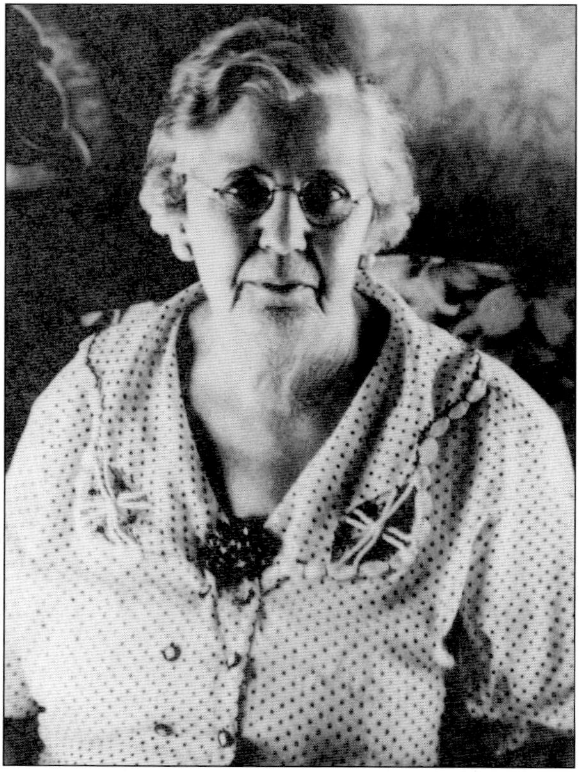

Carrie Hardin Logan Hood, affectionately known as "Miss Carrie," was the first woman to serve on the Trimble County Board of Education and, in 1913, the first woman hired as superintendent of schools in the county. A daughter, Louise Logan, was the first female bank cashier in Kentucky. A son, Keith Hood, was a linotype operator for the *Trimble Democrat* and a mail carrier. (Courtesy of Mildred Pardo Pruitt.)

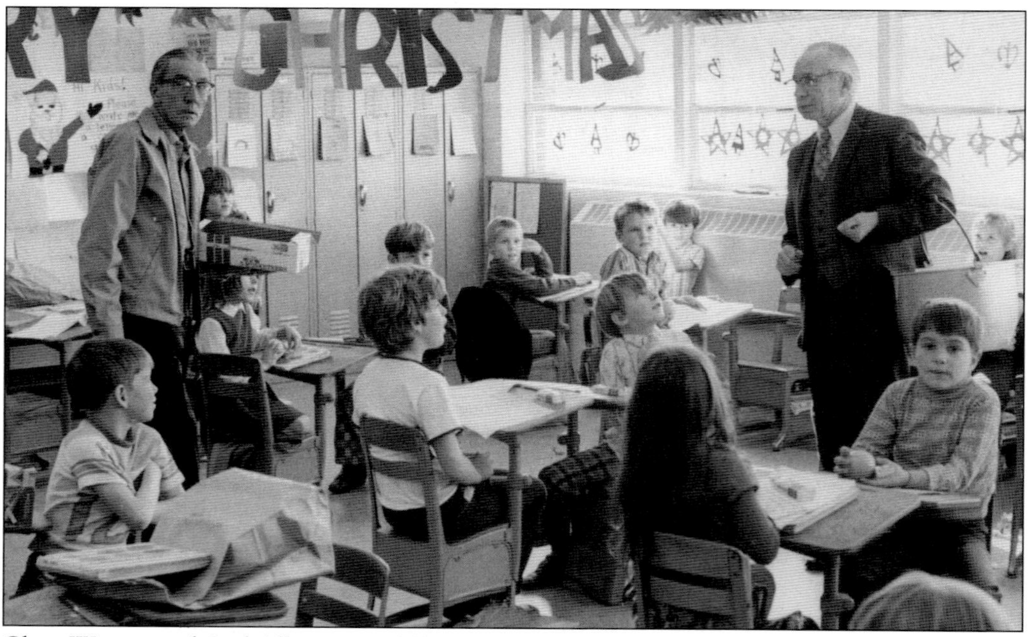

Chan Watson and Carl Allen visit a fifth-grade class at Milton Elementary School on the hilltop in the 1960s. Allen, who died in 2013 at age 103, was principal of the school for five years. A volunteer driver for the American Red Cross and president of the Tri-County Community Action Board, he was named Kentucky Volunteer of the Year in 2007. He taught Sunday school until age 101. (Courtesy of Gary Greenwood.)

Six

FLOODS AND OTHER DISASTERS

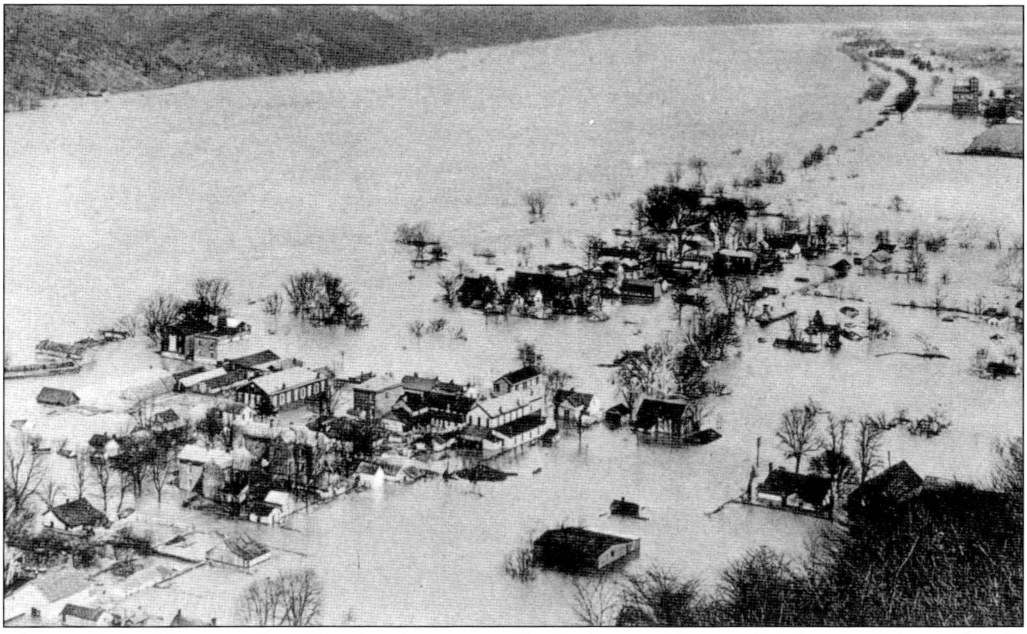

The city of Milton was hard hit by the Great Flood of 1913, the result of several days of early spring rains that followed a deadly winter storm. One of the worst floods on record, climatologists stated that "every major river and stream in Kentucky" overflowed its banks. The US Weather Bureau described lowland areas as "vast inland seas," as this scene of Milton, probably taken from the hillside at Moffett Cemetery, illustrates. In Cincinnati, the river crested at over 62 feet. (Courtesy of Darrell Henderson.)

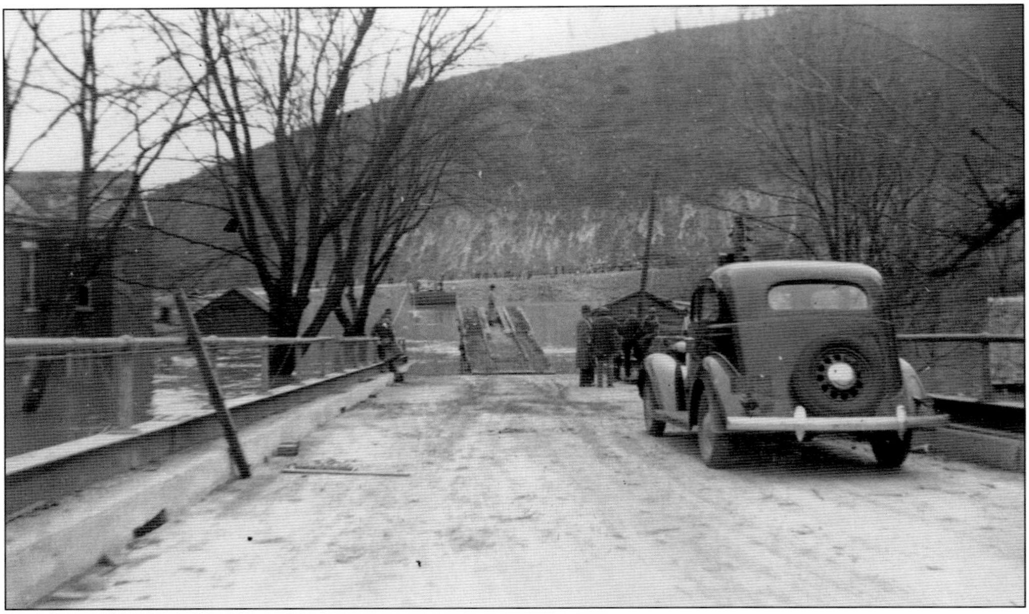

Insurance agent and amateur photographer Harry Lemen of Madison captured the severity of the devastating flood of 1937 in a series of photographs taken in Jefferson County, Indiana, and Trimble County. Here, he shows how cars crossed the Milton-Madison Bridge to the water line and lined up, waiting for a barge to transport them across the floodwaters covering the town of Milton to the road up Milton Hill. In the background below is the line of vehicles waiting to cross over to Madison. (Both, courtesy of Madison Jefferson County Public Library/Lemen Collection.)

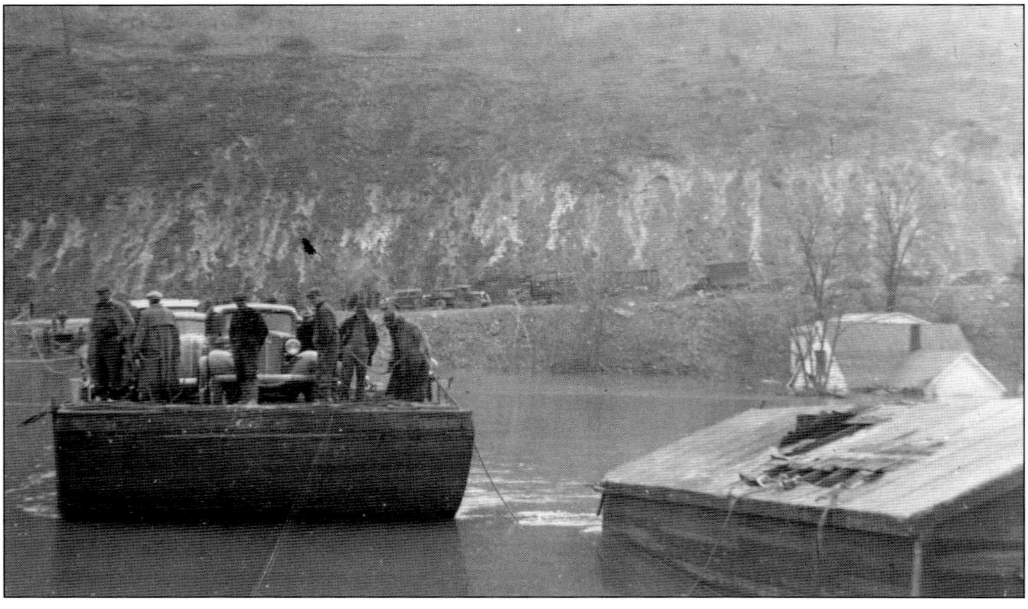

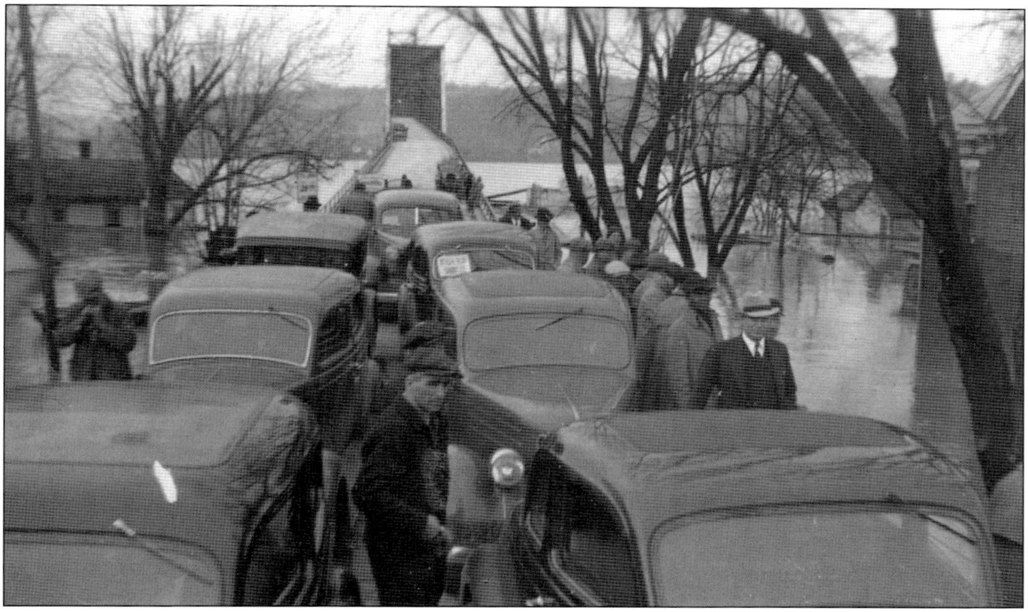

A barge carries the photographer and drivers with a load of vehicles to the Milton Hill road, where travelers can continue their drive to other parts of Kentucky. The flood occurred in January that year, when rain combined with melting snow brought the Ohio River to almost 80 feet, nearly 30 feet above flood stage, and forced tens of thousands from their homes. Nothing in Milton escaped the deluge, and many homes and businesses were destroyed. Most of the buildings seen in Lemen's photographs no longer exist today. (Both, courtesy of Madison Jefferson County Public Library/Lemen Collection.)

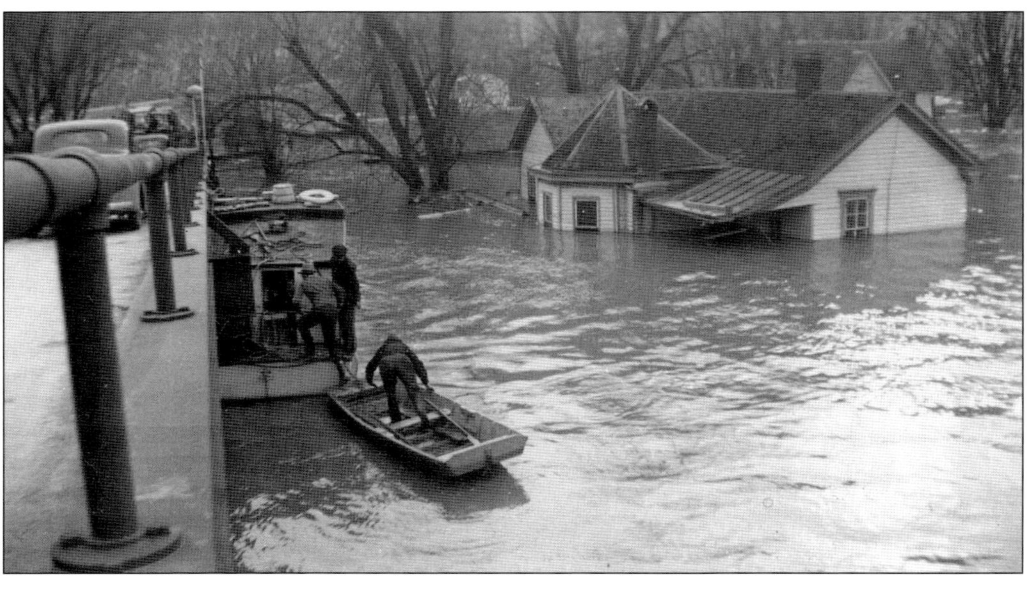

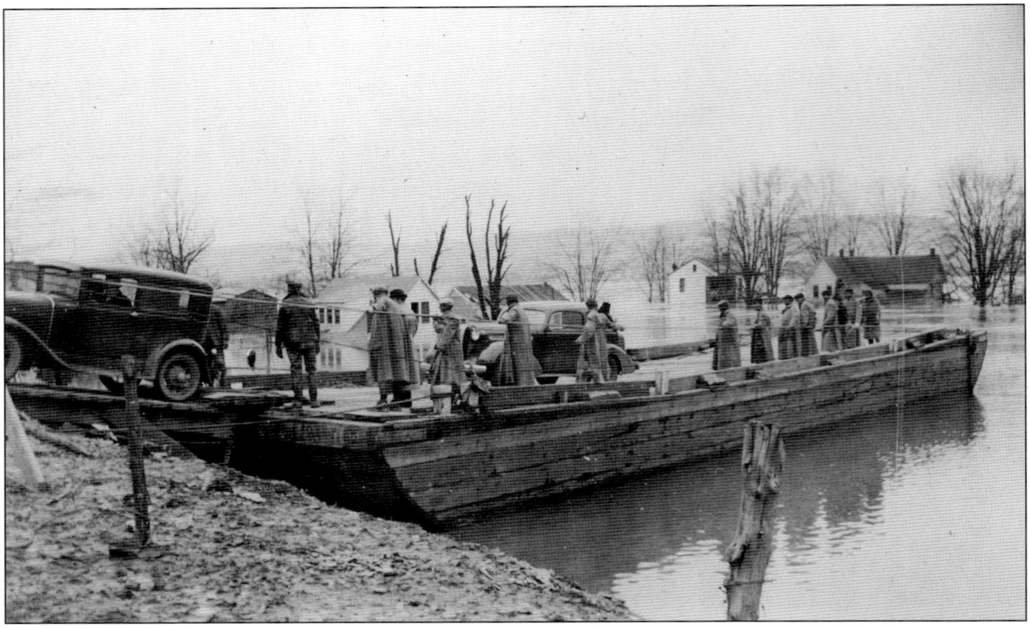

An automobile drives off the barge at its destination at Milton Hill above. Below, as the floodwaters recede, buildings set adrift upriver by the swollen Ohio River are lodged underneath the Milton-Madison Bridge, only feet away from homes and other buildings that survived the devastation. (Both, courtesy of Madison Jefferson County Public Library/Lemen Collection.)

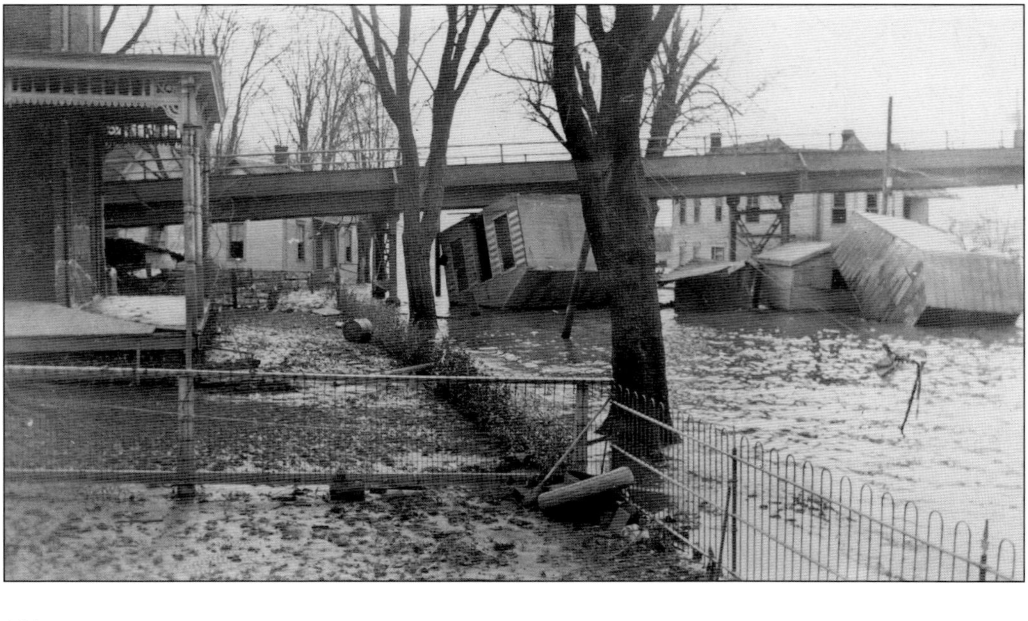

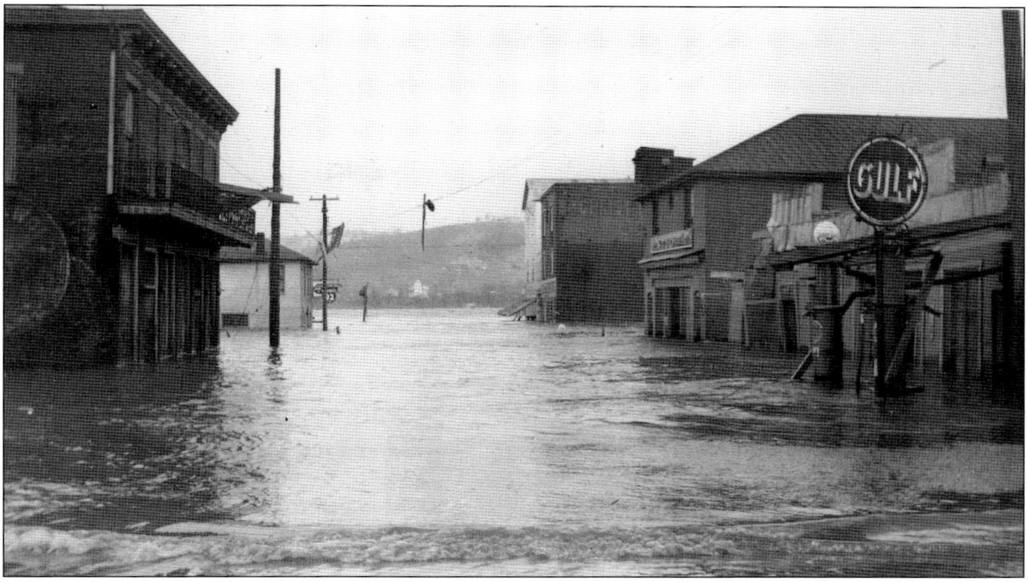

From the water's edge, the photographer looks down Ferry Street toward the Indiana side of the Ohio River. Floodwaters appear to have receded some. Historians note that the water level reached midway up the second floor of the white building at center left above. Below is a shot taken from behind the buildings on the east side of Ferry Street. Debris, including what appears to be a small outbuilding, caused severe damage to the wood-frame building near the flour mill. (Both, courtesy of Madison Jefferson County Public Library/Lemen Collection.)

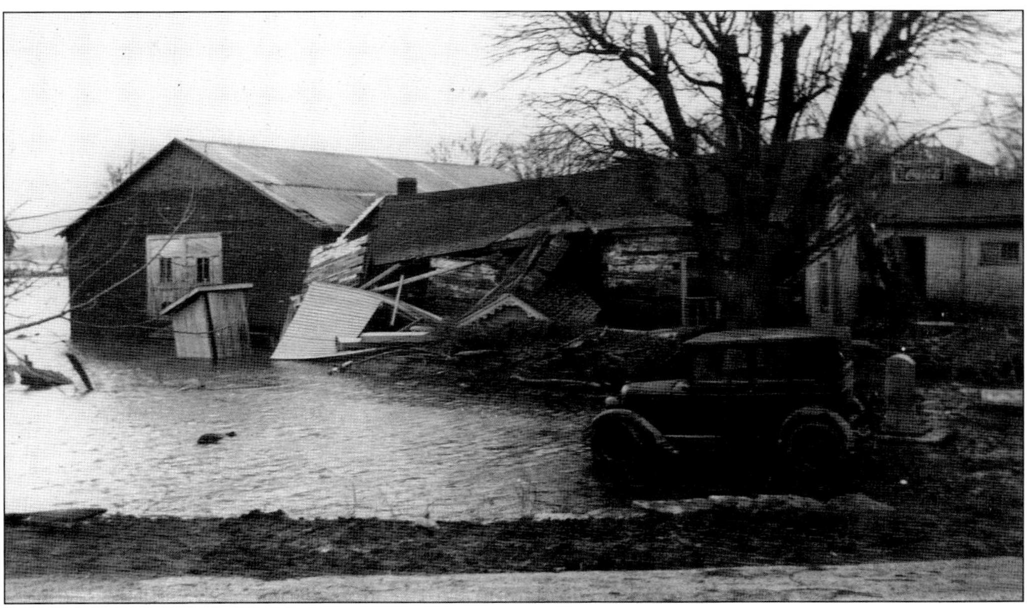

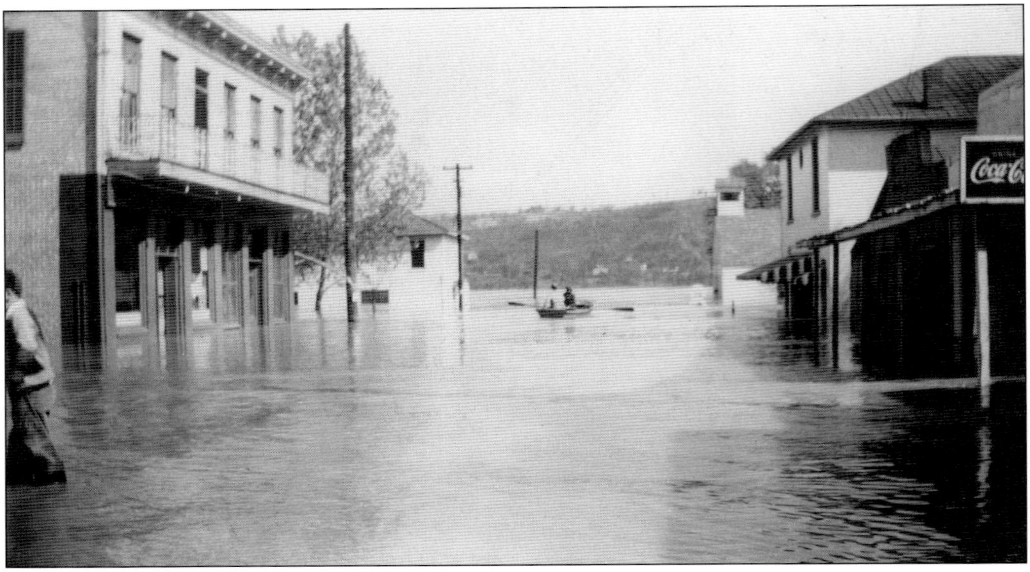

Though not as devastating, the flood of 1945 required Milton residents to travel by rowboat through the streets. Three weeks of higher than normal rainfall led up to this flood, which occurred in the first week of March. The period of February 20 through March 8 that year is the second wettest on record for Louisville, according to the National Weather Service. It would be nearly two decades until the next devastating flood occurred, in 1964, but the record flood of 1945 wasn't topped until 1997 (below). (Above, courtesy of Robert Bruce "Bob" Stewart Jr.; below, courtesy of Darrell Henderson.)

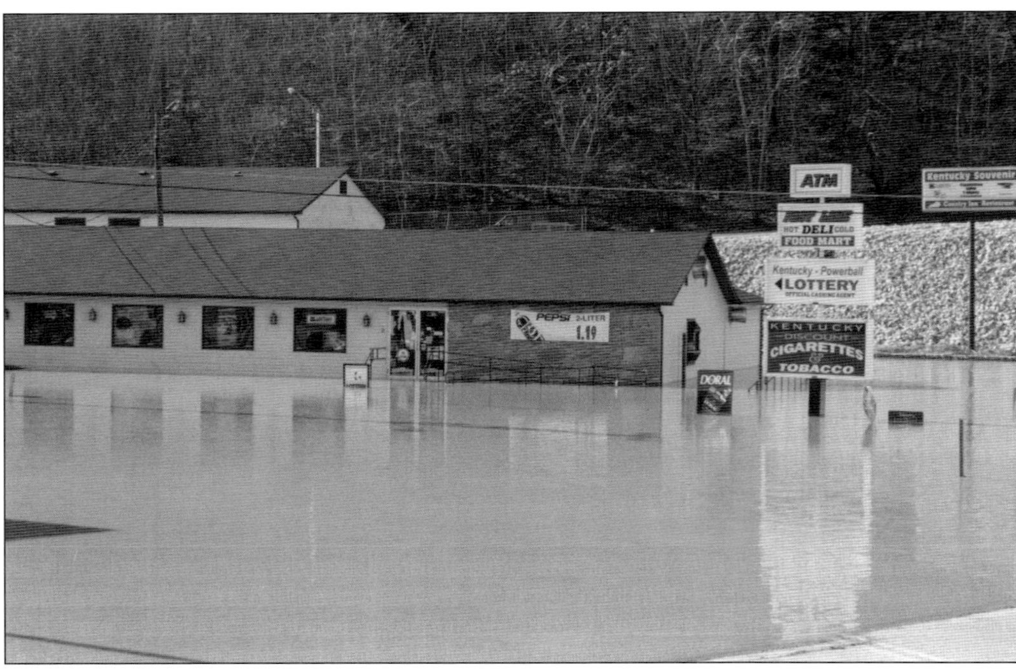

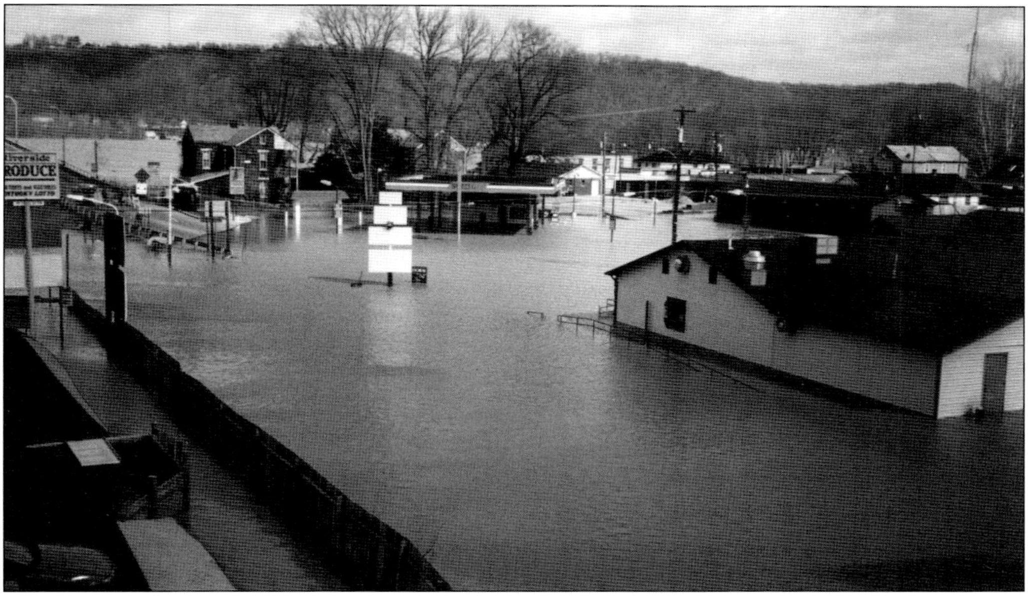

Three decades after the flood of 1964, the Ohio River again was unable to contain large amounts of rainfall in 1997, and flooding again ravaged the city of Milton. This time, there was no barge to help motorists across the Milton-Madison Bridge. Devastation also was felt inland from the Ohio and Kentucky Rivers due to "backwater" flooding of major creeks and other tributaries. Below, residents gather near the Dairy Queen to survey the damage to downtown. (Above, courtesy of Lucy Webster Smith; below, courtesy of Darrell Henderson.)

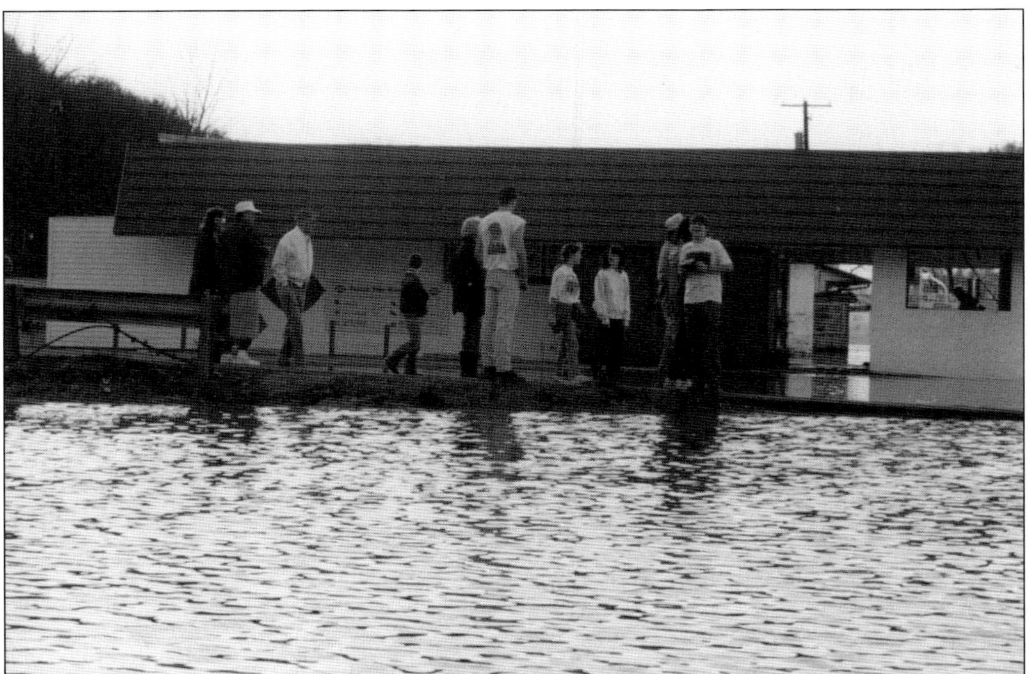

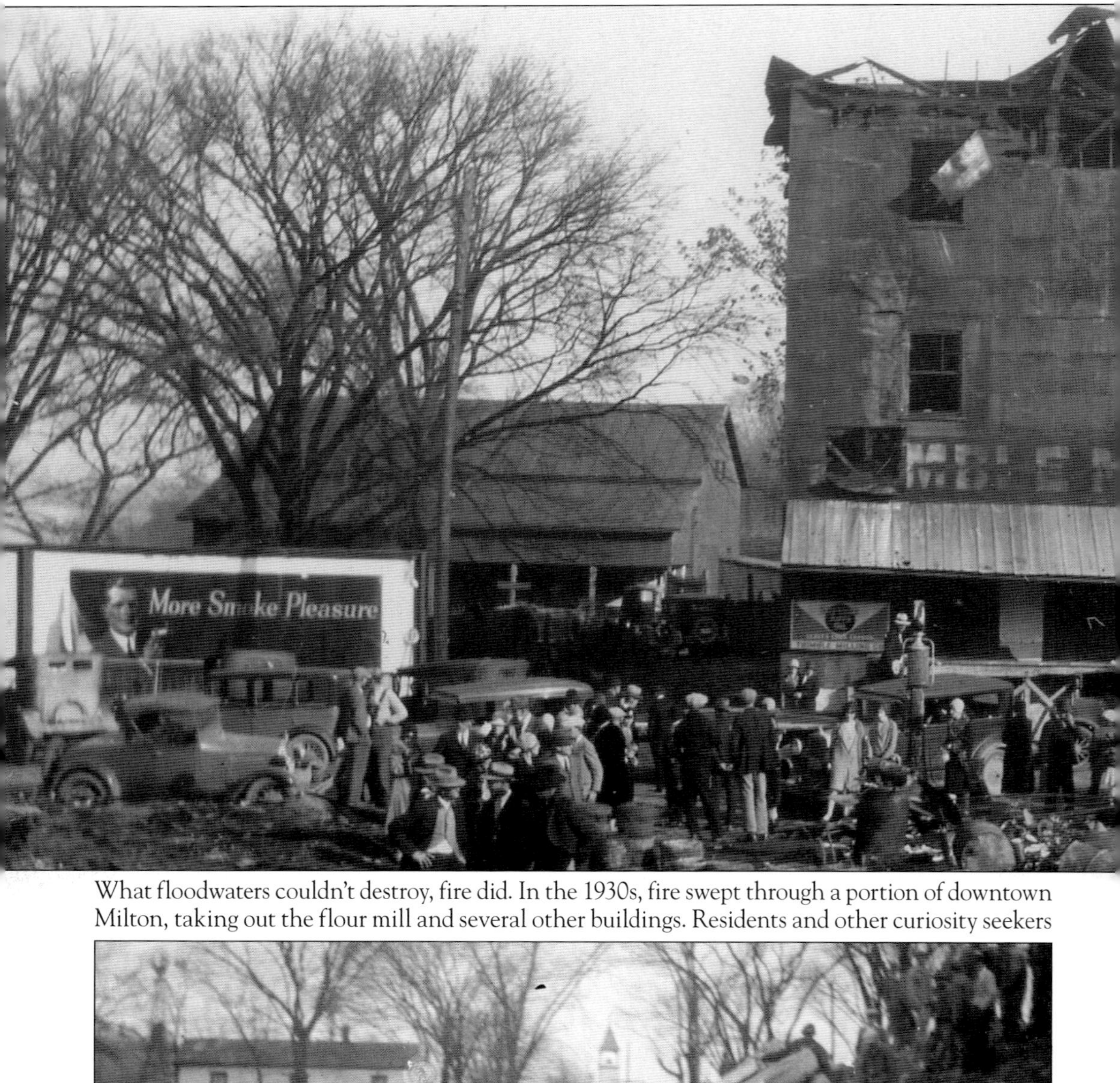

What floodwaters couldn't destroy, fire did. In the 1930s, fire swept through a portion of downtown Milton, taking out the flour mill and several other buildings. Residents and other curiosity seekers

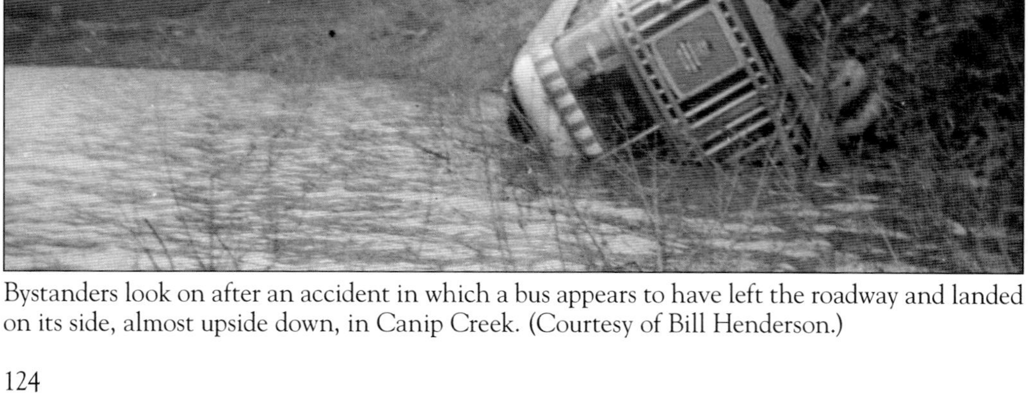

Bystanders look on after an accident in which a bus appears to have left the roadway and landed on its side, almost upside down, in Canip Creek. (Courtesy of Bill Henderson.)

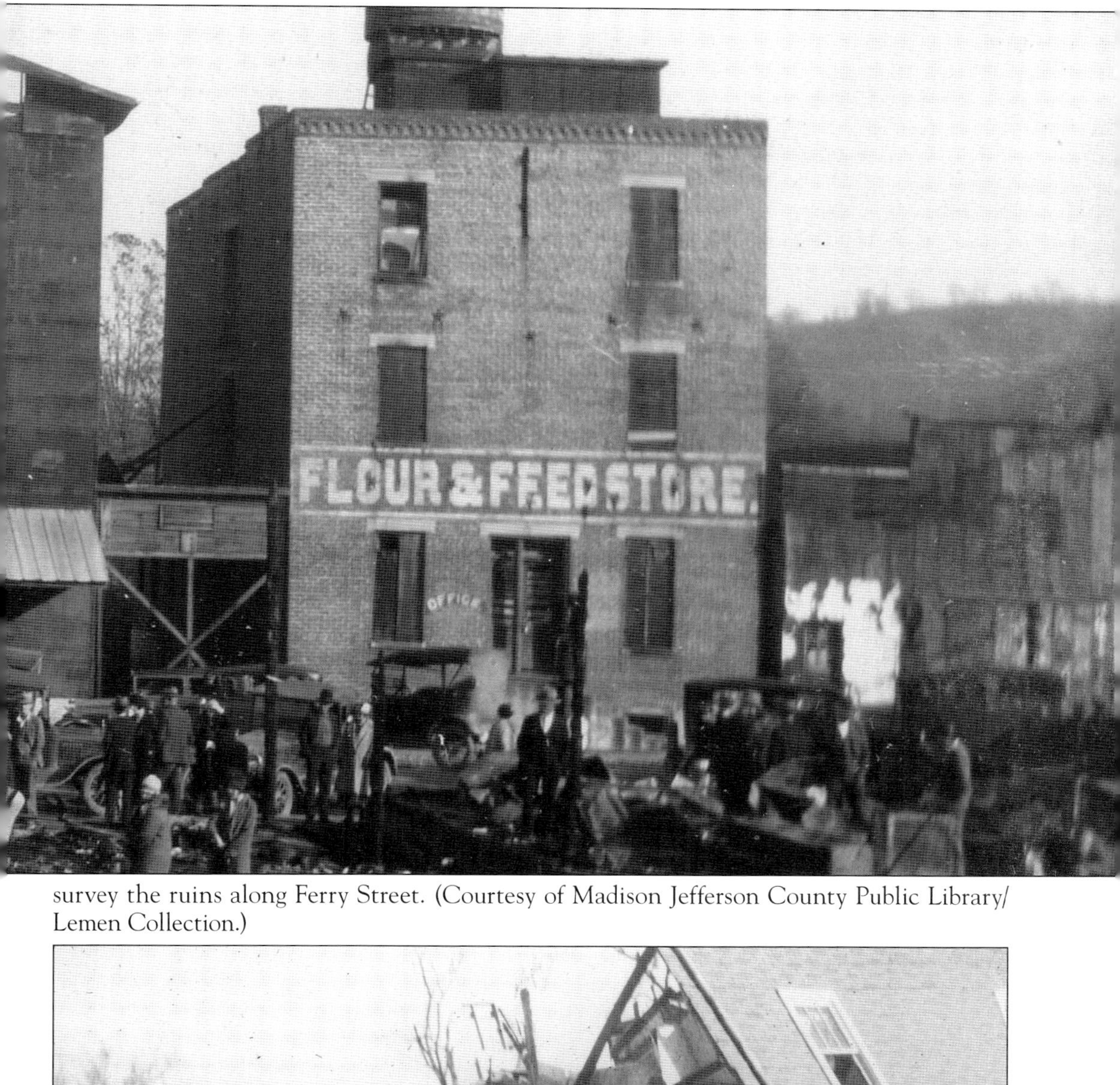

survey the ruins along Ferry Street. (Courtesy of Madison Jefferson County Public Library/ Lemen Collection.)

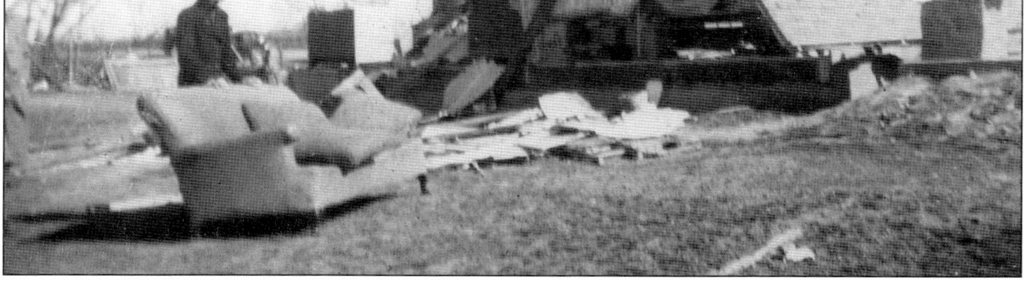

A woman surveys the damage after a tornado ripped through the Wheeler family home on Hickory Grove Road near Bedford. The storm occurred on an Easter weekend in the 1940s. (Courtesy of Mildred Pardo Pruitt.)

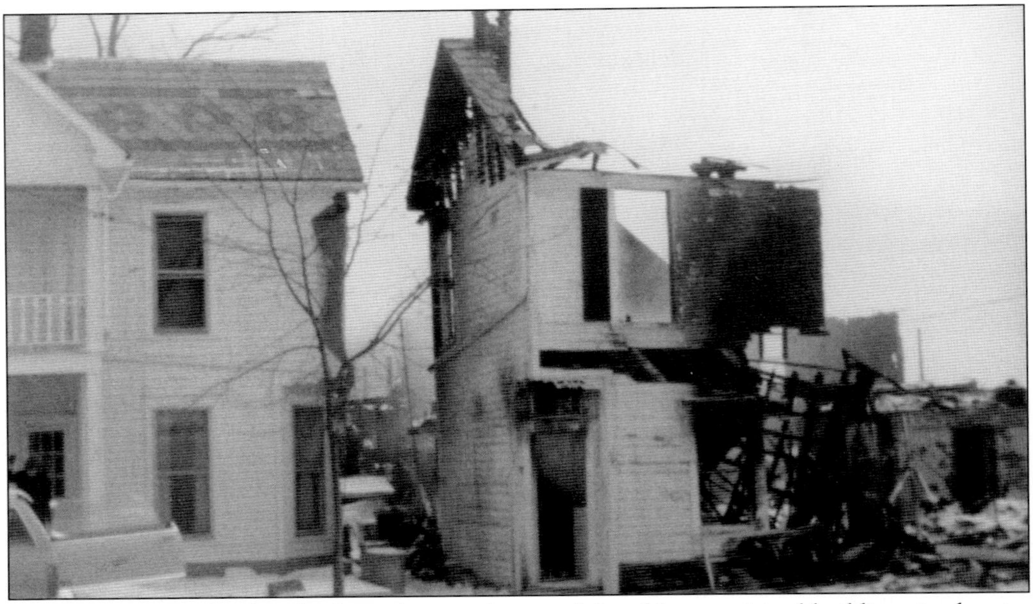

Several fires over the decades have destroyed most of the older or original buildings in the city of Bedford. This fire in the 1970s struck a Bedford landmark building that at one time was home to the Bedford Sweet Shop and the Tip Top Restaurant. The fire spared the Ransdell Funeral Home next door. (Courtesy of Frederica Congleton.)

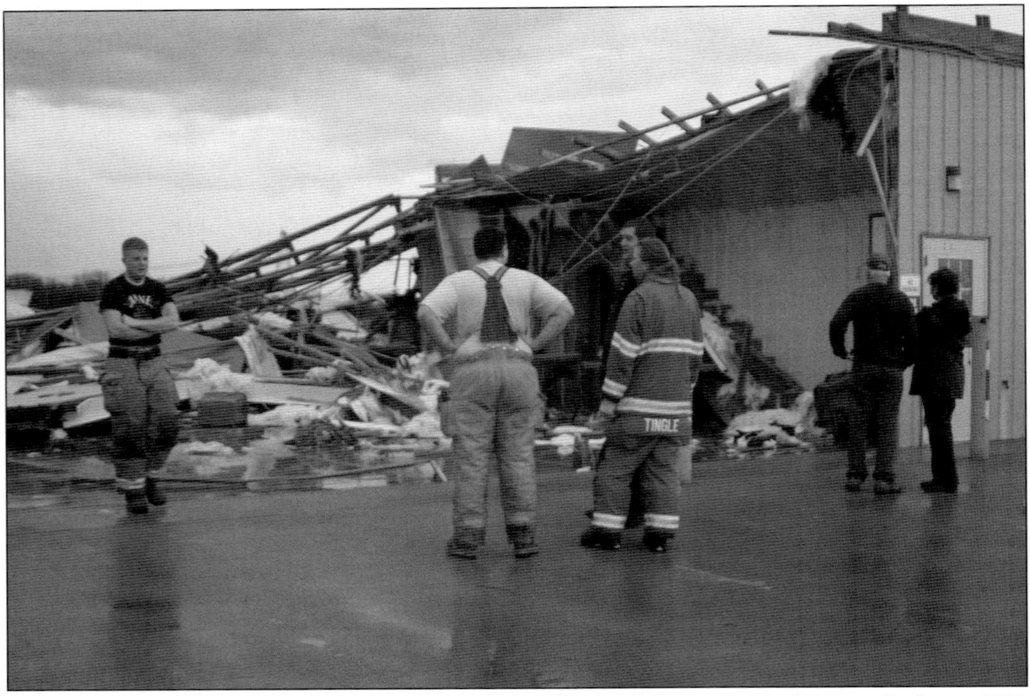

Members of the Milton Volunteer Fire Department gather at what remained of Station 2 after an EF-3 tornado ripped through the building. The twister destroyed fire trucks and other equipment on March 2, 2012. Three smaller tornados also tore through the county on the same day. Numerous homes and buildings were damaged, but only minor injuries were reported. (Author photograph.)

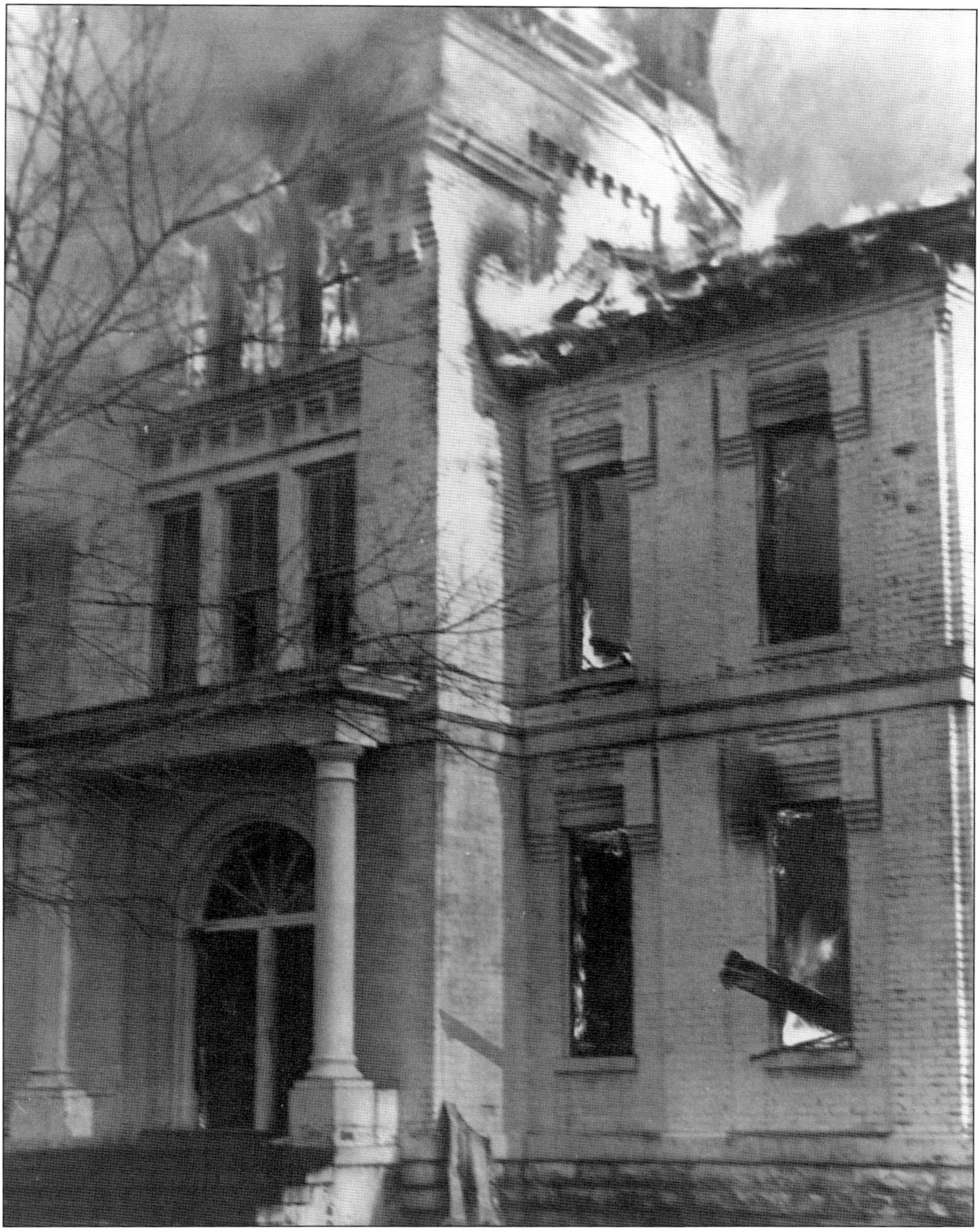

The Trimble County courthouse was gutted in a fire that started in the attic around 5:30 a.m. on March 5, 1952. This photograph was snapped by Sarah Bray Rand that morning, as flames shot out the upper-story windows. Residents, county employees, volunteers, and firefighters from Carrollton worked to salvage most of the county's records and original documents stored in the building. The walls of the original first floor survived, and the courthouse was rebuilt. (Courtesy of Jean Rand.)

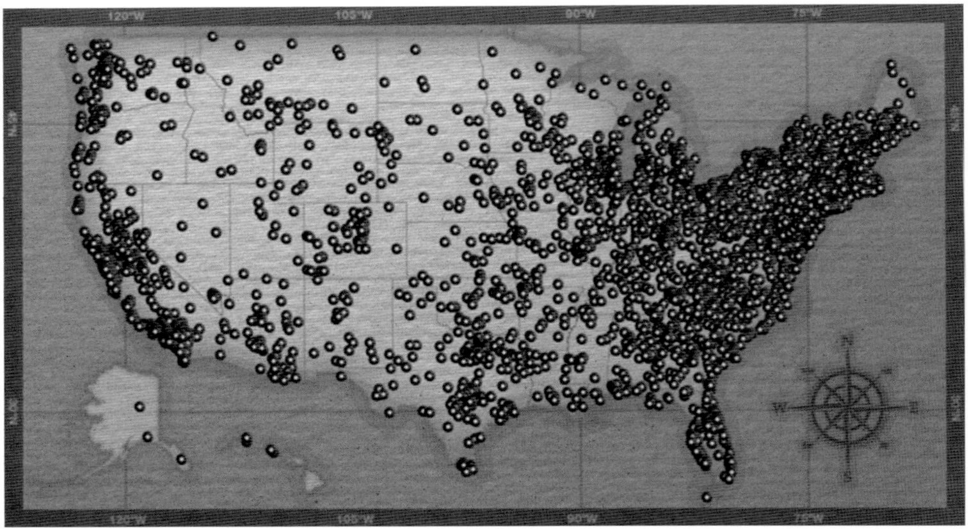